A Time of Awakening

Homayoun Amin

Copyright

Production: Joe Goodwill
Lead Editor: Joe Goodwill
Editor: Nima Mazinani
Graphic designer: Renee Mak
Cover designer: Vivien Anayian

Disclaimer

ISBN: 978-1543140248

Life is Unity Publishing
Vancouver, British Columbia, Canada

Contents

Dedication

This book is dedicated to the memory of my sister Telly. My love for her motivated me to leave an organized crime family so I could continue to give her energy and save her life. I would not be where I am, if not for her. This picture was taken in June of 2006, three months before she passed away. She never lost the sparkle in her eyes and always managed to smile, even though she was receiving massive doses of chemotherapy at the time.

Foreword

This is the story of my awakening. As you read this book, you may well find that this is the time for your own awakening.

I was a man on the brink of a catastrophic life decision: about to plunge into the seedy underworld of organized crime. Just as I was poised to make this leap, sitting in a smoky stairwell in a noisy nightclub, a miraculous thing happened. I was stopped in my tracks by the intervention of an almighty force that cannot easily be described in words. I choose to call it Life, or All That Exists, but some might call it God. Whatever you choose to call it, this inexorable force opened my third eye, precipitating me into a dizzying spiritual journey of enlightenment. I invite you to share my journey by reading all about it, and to benefit from the powerful lessons that Life has generously shared with me.

You live in fear because you cannot get away from your negative thoughts. Your anger consumes you, when you get upset. You may have difficulty manifesting your ideas into reality, because you are overwhelmed by useless thoughts. I want to share with you how you can live a life without anger and fear. I want to show you how to control your mind, so that your creativity can flourish and you can manifest the life that you want to live. You were meant to experience such a life.

I have evolved from a gangster into an enlightened man and a healer. In this book, I share with you how to connect with Life itself through meditation. Learn how to embark on your own spiritual journey, and potentially open your own third eye and be transformed, as I was. Our life on this earth of ours is in fact a spiritual journey, and I hope that my experience will provide a road map to help you travel along it wisely, so that you can actually achieve the true purpose of life.

What *is* the true purpose of life? Why are we here? It's hard to put it into words, but I have tried my best to share my perception of it in this book. If you are searching for meaning in your life, this book could help you in a truly life-altering way.

The book combines spiritual lessons with the story of my own arduous journey, which included escaping a life of drugs, alcohol, and crime; both healing and losing my sister; and an extreme fasting experience that ultimately took me across the barrier between life and the afterlife.

I hope that my story will entertain you, but more importantly, it is my hope that it will change your life. There is a time for everything, and right now, it is a time for dynamic, brand new spiritual insights. Many of the spiritual insights in this book have never been shared by any other spiritual master, and it is my hope that they will contribute to human evolution. I warmly invite you to read my story and share my journey.

I bow respectfully to every brave soul who has taken it upon themselves to embark on this journey of life. I feel you, I am with you, and I will do my best to reach out to you in any way possible to help you in your spiritual journey. Let us come together and write this next phase of our journey as one soul, as one consciousness.

God bless,
Homayoun Amin

INTRODUCTION

This is the story of how All That Exists saved me from a life of crime with an organized crime family and communicated with me through direct contact and events. In 2003 I was in the process of being recruited by an organized crime family. This was a complicated process that took about two years. I was being tested in different situations to determine my loyalty, honesty, and integrity. Organized crime families are very selective about who they recruit. However, they were not the only ones testing me at that time. God was also testing me to see if I was worthy of saving. One day in December of 2005 I was finally welcomed into the organized crime family. But on the day of my initiation, God connected with me directly and allowed me to experience enlightenment. Life then gave me a choice: I could forget what I had experienced and continue with the organized crime family; or I could change my ways and follow the path that Life had put before me. I chose the latter.

It was difficult, but I was finally able to leave the organized crime family and commit myself to the path of enlightenment. Within three weeks, I quit smoking, drinking, and doing drugs. I donated and gave away all the money that I had saved from my illegal earnings. I became celibate and dedicated my life to serve All That Exists. I began to meditate from morning to night to purify and crystallize my energy field, and I also worked with my father as a janitor to help support my family.

After about three months, while I was meditating, I felt a pinch in the center of my forehead and a vortex opened up. As I focused on the middle of my forehead, a tornado-like vortex formed and connected me to a spiritual realm. I was drawing energy with a higher vibration from this spiritual realm of consciousness. This experience continued to occur when I was meditating. At the time I did not know what was happening.

1

Later, I spoke with a chi gong master, who explained that my third eye had opened. Life connects to me directly through the third eye, and I have been given insight into the inner workings of our physical and spiritual bodies. Life has also given me knowledge and insight into our reality and the universe that we live in.

There are thousands of books and articles about spiritual and personal development, but almost all of them only give you pieces of the puzzle. Life has asked me to write this book so that I can share with you what I have learned since that fateful day in December of 2005. Collecting all the pieces is extremely important, but more important is the knowledge to understand how to apply those pieces in your daily life. My goal is not to give you a set of beliefs and tell you what the **truth** is. I want to show you how you can raise the vibration of your spiritual energy and experience the **truth** for yourself. We have all heard that **"we are all one,"** but what does that mean?

To become one with the universe, you have to become one with all its parts. To achieve that goal, you have to break all the divisions. You have to be a witness without any judgment. You have to learn how to truly love people unconditionally. You have to become the master of your mind and the master of your emotions.

Organized religions like Christianity, Islam, and Judaism have created divisions among people all over the world. Instead of uniting and bringing people together, they have caused division among the different segments of the population of this planet. In order to reach God, you have to transcend beyond the duality of this world; you have to transcend beyond religion. What I have to say has nothing to do with any of the organized religions, but I feel it is necessary to discuss some of the verses in the old scriptures that have caused divisions among people. I will also share with you what Life has shared with me regarding the role of male and female energy in heterosexuality and homosexuality.

For years I have taught meditation techniques to many people. To my surprise, I found that most people think meditation is about relaxation. Nothing could be further from the truth. Meditation affects every aspect of your life, so I'm going to describe the effects of mediation in detail, and share my knowledge of how meditation increases the frequency of your vibration. Ultimately, I hope to teach you how to meditate. Learning about different types of thoughts and thought patterns will help you understand your mind and what you need to do to gain control over it. I will also explain how to progress from simple, closed-eye meditation techniques to more complex, open-eye meditation techniques, and eventually how to turn any activity into meditation. I believe that the most important power is the ability to control your thoughts and your emotions. And if you can control your thoughts, you will be able to control your emotions.

The holistic approach to spirituality includes diet, physical balance, and emotional health. You cannot separate the physical body from the spiritual body, because all physical things are the extension of the spiritual energy, and they directly affect one another. So I have included discussions about diet and the importance of the physical balance in our spiritual development.

The very first step of my spiritual journey was to overcome my addictions. Many people struggle with addictions or know someone who does. I would like to share with you my experience with addictions and how I was able to successfully overcome them.

My insights are the universe's insights, so I want to share with you my insights into love, sex, relationships, and parenting. I have written this book for all people. Depending on where you are in your spiritual development, some of the material may or may not resonate with you. My advice to you is to run with the parts that resonate with you, and discard the parts that do not. Just because some parts may not resonate with you today does not mean they will not resonate with you two, five, or ten years from now. As you meditate and increase the frequency of your vibration, Life will give you new experiences to help you comprehend more of the material. Keep an open mind and be ready to abandon some of your beliefs. Your previous beliefs can hold back your spiritual development. Spirituality is always evolving, so if you are stuck in certain beliefs you will not be able to move forward when Life gives you new experiences. Always remember that there are no coincidences – everything that is happening to you has a purpose. Don't just explain away events that are happening in your life; those events are trying to tell you something. The best way to grow is to learn from your own experiences.

My Early Years

Growing up, I struggled in school from Grade 1 to 10, because I had undiagnosed Attention Deficit Disorder (ADD). While I was in class, I could never focus on the teacher. At home, I could not focus on the material I was supposed to be studying. I was continuously daydreaming. The thoughts in my mind overwhelmed me, so my grades were always just above 50%. For a long time I thought that I was not very intelligent.

My low grades in school created problems with my mother. She was very strict and education was very important to her. As punishment, I was grounded every summer and forced to study in order to catch up. Once I became a teenager, she would not buy me brand name clothing and shoes, even though we could afford it. She would also deliberately give me bad haircuts, so that I would not look attractive to girls. She thought that if I didn't look good, girls would not be interested in dating me, and I would have more time to focus on improving my grades. This obviously did not work. There is nothing you can do to prevent a teenage boy from thinking about girls; if anything her attempts exacerbated the problem.

Looking back, I am happy my mother did what she did, because it made me an extremely driven person. In my adult years I worked extremely hard to have the means to buy better and more expensive material possessions. I understand now that it is not important to acquire the means to buy more expensive material possessions, but being focused on obtaining the finer things in life gave me a great work ethic, no matter what it was that I was pursuing.

I loved playing all different types of sports. When I was fifteen years old I played in my school's ping pong, soccer, and basketball teams. Playing sports helped me to learn to focus myself, and I started to do better academically. Once I was doing better in school, I was able to come to some compromises with my mother. She finally bought me brand name clothing, and even allowed me to have a girlfriend. There were strict rules that I had to follow, such as always leaving the door of my room open when I had a girlfriend visiting. She would periodically bring snacks to check up on us. Apart from these rules, I was given more freedom to do the things I wanted to do.

My father was a great provider, but he was not involved in any aspect of parenting except disciplining. When I did something wrong he was very rough with me. I was beaten severely with any object that he could lay his hands on. Once he hit me so hard with a thick broomstick that it broke in half. I cried so hard that he immediately regretted doing it, and began to cry with me. I admit that I was no angel, but I did not deserve to get punished so severely. This continued until I was eighteen years old, by which time I had started weight lifting and was bigger than my father. He became angry when he found out that I had taken a driver's license test instead of taking a final exam at school. He began beating me up, punching and kicking me. My older sister Telly threw herself in the middle to try to stop the beating, but without success. I became so angry that I felt like I was going to hit my father back. To prevent that from happening, I threw myself through the glass patio door. At that moment my father realized that he could no longer continue to use corporal punishment on me, and that was the last time that he hit me.

After years of meditation, I have got to the point where I have no resentment towards my parents. My parents were not bad people. They simply thought they were doing the right thing in the circumstances, like most parents. Their parents had treated them the same way, so naturally they did not know any better. In fact, we are all doing the best that we can, given our past experiences. However, this does not mean that we should not work on ourselves and evolve. Every parent should try to grow spiritually and break negative cycles, instead of perpetuating them. Every generation has the potential to profoundly change the course of life for the following generations.

My parents were not especially religious. Both of them believed in God and in a higher power, but they did not follow a particular religion or faith. We were allowed to explore all of the religions, including Christianity and Islam, and decide if we were interested in following any of them.

When I was a teenager, I pondered about spirituality and our place in the universe. I was especially curious about space and the planetary systems. How was our universe created? I studied the Koran and the Bible, and tried to find satisfactory answers about our purpose here in this world. However, what I read made no sense to me. How could God banish Adam and Eve to Earth just for eating the forbidden fruit of the tree of knowledge? I could not believe that the God described in those scriptures had created this universe.

Telly was more like my parents: she believed in a higher power, but did not believe in any of the religions. My younger sister Naz ultimately chose Christianity. I soon lost interest in religions, but I always believed there had to be more to this life than there appeared to be. I always thought someone was watching over me, because I had many near-death experiences and survived against all odds.

Near-death experiences

My first near-death experience occurred when I was four years old. I was on vacation with my family on an island near Istanbul, Turkey. One day we all went to a public swimming pool, even though I did not know how to swim. My parents had bought me a small inflatable tube so I could stay afloat. I was playing in the water by myself, while my parents were talking to my uncles just outside the pool area. I decided it would be fun to submerge myself under the water, while holding onto the tube with just one hand. No sooner had I submerged myself, than I lost my grip on the tube and immediately sank to the bottom of the pool. I held my breath for as long as I could, staring at the surface of the water, but I quickly ran out of air and started to swallow water. Just as I was losing hope I felt someone lifting and bringing me up to the surface. I started to cough water out of my mouth and nose, and looked back to see the large, black man who had pulled me out of the water. He placed me on the edge of the pool and fetched my tube and brought it to me. He was saying something to me in a language I did not understand. I looked at him with gratitude, and then ran off to find my mother.

On another occasion when I was seven years old, I took the electrical cord of our vacuum when nobody was around and put the cord end partially into the plug. I wanted to find out what would happen if I put my finger between the two leads, because my parents had warned me that it was extremely dangerous. So naturally I was curious to know what would happen. I can't remember anything after touching the lead. I opened my eyes ten minutes later to realize that I had been thrown across the room and knocked unconscious. I should have died that day.

Premonitions and thought manifestations

Throughout my teenage years, I always knew when bad things were about to happen to me. I began to have premonitions about the future at the age of eighteen. The first time I had such an experience I was in a car with four other friends, on a ski trip. I had a vision that our car was flipping over. This vision manifested as a deep knowing about what was going to take place. I told my friends several times, trying to convince them that our car was going to flip over, but they all just laughed at me. About an hour into the trip, while my friend was driving in a curvy section of the mountain, a car in the opposite lane swerved into our lane and my friend made a hard right to avoid a collision. He lost control of the vehicle and it went off the road, down the steep ravine, flipping over several times before coming to a stop upside-down. Once we got out of the car, we saw that it had come to a stop at the edge of a cliff. My friends and I couldn't believe what had happened. This experience opened my eyes, and I began to truly trust my instincts.

These unusual experiences were not limited to premonitions about the future. On many occasions my thoughts manifested into reality, sometimes within seconds. Shortly after the incident where the car flipped over, I was driving with another friend on a stretch of highway in his old Renault. We were driving in the slow lane and a young man passed us in a brand new Buick, giving us a dirty look. He was looking down on us, as if he was saying, "I am better than you!"

So I shouted, "I hope you hit a wall!" Within fifteen seconds and for no apparent reason, he swerved to the left and hit the curb. He completely lost control of his vehicle and hit the wall of a nearby university. Other than in that section, there were no other buildings on the entire highway. My friend and I looked at each other in amazement, and he said to me: "Please, never think anything bad about me!"

It is very important not to disregard such experiences. We tend to explain away these types of experiences as coincidences, but life is far too intricate and connected to allow room for coincidences.

My nightclub years

In my early twenties, I was working hard managing our family business, and I was also focused on bodybuilding and weight lifting. I would work from 7:00 a.m. to 5:00 p.m. and then work out at the gym for two and a half hours. My mind was consumed by fast cars and meeting women. On weekends, I would go to a busy nightclub with a bunch of people to drink and party. At first I would get drunk by just having a few tequila shots. Then slowly two became three, three became four, until I had to drink 20 shots before I got drunk. I began to notice that during the week I was counting the days until the weekend so I could go out and drink. I soon began to realize that my drinking habits were becoming a problem, but I was having too much fun to do anything about it. Not too long later, I met a man in the gym who worked as a bouncer at one of the busiest nightclubs in Vancouver. He told me that they were hiring and looking for men who can handle themselves in fights and that I should apply. I had taken Kong Fu classes during my teenage years, so I thought this was a great opportunity to make some cash while remaining in the party scene. But I made a promise to myself to never drink on the job because I knew I could easily become an alcoholic. I went for the job interview the following week and was hired.

My best friend Sammy applied for a bar tending position at the same nightclub and was hired as well. We both quickly excelled in that environment and within two years I became the head of security for that nightclub and Sammy became the top bartender. Unfortunately, shortly after, my family lost their business due to a contract issue. This was particularly hard on my family, and my father had to pick up janitorial contracts in order to support my mom and Naz. Telly had just got married and was living with her husband, Moe. I did not know if the head of security job was going to last long, so I applied to the British Columbia Institute of Technology to become an electrical engineer and was accepted. I would go to school and study Monday through Friday, and ran the nightclub Friday and Saturday nights. I was making enough money to pay for all of my living and school expenses just working two nights a week, so I took the job very seriously.

At one point, the nightclub was having difficulties with gangs and organized crime families fighting in the club. There was a meeting with a master police Sergeant and we were informed that if this issue were not put under control, the police would come down hard on the nightclub. The problem was that average men would unsuspectingly pick a fight with one of the organized crime family's members, and before knowing what's going on, would get pummeled by twenty men. I sat down with my partner to figure out how we could solve this problem, and we came to the conclusion that we could not control every single member in the family. The only way to stop these fights from happening was to get to know the top men in each group, and have them control their men. The organized crime families operate like terrorist cells. There could be as many as 2,000 members in the big umbrella in each city, but they are literally made up of smaller families with aunts, uncles, cousins and so on. These smaller groups know of each other, but they do not always directly work together on a large scale. Instead, to minimize the risk of getting caught, one or two people from each group act as the contact point to make connections between other groups. One of the other nightclubs in Vancouver had very busy Thursday nights. Many of these groups gathered there to party, and we decided to go there with our crew to have drinks and get to know these men better. I had a crew of seventeen men, all of us tough and capable. I had men who were training for UFC and had multiple black belts- we all could handle ourselves when it came to fighting. I've always had a respectful relationship with organized crime families, but it was always a balancing act. I had to be stern enough so they knew I would not tolerate fights and bad behavior in our club, at the same time not to go too far, because I could have got shot and killed. I always wore a bulletproof vest when working since I had so many death threats. No matter how hard I tried, there was always somebody who was not happy.

I began to have a closer relationship with all the different groups. I got along with most of them and it got to a point that if they had a problem with anybody, instead of beating them up, they would let me know and I would take care of it. We went through a period of two years with only a single fight. The club was bust and making money, I was making good money, everybody won, and everybody was happy.

One Thursday night when I was out with my crew, I met a beautiful woman called Mara through a mutual friend of ours. I immediately felt a deep connection with Mara, and we started spending time together every night. I made a huge mistake by doing something I had never done before: I let Mara move in with me. We lived together and went out to the nightclub to party every Thursday. I was having a blast. I quickly fell in love with Mara; I knew that she had previously dated some of the members of the organized crime family, but I didn't care. I loved the way she made me feel; we would dance all night, getting lost in the moment. I loved her more than I had loved anyone before – but it was a toxic relationship.

I always had strict rules about not doing hard drugs. All the men in the crew would get together after work on Friday and Saturday nights and smoke a joint, but I never touched hard drugs. The following September on my birthday, my friend Romeo suggested, "Let's pop ecstasy tonight."

I replied, "There's no way I'll touch that stuff!"

He was persistent and insisted, saying, "Come on, it's only one night. It's your birthday, why don't you just let loose for one night?" I caved in and popped ecstasy for the first time. I had never felt so alive in my life, it felt so good just listening to music and dancing to the songs. I enjoyed it so much that popping ecstasy became our ritual every Thursday. But it crept up slowly, just like alcohol. After three weeks, one pill was not enough, and one pill became two, and two became three, and so on.

Despite my lifestyle, I continued to make progress in my life. Even though I was working on the weekends and partying on Thursdays, I was still able to finish my education and receive my diploma in electrical engineering and industrial control.

I was making such good money at the club that I did not bother looking for a job in the field I had trained for. Several times the heads of the different organized crime groups invited me to their meetings, and I knew they were actively trying to recruit me into their groups, but I was not interested in that lifestyle.

Unfortunately, all good things must come to an end. The manager of our nightclub began to steal money from the club. I repeatedly warned the main shareholder, but he did nothing to stop it because he was in on the take. Eventually the club went out of business, but by that time I had earned a reputation with other nightclub owners as someone who could handle tough crowds. So I was immediately hired at another nightclub and promoted to head of security; however, the money was not nearly as good as the previous club that I worked at.

Mara wanted to be spoiled, but after the drop in my pay, she had to contribute to our living expenses. Money got tight and that started to cause a rift between us. At the same time, everything that could possibly go wrong, went wrong. Telly, who is four years older than me, was diagnosed with breast cancer, which was devastating for my family. On top of my other expenses, I began to help my Telly and Moe with some of their expenses. I was extremely close to Telly; while growing up she had always protected me when I did something wrong and was being punished by my parents. I felt helpless when I visited her.

Fortunately, after extensive chemo and radiation sessions, Telly was able to beat the cancer. Once when I was visiting Telly, a woman was giving her Reiki energy healing. After the woman finished the session, she looked at me and told me that she could feel my energy field and see my aura. She told me that I had a very strong energy field, and that if I practiced and took courses, I could become very effective at healing people. I did not think much about that encounter; I was far too busy dealing with all the commotion that was going on in my life.

I noticed that Mara started to stay out late some nights, and she gave me excuses as to why she was coming home late. But I always know when someone is lying to me, and I quickly found out that she had gone out on a date with another man. This was devastating to me; none of my previous girlfriends had ever cheated on me. To make matters worse, I found out that she was going out with a man who belonged to one of the organized crime families. This was extremely unexpected, and the trauma was so great that for the first time in my life I had a panic attack. I felt terrible that day, and I knew that I never wanted to feel that way again. But instead of learning from my mistakes and changing the direction of my life, I sank deeper into the abyss. I got a job working the door for the only legal after-hours nightclub in Vancouver. I started to make really good money again, but this time I broke my rule about not drinking and doing drugs on the job. The owner did not care if the staff members partied, which was great. I was taking a different woman home every weekend, sometimes two women at the same time, but nothing could fill the hole that had been left by Mara when she had cheated on me. I kept partying and gradually my moral standards declined. One night while I was working at the after-hours nightclub, I met a beautiful woman who happened to be a stripper. When I asked her if she had a boyfriend, she told me that she was dating three different men. I liked that she was honest with me. We started dating frequently, and I liked this no-obligations arrangement. I didn't have to worry about her breaking my heart because there were no expectations. My life had become about making money, doing drugs, and having sex.

One Sunday afternoon, Telly called and asked me to go and visit her at our mother's apartment. When I got there Telly told me that her cancer had metastasized into her liver. I cried uncontrollably; I could not bear the thought of losing her. I knew that liver cancer patients have a very small survival rate. I pulled myself together and told Telly that she would beat this, and that we were going to support her, no matter what.

That night I was overwhelmed by my emotions and just wanted to escape my thoughts. I popped ecstasy and went to an after-hours nightclub by myself. That night the club was full of gang members and the members of a particular crime family; there were no regular people there that night. I could tell they were surprised to see me there all by myself. That night, I decided that I wanted to join them.

We all want to belong to something bigger than ourselves. Unfortunately, my desires were taking me to the dark side. Instead of wanting to belong to something good and positive, I was choosing to belong to something bad and destructive. I spent time with all the different groups that night. Normally no one would dare to mix with them, but somehow I felt at home, and I could tell they did not mind my company.

I had developed a close friendship with many of them throughout the years working in different nightclubs, but I had never asked about their business. That night I started talking with a high-ranking gang member who I knew really well. He told me that he would help me out and give me products at very low prices. Without much effort I had got to the top of the food chain. I finally realized why the different groups had been trying to recruit me for so long: I knew members of all the different organized crime groups, and that was a great advantage because different groups had access to different things at different prices. All I had to do was to find out who had what and at what price, and make the connection. It was easy money.

I soon realized that they were putting me in various circumstances to test me, and see how I would react in different situations. They were testing my honor, honesty, and loyalty. They were also putting me in situations where I had to anticipate when things were about to go wrong, and prevent them from happening. During all that time I was loyal and never lied or cheated anyone.

While I was involved in the recruitment process, Telly continued to get worse. Her doctors were trying various chemotherapy treatments, but she continued to deteriorate. I somehow thought that if I made enough money, I could fix things, and everything would turn out all right.

Over a period of year and a half I met all of the people within the families. Sometimes I was aware that I was meeting them, but sometimes I did not know they belonged to a family. It appeared to me that I was meeting them randomly in the nightclub, but in fact they were all assessing me. They all had to give the okay for me to become one of them.

There is a significant difference between gangs and organized crime families. Gangs are a group of people who get together and carry out illegal activities, while organized crime families are actual families that have been working together for centuries. Each ethnic group has its own organized crime families; sometimes multiple families from different races make up these organizations. The souls of people in these families reincarnate into the crime families after they die, repeatedly until the end of time. There is no chance of evolving in your next life if you join these organizations. However, gangs are not the same way – the commitment for the gangs is for just one lifetime. I was not aware what I was getting myself into when I decided that I wanted to join that organized crime family.

I began to go out to different nightclubs five nights a week, because that was where business was done. All of the gangs and organized crime families party in the clubs because they offer safe environments to do business and make plans. Undercover police try to keep an eye on them, but it's impossible for the police to really know what's going on.

For the most part, the different organized crime families got along with each other and worked together on different projects. As I said before, different crime families had access to different things. For example, one group might have people who worked in the ports, while other groups would have access to other logistically advantageous areas. I tried to keep a low profile as much as possible, because I knew that the police were always watching. However, doing shots is how members bonded with each other and made connections. I was spending time with the big boys, and the police were taking notice. I began to realize that I was being followed, and knew that I had to be very careful.

Most people don't know that when the police put someone under surveillance, it is not just a single car that follows the person; the surveillance team is made up of four or five alternating cars, so the person doesn't know they are being followed. I knew that unless they had concrete evidence of me doing something illegal they would not put me under surveillance for an extended period of time, as it is extremely expensive. Nonetheless, I was always vigilant about watching my back and making sure that I was not being followed.

From the very beginning I was granted different connections by the organization to do different things; it was a kind of job training. They were very protective of me and wanted to make sure that I was safe, but I knew I was being tested to see how I would react in different situations. I noticed that on many occasions, they wanted to see if I could foresee if something was going to go wrong, and take steps to avoid or mitigate the damage. I was surprised because sometimes the tests were very elaborate, but eventually I realized that Life was also testing me. I don't know how, but most of the time I could feel deep inside me when something was up. For example, one night I invited Sammy and his girlfriend to a party being hosted by one of the women in the family. The party was in a new nightclub that had recently opened. All the different factions of the crime families were in different sections of the nightclub, and as we walked in I had a feeling that something big was going to happen that night. I turned to Sammy and said: "Something big is going to happen tonight. There is going to be a big fight tonight, I can feel it. They're want to see how I will react if a fight starts."

While we were at the bar, my main connection to the families arrived. We were all having a good time. A group of seven men went past us; they did not have all their members with them, but I knew they were from a large family. One of them knew me. He jokingly grabbed me and rubbed my shaven head; we both chuckled and they moved off towards the corner of the nightclub, where another large group had gathered. I saw them greet each other in a very friendly way, but within five minutes I saw a huge fight break out in that corner. Somehow the seven men had got into a fight with that large group – it was about thirty men against seven. Six of them managed to get out, but the one who had joked with me was trapped and could not get away. They were throwing so many bottles and glasses at him that he was completely disoriented, and they weren't going to stop.

Once a situation like this happens they don't stop until it ends; those men were going to kill him. People were running away from the fight, but I ran to where he was. I was his only chance of getting out of there alive. I knew the large group and had a good relationship with their leader, and I was hoping that they would not aim directly at me. With all the bottles and glasses flying all over the place, I did take some hits to my head and my neck, but miraculously I did not get cut. You never know what can happen in these situations: they might get angry if you try to help someone they are attacking, so I just grabbed him and dragged him towards the back door. The bouncers stopped the group from following us outside, but some of them ran out through the front door.

He had deep cuts all over his face and his body. I dragged him towards my car, planning to get him to the hospital. Another man from the large group appeared in front of us holding a gun, and shot five times at the man I was trying to save. Thankfully he missed both of us. We all scattered, and I heard the sirens of police cars. I ran towards the front door of the nightclub, where I saw Sammy and his girlfriend coming out. I wanted to get out of there as quickly as possible; I had the man's blood all over my shirt and my jeans. I knew if I didn't get out of there before police arrived I would have to explain all that blood, so we got away very quickly.

Sammy was furious. "Are you crazy?" he yelled at me. "Everybody is running away from the fight, and you run in, do you want to get yourself killed?"

I thought that this could not have been prearranged; how had I known what was going to happen?

The following Friday I was asked to go to an event where multiple trance music DJ's were playing. The head of the families was there that night, along with all the groups in the organization. It just so happened that my Mara was also there, with her new boyfriend who was a member of one of the groups. There are many people who work for organized crime families but are not officially part of the family. I was not sure where I would fit in, but one of the rules that I learned right from the beginning was that you never ask questions. If there is anything to be known, they will tell you. This night was different. I hung out with the man in charge and the heads of the families. I had taken my rightful place among them; I was finally one of them, and I realized that they had officially taken me in.

Unfortunately, not everything was going well. Telly was dying. Moe called me in despair; the doctors had told him that she would not survive much longer and he should make preparations for the funeral. I visited her the next day and sat with her, crying. She looked like a balloon because her body was retaining water. The cancer had spread out throughout her body, her liver was failing, the chemotherapy medications were no longer working, and her cancer indicator count was going up continuously.

Later that day I got a text to go to one of the nightclubs that was owned by one of the organized crime family members. As I entered I saw that all the families in the big organization were there; in fact, every single person I had met in the past year and half was there. I realized that many people I had casually talked to in the nightclubs for the past year and half were actually part of the organization. They were all smiling and congratulating me, welcoming me into the family. I felt very proud to belong to something bigger than myself. I was now part of an international organization that spanned the entire planet. I now had an army behind me, and I felt untouchable. But I had mixed emotions: I was extremely sad because Telly was dying, but I was relieved that I had finally achieved my goal of belonging to something bigger than myself. I had found my purpose.

Some of us went to the legal after-hours club where I used to work, and I called my Sammy to come and join the celebration. Mara also arrived, with her boyfriend. After a few hours I went to smoke a cigarette on the stairs. Mara joined me, and we started talking. I told her that I no longer held any resentment towards her; after all, her leaving me was the reason why I had pursued joining the family. After hearing this, Mara left.

MY EXPERIENCE OF ENLIGHTENMENT IN DECEMBER OF 2005

What I'm going to tell you next is very difficult to understand. I can only tell you half of what I experienced, because words cannot possibly describe the other half. Unless you experience those events yourself, it is impossible to comprehend. In very simplistic terms, I experienced enlightenment; I was one with All That Exists for a period of time.

Defining God

Before I begin, I need to define God. God is the single consciousness that is all of us. In fact, nothing but God exists, and God includes all physical and non-physical entities in this universe. Unfortunately, I have to try to use words to describe this spiritual event. I have no choice but to use words like "I" and "you" or "God" or "Life," but for a period of time, I was one with All That Exists. There was no "you" and "me," only absolute unity and pure understanding. Words specify, distinguish, and isolate – that is the very function of words; and because of this, words cannot possibly describe this experience. The moment we use words to explain any event, those words introduce specificity and hence separation – but God is unity. The following is the best I can do to describe this experience, but unfortunately words cannot do justice to what happened that night.

I was sitting on the stairs thinking about all that had happened, when I suddenly felt a surge inside of me; I became aware of a part of me that I did not know existed. Imagine that all your life you knew yourself to be the pinkie finger of your hand, and then suddenly you feel a surge within you and realize that you're not just the pinky finger: actually there is an entire body attached to that pinkie finger, and that is also you.

I heard a voice coming from inside of me: *"Do you know why you are here?"*

"No," I replied.

"Do you remember the times when you could see events before they happened?"

In that moment, the time when my friend's car had flipped over, and the shooting, flashed before my eyes. I understood that all the major negative events that had happened in my life were due to some action that I had taken before. I had never got away with anything in my life: I was shown all the negative events, and then I saw what I did to cause them. Life connected all the dots for me to see. I had clarity about everything, I was communicating with All That Exists, Life itself. And I felt loved in a way that I cannot describe with words. I understood that Life had been watching over me throughout my entire life.

Ashamed, I said: "You have always known about everything that I have ever done wrong."

"Yes," Life replied.

Then I saw the events when I should have drowned in the swimming pool, and when I had been electrocuted. Life had saved my life and brought me back to life. I was filled with joy.

"Do you want us to be together?" Life asked.

"Yes," I replied joyfully.

"Are you sure?"

"Yes", I replied again, "Yes."

"If you want us to be together you cannot pop ecstasy."

"Okay," I replied.

"You cannot drink alcohol."

"Okay," I replied.

"You cannot smoke weed."

"That's not fair!" I replied. In frustration I asked: "Can I smoke cigarettes?"

In that moment, I felt a sharp pain at the bottom of my right lung, and I saw a vision of where it had become cancerous. I got up and started pacing back and forth, thinking about these conditions and what I should do. Then I suddenly remembered something I had heard in the past: no matter how late in life, if you pray with sincerity before you die and ask for forgiveness from God, no matter what you have done, you will be forgiven.

Life communicates with me through my friends

I thought that's what I would do: I would continue as is until I got older, and then I would ask God for forgiveness. No sooner had I finished that thought, than I found myself standing next to a woman and her boyfriend in the club. Suddenly the man looked at the woman and said: "It's getting late; you have to decide what you want to do."

I thought this must be a coincidence; Life could not be communicating with me through him. I walked away from them, continuing to think about the idea of continuing with my current lifestyle, and then asking for forgiveness just before I died.

A friend walked towards me and casually said to me: "It's getting late; you have to decide what you want to do."

I stared at him in shock. "Why did you say that?" I demanded.

He looked baffled by my question and replied: "I don't know. It's getting late and I want to know what you're going to do next."

I understood that Life was now communicating with me through my friend. It became clear to me that I could not go on as I was and ask for forgiveness from God before I died. I needed to make a decision that night.

Without saying anything more, I walked out of the corner room. As I walked out I heard the voice from inside of me: *"Are you willing to sacrifice yourself for your family?"*

"Yes," I replied. I looked up, saw Sammy standing in the corner, and walked towards him.

"It's just like the movie *Matrix,* isn't it?" he suddenly said, before I could say a word. "Are you going to take the blue pill, or are you going to take the red pill?"

In that moment, I realized that God was communicating with me through everyone.

"Why did you say that?" I asked Sammy.

"I don't know; I just felt like saying it," Sammy replied.

Without saying another word, I walked away from him. I was freaking out. There was no place for me to run; there was no place for me to hide. I had to make a decision right then and there.

"Okay, I agree, but what am I going to be doing?" I said, reluctantly.

"You are going to make a difference in this bad world," Life said.

"Okay", I said.

"Are you sure?"

"Yes."

"Remember what you are promising tonight, don't break your promise a few months from now and then say sorry, I was high on ecstasy."

The DJ was playing a vocal house song that I had never heard before, and God started singing the lyrics in my head two seconds before they came out of the speakers. I had had enough of everything. I grabbed my jacket and left the club immediately, feeling overwhelmed. As I walked to my car I looked across the street. I saw a Chinese man opening the door of his car, and realized I had dreamt this exact moment the night before. Life was demonstrating absolute control over everything. I drove home and took two sleeping pills to knock myself out.

I woke up the next day and pretended that nothing had happened the night before. I was supposed to go to my friend's birthday party at a nightclub that night. Upon arrival I did not drink or do any drugs, and as the night went along everything seemed to be okay. At the end of the night I noted that nothing out of the ordinary was happening, so I popped an ecstasy pill and went to an after-hours event where all the crime family members were gathered.

As soon as I arrived on the doorstep of the after-hours, I again felt the same surge that I had felt the night before.

"I wasn't expecting to see you here," I heard.

I quickly turned around and went right back home, absolutely terrified. I thought that I was going to die. As soon as I got home I felt a surge again, this time telling me: *"You can help your sister."*

My First Healing Experience, With My Sister Telly

I recalled what the woman who was giving Telly Reiki energy had told me. I went to my mother's home, as she was taking care of Telly there. When I arrived my sister was in a lot of pain. I cried and told her that I didn't know how, but I thought that I could help her.

I asked Telly to lie down on the bed. I started to vibrate and moved both my hands from the neck area towards her feet, over and over again for twenty minutes. When I finished her eyes lit up. She told me she didn't know what I had done, but that she felt no more pain. We both cried and I told her that I would come back in two days and repeat it. I was absolutely exhausted, as if someone had drained the life out of me. I went home and slept for fourteen hours.

I woke up the next day and promised myself not to drink and do drugs, but I was not ready to quit smoking yet. I went to Sammy's apartment, and explained to him what had happened to me over the past two days. He thought that I was being paranoid and going crazy, and we started arguing.

"If you believe what you are telling me, then why are you still smoking cigarettes?" he demanded. "Didn't God ask you not to smoke cigarettes?"

As soon as he finished that sentence his phone started ringing; it was his grandmother from back home. Later he told me that he had not talked to his grandmother in over a year. As he spoke with his grandmother, he looked at me with a stunned look on his face and told me, "My grandmother keeps repeating, 'Please don't smoke cigarettes, it's bad for you.'"

He hung up the phone after finishing his conversation, and I could tell that he was overwhelmed. He told me he was supposed to play poker that night, and he didn't want to talk about God or gangsters or anything like that. He just wanted to have a normal night, so he told me not to talk about this matter.

Within seconds his buzzer rang; Sammy was expecting a friend to pick him up to go play poker. He asked his friend to come up for five minutes while he got ready. When Sammy opened the door his friend walked in, overcome by emotions.

"You won't believe what just happened to me!" his friend burst out. "I was just in McDonald's getting food, and as I was paying for my order, a homeless man came up and said, 'Don't worry about it, I got this,' and paid for my food. What the hell, I'm all dressed up, I have a stack of cash in my pocket; why did that happen?"

He was absolutely bewildered.

"You wanted to have a normal night?" I said to Sammy. "Did you see what happened; do you believe me now?" I was convinced, but Sammy was having a tough time processing it all.

I went back to my apartment, thinking about all that had happened. What was my next move? Life had not asked me to stop spending time with the organized crime family members, but had just asked me to stop drinking, smoking, and doing drugs. Life had told me that I was supposed to make a difference in this bad world, so what did that mean? Was I supposed to make a difference in the world of the organized crime families? Or was I supposed to make a difference outside of the family? Maybe I was supposed to learn energy healing, and help heal people's illnesses? I did not know the answer to any of those questions, so I decided to continue everything as I had before, except without smoking, drinking, and doing drugs. With the lifestyle I had then, this was easier said than done; the following three weeks were extremely difficult.

Life communicates with me via the energy of my hands

I noticed that Life had a new way of communicating with me. At that time I was not aware of the different energies in our bodies. Every human being has both cold and hot energy, Yin and Yang. Normally you do not feel the cold energy by itself, but in some instances, such as when you're experiencing muscular or join paint, if you touch the skin surface in that area you can feel that it's slightly colder than other areas. This is due to the excess of cold energy. I started to notice that when I was not supposed to do something, Life released a lot of cold energy through the palms of my both hands. It was a very eerie feeling, but it was very distinct.

From my previous activities I had saved up $70,000 in cash for a rainy day. As soon as I tried to use it, Life released cold energy through the palms of my hands, and I knew I could not use that money because it had come from illegal activities. I had some money stored in a safe house and I left it there. But I took all of the money from my apartment and donated it to a shelter for drug addicts.

Life also released cold energy through the palms of my hands when I tried to have sex with my girlfriend Melanie, as well as when I tried to masturbate. It became clear to me that sexual activities could not be part of my life either.

I really struggled for the first three weeks. I still hung out with other members, but for the most part, I did not do any drugs nor drink any alcohol. I relapsed once, but came home and asked for forgiveness. All the members were surprisingly fine with me not doing drugs; they never once asked me why I had decided to quit or try to encourage me to do it. When we were all together passing around a joint, they would ask me, "Do you want to take a toke?" I would say no, and they would move on to the next person.

Many of the crime family members from different groups approached me about doing business. The offers were substantial. I could have made $20,000 a week if I wanted to, but I kept coming up with excuses. I realized that they knew what was happening to me: they had opened the door for me, but I had not walked through that door yet, I was just on the edge, looking in. I alone could make the decision as to whether to walk through that door or not.

Telly's health improves

After I had worked on Telly three more times, she went to her next session of chemotherapy, where they drew blood to measure the progression of her cancer. Unfortunately, we would not get the results back until the following week, but I could see the difference before and after my sessions with her. It was as if I re-energized her – just like after you replace the weak batteries in a flashlight with new ones, there is a clear difference in performance. I continued working on her until the following week, when she went for another chemotherapy session.

The blood test was a typical one: her blood was tested for levels of specific proteins to determine the progression of cancer. Telly's doctor told her that the count had come down for the first time in a long while. We also noticed that her body was no longer retaining water; slowly, she began to look normal again. This information really motivated me to continue walking the path that Life had set before me, but I had given all my money away and I was running out of funds to support myself. I did not have enough money to pay my rent, and was using my credit cards to buy food. After discussing my situation with my father, he asked me to move back home temporarily, until I figured out what I was supposed to be doing. So I agreed to move back home to my parents' apartment.

THE FIRST PHASE

I had graduated from the British Columbia Institute of Technology with a diploma in electrical engineering and industrial control. My brother-in-law had also graduated from the same program years earlier, and was working for Cummins Engines. He notified me that they were hiring, and that he was the person in charge of the hiring. My brother-in-law told me that if I was interested, the job would be mine, but I would still need to go for an interview, for the sake of appearances.

Beginning to learn to meditate

I mmediately after Life connected to me in December of 2005, I began to repeat the mantra, "Thank you God" to keep myself from going crazy. I was constantly overwhelmed by my thoughts and emotions. I had never meditated before, and I knew nothing about it. I decided to start meditating, as if I had been doing it for a long time. At first, I played meditation music on my CD player and took deep breaths, focusing on the sound and my breathing. I started with just ten minutes at a time, and slowly increased the time in two-minute increments until I reached thirty minutes. I continued using these techniques as many times as possible throughout the day.

Becoming a janitor

O nce while I was meditating, I felt a surge inside of me again. This time, Life asked me not to work as an engineer, but to go to work with my father and become a janitor.

I did not know if I could give up everything in my life to move forward on that path. I had been going out with a beautiful woman, Melanie for about a year and a half. She was a stripper, and I was very much in love with her. Ending my relationship with Melanie, and giving up parties and all my cash, had been hard enough. On top of all that, going to work as a janitor was a big hit to my ego. I went out that night to hang out with the family members again, and I had another relapse.

The next day I got a phone call from a friend who I had not talked to in over a year. She called to see how I was. I did not tell her about any of the events that had happened to me; it was just easier that way. Then suddenly, without any context, she told me that the previous Sunday she had gone to church, after not going for a very long time. She told me that she had talked to her pastor, and he had said, "If you ask God for forgiveness, you will be forgiven. But if you wait too long, it might become too late."

I was no longer surprised to get a message from Life in this way. Life uses this method to communicate with all of us all the time, but sometimes we just don't want to hear it, so we ignore our instincts and the paths that are put before us. I still did not mention anything that had happened to me, but I got the message: that was the last time that I relapsed.

I continued working on Telly, but I was still spending time with the family members, without drinking or doing any drugs. I was also finally able to completely quit smoking. Every week, Telly's cancer blood marker continued to come down. Everything seemed to be working well until about five weeks into my journey, when Telly contacted me and told me that the markers had gone back up that week. I knew that something was wrong, so I meditated and asked for guidance.

"What is it that you want me to do? Just ask me and I'll do it," I asked Life. I felt a surge in me again, and I received a message.

"You cannot be told what to do, because you have to choose this path. In the same way that the organized crime family members could not force you to join them, I cannot force you to choose the light either."

Life also shared with me that if I chose this path I would have to make many more sacrifices, and there would be much pain and suffering before I would reach the light.

This was not just about me; Telly's life was also at stake. I would have given anything to save her life. Without any hesitation, I threw away my cell phone and disconnected myself from all the family members. I began to go to work with my father, and I quickly realized why I needed to do janitorial work. The first reason was to reduce my huge ego; the second reason was that janitorial work was a type of job where I could work by myself. I would try to focus myself while cleaning; it is literally a form of meditation. I could not have achieved the same thing had I worked as an engineer.

I had clarity as to what was expected of me: Life required my complete surrender. I knew that if I chose to walk that path I would have to surrender my will. I agreed and fully committed myself. I promised myself that I would walk the path that Life put before me, without any question or any hesitation, no matter how difficult it might be.

The first step on the path to enlightenment is separation and celibacy. I quickly noticed that Life released cold energy through the palms of my hands as soon as I tried to watch TV or listen to music, letting me know that I needed to cut them out of my life for a period of time. The reason separation is necessary is that we constantly occupy ourselves with something. When we are outside of our homes, we're doing something, then when we come home, we occupy ourselves with watching TV, cooking, cleaning, reading books, and so on.

Because our minds are constantly occupied with distractions, we never have to deal with our thoughts and emotions. But when we unplug ourselves from everything, we allow all our thoughts and negative emotions to come to the surface. With proper meditation techniques we can then release and transform these energies, even if we are not on the path of enlightenment. For this reason, I recommend to everyone to take some time each day, and sit silently to meditate. This will give you time to release and transform harmful energies.

The requirements are greater for someone who is on a path of enlightenment. For this, a minimum separation of two years is necessary. This is the most difficult time on the path to enlightenment. The moment you unplug and separate yourself from everything, all the fears and anger that you have built up throughout your life will tend to come up to the surface all at once. Sexual energy starts to build up inside of you, and you have to be in deep meditation to be able to transform all these energies. Most seekers give up during this time period.

To gain a better understanding of energy healing, I searched for an instructor and found a chi gong master. During our first meeting, I told her my story. Until then, only Telly had believed me. However, the chi gong master also believed me. She was amazed and extremely supportive. Without charging me any money, she enrolled me in her classes.

MY THIRD EYE OPENS

I was now fully committed to this path. Within two weeks, while meditating, I felt a pinch on my forehead. It felt like a vortex opening up in the center of my forehead. The best way that I could describe this feeling is this: it felt as if I had a tornado forming in a single spot in the center of my forehead. I noticed that my hands and feet were getting hot as well. I immediately contacted the chi gong master and went to see her. I described the sensation to her. She was happy and amazed. She told me that my third eye had opened. She explained that third eye is the sixth chakra, but it is usually dormant. This was truly a blessing.

Chakras are Energy Centers that draw universal energy both in and out of our physical body and spiritual energy field. Chakras are vortexes that vibrate at different frequencies. Different chakras with different frequencies connect us to different planes of consciousness with the matching frequency. The higher the frequency of the chakra, the higher the plane of consciousness it connects to. Chakras connect us to different dimensions of the universal consciousness. Each plane of consciousness represents different aspects of All That Exists – which includes you. We are multi-dimensional beings that exist beyond three-dimensional space; unfortunately, we are only aware of a very small part of ourselves. We have seven main chakras and hundreds of minor chakras. I'm going to describe in detail the function of the seven main chakras, with the corresponding layer of our spiritual energy field, later in the book.

I noticed that when I silenced my mind and focused myself on the location of the third eye, the vortex would open. From that point forward, no matter what I was doing, I was always focused on the third eye. As time went by I felt that the opening of the vortex was widening; the tornado-like vortex on my forehead was getting stronger and stronger. I have been able to widen this opening over the years with intense meditation; it has

29

sucked in powerful energy with higher vibrations. Through the third eye, I felt a deep connection with higher consciousness. Life was guiding me through direct contact, and the universe had become my master.

I knew exactly what I needed to do from that point forward. The energy that I was receiving had powerful healing properties: upon giving that energy to any painful area, the pain would simply go away. The healing sessions with Telly were no longer draining me. I also noticed that the third eye was guiding me through the healing sessions. During the sessions I would run my hand over Telly's body, and when I would get to the problem or painful areas, the opening of the third eye would widen, sucking in more energy and allowing me to release more energy through the palms of my hand. Since my third eye had opened, I did not need to continue learning chi gong; I had all the tools that I needed. I only did healing sessions on Telly, family, and friends. Life wanted me to continue working with my father as a janitor, so I did.

When I worked on Telly, I could feel exactly where the tumors were just by running my hand over her body. She got better every week; the cancer markers were decreasing by about 300 points each week.

I want to share an experience that I had while working on Telly. At the time, her cancer markers had come down to 2,372. She was still smoking cigarettes, and we were sitting together talking.

"You know that you eventually need to quit smoking," I said.

"I know, I have to do it," Telly replied. "I promise to quit smoking when the cancer markers get down to 1,000."

I worked on Telly three times as usual that week, and then we went to the hospital for another chemotherapy session. As usual, they drew blood to determine the level of her cancer markers. When we went back to the hospital the following week to get the results, she opened the letter and looked at me with amazement, and then handed it to me. I looked at the paper and saw that the number was exactly 1,000 – not 998, not 1,003, but exactly 1,000!

Obviously this was not just about cancer markers: Life was demonstrating absolute control over what happens in our bodies. Think for a moment about what was required for this to be the exact amount of cancer markers in her entire blood system. We had previously had a decrease of about 300 per week. But during this week there was a decrease of exactly 1,372 to reach a count of 1,000!

I have had hundreds of such experiences since December of 2005, I could write an entire book on this subject alone. You might then wonder, why is the world the way it is, if Life has absolute control over everything? This is a valid question, and I will address this subject in a future section.

Everything was going really well. I had a very strict regimen and was learning new material every day. Without anybody ever teaching me anything about meditation or reading anything about it, I was trying different meditation techniques. One day I was practicing a particular breathing technique where I would take a very deep breath and hold it as long as I could. Then while I was holding my breath, I would focus my attention on a single point to keep my mind as silent as possible and to lower my heart rate. I had become so good at this that I could take a breath and hold it for about fifty seconds, for a period of half an hour continuously.

During one of these meditation sessions, I felt my mind becoming very silent and could not feel any tension in my body. The amount of time between each breath kept getting longer and longer, and suddenly I felt my consciousness lifting out of my body for a moment. Unfortunately, I did not know what was happening, so I took a breath, and stopped the meditation. I had to go to work with my father, but I noticed something different right away: there were absolutely no thoughts in my mind the entire night, without any effort; it was absolute bliss.

There were no thoughts, no negative feelings, nor any tension whatsoever. I was not in the future, nor was I in the past; I was present and alert. I felt so blissful that it did not matter that I was cleaning toilets and doing janitorial work. It was by far one of the best nights of my life. The universe wanted me to experience pure silence. In Buddhism they call this "nirvana" and in Sanskrit they call it "Samadhi."

I had been able to silence my mind for short periods of time before, but this had always required tremendous effort, and I could never rid myself of tension. I was so happy that I thought I would go back and repeat that experience again.

The following days I tried repeatedly to experience the same event by practicing the same meditation technique, but no matter how hard I tried, it did not happen again. In frustration I sat silently and asked for guidance, and I received a message:

"A drop of water can reach the ocean through the rain, but it can also reach the ocean through the river. The path of the river is dangerous and has many curves, ups and downs. A drop of water that reaches the ocean through the rain will never learn the path of the river."

I realized that I needed to learn how to reach that state of consciousness through an inner journey; I needed to learn how to silence my mind. Life communicated to me that in order to reach that state of consciousness, I needed to rid myself of all greed and desires. I needed to fully surrender myself without any fears, and free myself of all negative emotions.

Desire is a negative emotion

Desire is a negative emotion because when you desire an object (or even love), the focal point of your happiness is always in the future. When your happiness is dependent on obtaining love (or a desired object), you are not looking for someone to love because you're ready to give, you're looking for someone to love you because you are missing something. You feel incomplete, and that is not true love. True love can only be experienced when you achieve complete contentment in your life. When you're not missing anything, you can give without expecting anything in return; your love is unconditional.

A desiring mind can never become silent, because the object of any desire is always in the future. You're always thinking about the time when you have obtained the desired object, or you imagine different scenarios that might happen when you have achieved your desire. For example, if you desire to be with a beautiful woman, or a handsome man, you imagine going out on a date with them, or having sex with them, and so on; you're always dreaming about the future.

How to silence your mind

The only way your mind can become silent and achieve true bliss is to be content with what is now, not with what could be. This is not to say that you cannot be creative, but creativity should come from a place of contentment, not from your fears or desires. I explore this further later in the book.

Surrender can mean different things to different people, depending on where they are in their spiritual development. A seeker who wants to become enlightened has to surrender him or herself to a master. The master takes responsibility to direct the seeker in the right direction. I surrendered myself to the universe, so I follow the path that the universe has put forth before me. To reach that level of understanding, you need to have had a significant experience with All That Exists. Tremendous trust is required to give up making decisions in your life, but something amazing happens when you do. Most human minds are always working, and assessing different scenarios in order to make any decisions. Once you give up making decisions, your mind has nothing else to do, so it becomes silent. But you do need to have the ability to see the patterns of the events that are happening in your life. You need to be able to recognize the direction that the universe has put before you, and be brave enough to follow it. Not everyone who sees the path will walk along it.

When making any decision, put aside all your fears, and listen to everyone who is talking to you. If multiple people are telling you the same thing, or you see a sign on the street as you're passing by, or you are flipping through TV channels and suddenly there is a program or a movie relating to your situation, the universe is trying to tell you something. But more importantly, trust your instincts – remember that all the answers are within you. You are God's consciousness, so trust yourself.

I continued to focus on my meditation, from morning to night. I had made great progress in silencing my mind. Besides my strict regimen, I took Telly to the hospital once a week for her chemotherapy session. At one of these sessions, we got the good news from her doctor that her cancer markers had come down to 360. At that rate, she was likely to be cancer-free in one or two more weeks.

Telly's health declines

I always gave energy to Telly the day after her chemotherapy session, because the session always made her very weak. But when I did our next energy session, I got an unpleasant surprise. As soon as I went to run my hand over her body, Life released cold energy through the palms of my hand.

I could not understand why this was happening, because Life only released cold energy through the palms of my hand when I was not supposed to do something. I went to my room and meditated, and asked for clarification. I received a message from Life that I was never meant to save Telly, she was meant to save me. I was also informed that she would not survive the cancer. Life knew that I would not have had the strength to make those changes for myself; I only had the strength to do it to save her life. My love for Telly pulled me through my darkest days, but I was now ready to walk the path on my own.

This was a very hard pill to swallow. Part of me felt cheated; I had done everything that was asked of me. I could see no reason why she had to die, but part of me knew that there is a reason for everything. Life was also testing me to see if I would follow the specific instruction given to me, even if it meant Telly's death. I had been given access to the energy of the sixth plane of consciousness, and I had to prove that I would follow Life's command before I would be given access to the seventh plane of consciousness, which is the ultimate.

I battled with my thoughts day and night. There was nothing I could have done; I could not go against Life's command. I did the best I could to keep my mind silent. There was no doubt in my mind that regardless of what happened, I was going to continue on this path. I obeyed and did not give energy to Telly any more, but part of me was bitter, and angry.

The following week when we went to the hospital, we got bad news: the doctor told us that her cancer markers had gone back up by about 300 points. From that point on, the count continued to increase every week. I was hoping that this was just going to be a test, and that somehow at the end, Life would miraculously save Telly's life, but it was not so. She died in September of 2006, on a day that was by far the worst day in our family's life.

Life gives us challenges

I had suffered a major back injury in 1996, but after extensive rehabilitation, I had not experienced any pain since 1999. But the very next day after Telly's death, my back pain returned. I had a

As I said at the beginning, I have dedicated this book to the memory of my sister Telly. My love for her motivated me to leave the organized crime family so I could continue to give her energy and save her life. I would not be where I am, if not for her. This picture was taken in June of 2006, three months before she passed away. She never lost the sparkle in her eyes and always managed to smile, even though she was receiving massive doses of chemotherapy at the time.

realization as to why these events were happening. As we go through our life, we suppress our hate, fears, and anger. Life gives us opportunities to bring these energies up to the surface through negative experiences, so we can learn to deal with them. Over time we get better at dealing with some challenges, and we suppress them again, eventually getting to a point that the events are no longer challenging. Life responds by raising the level of the game – by giving you new challenges. These events could be physical injuries, financial difficulties, or any type of negative experiences.

Imagine you are a glass of water, with the glass being your body, and your energy field being the water. But imagine there is dirt mixed with this water and the water is murky. Now if you wait long enough, the dirt that is mixed with water is going to sink to the bottom of the glass, and the water is going to seem very clear, but the dirt will still be there. To get the dirt out, Life takes a stick and stirs the water to bring the dirt back up, so we can work through those issues and remove the dirt for good. This is why every time we think our life has settled down, events happen to turn everything upside down again. The only way we can get the mud out of the water is by bringing it up to the surface. It is the only way our souls can become crystallized.

Unfortunately, we constantly add mud to the water, by being fearful and getting angry in our daily life. It's a vicious cycle that can go on for thousands of lifetimes. The good news is, there is no time limit for us to reach the light: we will all get there. However, you can learn techniques to prevent adding additional mud to the water, and help to get the existing mud out of the water.

MEDITATION IS THE KEY TO LIVING A HEALTHY LIFE

Meditation is the key to living a healthy life. Most people associate meditation with relaxation, but this could not be further from the truth. Relaxation is only the by-product of meditation. In fact, meditation and focus affect every aspect of your life.

Meditation is a state of consciousness, where there are no thoughts. Without any effort, you are fully aware, alert, and present. You're not in the past, nor are you projecting into the future. Fully alert, you are ready to experience whatever comes your way. You have transcended beyond the positive and negative. All the negative emotions such as fear, anger, and hate have transformed into faith, fearlessness, compassion, and love. Your creativity is overflowing, even though you're not projecting by thinking about the future. This is Nirvana, this is God's consciousness, absolute bliss.

The goal of meditation

The goal of meditation is to give you the ability to silence your mind and focus your consciousness. Let us look at the effect of focus and meditation in our daily life.

Recall a time when you were studying or preparing for an exam. How many times did you have to re-read a paragraph because halfway through you realized you had no idea what you had just read. This happens because you were thinking about something else, so you had to go back and start from the beginning again. Could you imagine how much faster you could have got through the material if you had better focus, and were able to silence your mind?

37

I am amazed that our school systems do not teach children and teenagers how to focus themselves. Attention deficit disorder, or ADD, is one of the most common problems in younger students. But instead of teaching these children how to focus, they are put on medication; in fact, all they need is to learn techniques on how to focus themselves. Having a better focus could be very beneficial through high school, college, and university.

Playing sports can really help the focus of children and teenagers because it is a natural form of meditation. And having better focus can help elevate their game in any type of sport. Unfortunately, children and teenagers are more interested in spending time on social media and video games, rather than involving themselves in sports. It is the responsibility of all parents to help their children to better balance their lives.

When you develop the ability to silence your mind, you can give all your attention to the task at hand. This applies to almost everyone who is doing almost any type of work. Focus affects every aspect of our daily life, and this is not a coincidence.

Consciousness manifests the physical word through focus. From the time that we are very young, we start thinking and projecting ourselves into the future. Unfortunately, our focus is very weak when we are younger. This is why if you ask a six-year-old what they want to do when they get older, you find they are constantly changing their mind. One day they want to become a pilot; the next day they want to become a firefighter or a doctor.

As we grow older, our focus improves through playing sports, studying at school, and various types of activities that require close attention. However, not everyone improves at the same rate. Some very young teenagers have a clear idea of what they want to do as adults; they are better at organizing their thoughts into action. Others with weaker focus struggle through high school and as young adults. This issue usually resolves itself in the late twenties, but sometimes it continues into the thirties and forties. We have all come across people who just can't get it together, which is why it is critical for parents to teach their teenagers how to focus and meditate.

You have to understand that we manifest our physical life through consciousness. Once you focus your consciousness on a single matter, your energy begins to vibrate that idea to the universe. Focus is like a magnifying glass: if there is no focal point, the universe cannot lock onto that vibration. However, if you can keep vibrating that idea, the universe will put in place the sequence of events where that idea can become reality, but it takes time for this process to take place. You need to remain focused and put sufficient effort behind the idea to make it into reality.

In order to successfully manifest an idea into reality, you must first evaluate yourself to see if you are physically and mentally ready to take up the challenge of that particular goal. It is very important to be one hundred percent honest with yourself. Meditation and focus will give you the discipline and the work ethic that you need to bring your ideas into reality.

One last thing to consider is that what we want to manifest must align with our life path. Try to focus on things that will help you evolve, rather than focusing on financial gain. If you are passionate about something and are focused on evolving yourself, you will become successful and the financial gain will be the by-product of your success.

The six different kinds of thoughts that you need to become aware of

You must first learn about the different types of thoughts and your own distinct thought patterns, in order to have a better understanding of how your mind works.

I call the first type of thoughts random thoughts, because you randomly jump from one thought to another thought without any particular pattern. Any object, person, or a situation can trigger the start of these thoughts. For example, you're walking down a street and you suddenly see a vehicle, which is the same color, make, and model as your friend's car. This triggers a thought about an event that you both went to together, which might make you think about something that happened at that event, and so on. These random thoughts are the most useless type of thoughts, because they serve no purpose and go nowhere in particular.

The second type of thought pattern relates to the things that you're supposed to be doing within a week of the present time, called daily activity thoughts. You might have some thoughts about having a conversation with someone, going to work or school, or errands that need to be done at home. You might have up to fifteen or twenty thoughts that recycle in your mind over and over again until the task is done, by which time you have probably added new ones. There is no point in having these thoughts either. You already know the tasks that need to be done, thinking about doing them twenty times is not going to change anything.

The third type of thoughts are interactive thoughts. This type of thought could be either beneficial or menacing to your mind. For example, if you are going to an interview, you imagine what questions might be asked of you, and you answer them in your mind. You imagine interacting with the interviewer. You go on interacting with your thoughts for many hours, in order to prepare yourself, which could prove to be very beneficial as it will prepare you for different scenarios.

On the other hand, if you get into an argument with someone at work, after the initial interaction, you start thinking in your head that I should have said this or I should have done that. You might imagine different scenarios where each one of you would say or do a different thing. Then you might remember a past event and think that you should have brought it up. The initial interaction could have been just a minor disagreement, but because you interact with your thoughts in this way, you give more energy to these negative feelings and the anger keeps growing inside of you. These energies are stored in different parts of your body and create blocks that prevent the movement of energy, which is detrimental to your overall well-being. With the help of meditation and focus, you can immediately stop and redirect your thoughts, before they become inflamed.

The fourth type of thoughts are creative thoughts. Creative thoughts are very important in the creative process. For example, you're planning to open a new business. You start thinking about what is required to get it done. You think about materials, people that you need to see, plans, and so on, and put them together in your mind. One thing to know is that every human being is creative in their own way. A person's creative talents may lie in business, work, poetry, writing, sports, or many other things.

The reason so many people are not successful in their life is due to the fact that they spend most of their life in the prison of their own mind. This state of imprisonment persists because they're not able to control and manage their thoughts. You have to develop the ability to direct, control, and manage your thoughts. The biggest power a human being can acquire is the ability to silence their mind: shut down all the random thoughts, the daily activity thoughts, the negative interactive thoughts, and all thoughts that arise from fear. Only when these disruptive thoughts are controlled can you then focus all your energy into creative thoughts, allowing your creativity to have a chance to flourish. Any time spent on those other thoughts is a complete waste of time and energy.

Your creativity comes from the source itself. These thoughts are not generated from any part of your brain, they come from your direct connection with your higher self. Once you silence your mind, the fourth chakra becomes hyperactive and strengthens this connection, and your creativity can flourish in that environment. I will be discussing the functions of the seven main chakras later in the book.

Creative thoughts come from a universal field. Our core energy is vibrating at a specific frequency at a specific time. Just like a channel that tunes on a specific frequency on a radio, you are also tuned to receive your creative thoughts directly from the source.

The fifth type of thoughts are daydreaming thoughts. These thoughts are by far the most detrimental to your wellbeing, because they directly affect your happiness. Creative thoughts and daydreaming thoughts both use the power of imagination, but with one big difference. Creative thoughts are used to manifest ideas into reality by going through the creative process from the bottom to the top. This is similar to building a concrete building from the first floor to the top. The daydreaming thoughts are thoughts that you have about something without going through the creative process, which is the cornerstone building block of creating anything. You daydream about being rich and driving a nice car, or being with a beautiful partner, or being in a powerful position – but all without seeing yourself taking the necessary steps to get there. These daydreams are just illusions that you use to escape from the reality of your life. Your life cannot possibly compete with these illusions, so you always have to come back to reality – and that can cause discontentment, unrest, and sadness in your life. You have to learn how to use your imagination productively by focusing yourself on the process, rather than focusing on the end result. This is why so many people cannot manifest their ideas into reality. Metaphorically, you have to see yourself take one step at a time and build the concrete building from the first floor to the top.

The last type of thoughts are the thoughts that come from your center, which is your higher self. These are called central thoughts. When you are in turmoil, or dealing with a significant situation, or having an epiphany or suddenly come to a realization, you might be thinking out loud, or you might start talking to yourself. Listen to the voice that is coming from inside of you, because it is coming from your center, from the source itself. We often don't pay attention when we are thinking out loud inside. We may not utter any words, but if you pay attention, even though no sound is coming out, your tongue is still moving. You are literally talking to yourself. These thoughts are coming from your center, not your head. So when you are thinking out loud inside, pay attention to what it is that you are telling yourself, because your higher self is communicating with you, and your higher self is God's consciousness.

The inner workings of our minds

Your soul has lived many lives, and carries with it the combined experiences of all those past lives. Your soul vibrates through your center; you can feel its presence with your entire being. If you learn to connect to that part of yourself, you do not need any guidance from anybody else. This force trumps all else, so listen to it. When you have a thought or experience an event and feel the hairs on your arm rising, your center is vibrating that thought.

I now want to discuss the inner workings of our minds and how we project into the past and the future. Your eyes act like the mouse of a computer. Depending on if you are thinking about the past or imagining something in the future, your eyes will look up to a different part of your brain to access consciousness relating to that experience or thought. For that reason, when you talk to someone, they are constantly moving their eyes. Even if you watch someone who is dreaming, their eyes are constantly moving.

Consciousness is connected to your physical body through your nervous system. Your past experiences are energies that occupy part of your consciousness. They are not permanent but depending on the event, you could hold onto these energies for a long period of time.

Let me give you an example: when someone is telling a story about a fight or terrifying experience that they have had in the past, as they begin to tell the story you can see them breathing faster, you can feel their anger and anxiety coming out. That experience has its own energy; it is a live event. The consciousness is literally projecting itself into the past when we activate thoughts relating to those experiences. It is similar to when you watch a movie in a theatre. We project those energies onto the screen of consciousness and we immediately store them back in the same location in our bodies.

When you're experiencing negative emotions on a regular basis for whatever reason, such energies can bond together and form a block that restricts the flow of energy in that area, which can result in emotional distress or physical illnesses. Emotional distress is the most common cause of physical illnesses. Physical illnesses can be resolved with medication and physical therapy, but if you do not address the underlying conditions that cause those illnesses, they return or manifest themselves in a different form of illness. This is why meditation is so important for both your emotional and physical wellbeing.

We are emotional beings by nature and unfortunately controlling our emotions, particularly negative ones, is extremely difficult. All negative emotions are caused by our conditioning and feeling of separation from one another, and from All That Exists.

We always respond to every situation with an emotional reaction, which is to be expected because our conditioning starts from the moment that we are born. The only way an infant can communicate when he or she needs something is through crying to show distress. Unfortunately, children never truly let go of this bad habit, even after learning to communicate through language, it continues through our adulthood. So the next time you're in a situation where you're not happy about something that is happening, remember your negative emotion response is due to your past conditioning from your childhood.

Conditioning is a necessary part of our development. As we grow older, different forces in our lives shape our character – and genetics, parents, and siblings have the biggest effects. Our friends and teachers, as well as the influences of different cultures, make up the rest. All these forces help us to individualize ourselves from other people. To a certain extent they define who we are, but the truth of the matter is, we are not

defined by our past experiences. We are not the personality or the ego –
you are only experiencing this character. You can become alert and deny
your conditioning to control your responses. It is not necessary, indeed it
is detrimental, to have an emotional reaction in every situation.

While conditioning helps us to develop our individuality, it is also the
cause of our fears, anger, and other negative emotions. For example, when
someone dies, we see that everyone is crying and sad, so we become fearful
of death. If your family experienced financial difficulties throughout your
childhood, you may always worry about not having enough money when
you are older.

We see how our parents use anger when dealing with disagreements,
so as adults we have the same emotional outbursts when we disagree
with others. When you come into any situation, instead of allowing your
conditioning to control your response, allow your center to guide you in
that moment. Our conditioning is deep, and change will be difficult, but
by becoming aware in the moment and developing the right techniques,
you can change any aspect of your personality.

When you come across any situation, the most important thing
to remember is to control your initial reaction. Do not allow your
conditioning to dictate your response, become aware in that moment.
Awareness gives you the time to analyze the situation. Try to see other
people's conditioning – understanding their conditioning will help you
overcome yours. Let's look at some examples.

Imagine you are working at a company and your boss is rude and
disrespectful, and every day you come home upset because of his behavior.
Ask yourself, "Why is he behaving that way?"

He is behaving badly because of his conditioning. He is rude and
disrespectful because he feels weak and insecure in his own life. If he
felt strong and was assured of himself, he would not need to be rude
to assert his dominance. His attacks on you are not personal and have
nothing to do with you. He's literally transferring his negative energy of
being weak on to you by saying something rude and disrespectful. When
you get angry, even if you don't say anything, you receive that energy. You
may even go home and pass this energy on to your family, or you may go
to sleep upset every night.

Using mantras

U sing mantras in such situations is extremely helpful. The next time someone says something rude and disrespectful, say to yourself: "I am strong and unbreakable." Always make the mantra a positive sentence rather than a negative sentence such as, "I am not weak." This is just an example, make your own mantras and choose sentences that resonate and have the biggest effect on you. We are all different, so different mantras will work for different people.

Remember that you are God's consciousness, so you are strong and unbreakable. When you keep repeating that sentence you identify with your higher self, which is the bigger part of you, not the part that is in your head. Do not expect an immediate change, it may take some time to break your conditioning. Remain calm throughout the bad behavior, repeating the sentence several times. In doing so, you reflect his or her negative energy back to him or her. When people get angry with you, if you can control yourself and remain calm, they become even more frustrated and angry, because their negative energy gets reflected right back to them.

Remember that you cannot change anybody else's behavior. You cannot break their conditioning by arguing with them about their behavior. You only have control over how you're going to react in any negative situation, so instead of arguing with them or getting angry, change your experience of that interaction by remaining calm and silent.

The important part in any interaction is for you not to get angry. Be aware in that moment, see the flaws in the people that you are dealing with, see their conditioning, change your experience of that event and focus on breaking your conditioning. A tremendous amount of growth follows if you can overcome this obstacle. You can transcend experiencing negative emotions if you continuously work at it. This is the biggest hurdle you need to overcome in your spiritual development.

Always remember that the person you are upset with is you in a different form. We are all one, and there is no point being angry with yourself. This is why when two people are arguing, both parties always end up with bad energies at the end of the argument. Nobody has ever won an argument in human history, both sides always lose. So ask yourself, why fight a battle that you cannot possibly win? If someone is trying to pick a fight with you, let them get riled up, don't give them anything to hit back, and they will eventually tire themselves out. I am not saying not to defend yourself if someone is physically assaulting you, but if someone is rude and disrespectful verbally they cannot hurt you. The power goes to the person who can control themselves emotionally.

One of the most famous lines that Jesus said was: "Love your neighbors as you would love yourselves." Why do you think Jesus said that? Was it because he was a great man? He was in fact a great man, but that's not why he said it. He said it because he had come to the realization that he and his neighbor are one and the same. If you have realized this fact you have become enlightened.

How to overcome anger

To overcome anger, you need to understand where your anger is coming from. Anger is a type of energy that builds up inside of you from a very young age. The energy of all the events where you have had an argument is all inside of you. When someone does something that makes you angry, the event triggers the accumulated energy, and it all comes out at once. It is like opening a storage room door that has been overfilled with garbage. The moment you open the door, all the garbage spills out. Your anger reacts in exactly the same way.

Just as fast as the anger comes out, you pull it back in. You sometimes even surprise yourself with the amount of anger that has come out. You need to get rid of this accumulated energy through activities. Here are some of the activities you can do:

- **Intense physical exercise**. When you do intense physical exercise, your heart beats faster, and at the same time you take deeper breaths. This causes your chakras to open up and freely move universal energy throughout your body. This is like taking a pressure washer and cleansing your systems. This method will help with current and recent episodes of anger situations, but will not be as effective for the older events.
- **Self-healing techniques such as chi gong and Tai Chi**. These self-healing techniques have been specifically developed to help strengthen your energy field and help the movement of energy throughout your

body. You can focus and meditate while you are practicing these self-healing techniques. In addition, they are very effective in preventing different kind of illnesses. I have personally tried both and found that both have an incredible effect in the movement of energy.

- **Meditation**. It is only through meditation that you can go deep enough into the past and pull out all the conflicts that you have experienced since childhood. On many occasions when I have sat in deep meditation, I have suddenly recalled an event that happened when I was ten years old, and had an argument with another student, or felt anger towards my father for his strict discipline. You do not need to spend thousands of dollars on therapists and counselors if you meditate regularly. I will teach you specific meditation techniques to help release these energies.

There are also some techniques that you can use. If you have problems controlling your anger, the first thing you need to understand about anger is that it has a particular energy that can only become active if you're breathing faster with a higher heart rate. Your heartbeat and your breathing go hand to hand. If your heart beats faster, you breathe faster, and if you breathe deeper and slower, your heart beats at a slower rate. We have all heard people saying, "Take a deep breath!" when someone is getting angry, but it never works because one deep breath is not enough.

Take a deep breath, but don't breathe out right away. Hold onto your breath as long as you can (without it getting uncomfortable), then let it out, and repeat until your heartbeat slows down. You cannot be angry when you are breathing slowly, it is not possible. If you can control your breathing you can control your anger.

People who have serious problems with their anger should always carry a small paper bag in their pocket. As soon as you feel your anger coming out, start breathing into the paper bag. As oxygen gets depleted in the bag, your brain senses the oxygen deprivation and sends a signal to your heart, lung, and brain to slow down in order to conserve oxygen. Once you feel you are breathing normally, stop breathing into the bag. Do not wait too long; you just need to breathe at a slower rate. The same technique also works for people who suffer from panic attacks.

How to overcome your fears

Fear, anger, and sadness are the most dominant among negative emotions. Fear of death is the mother of all of our fears. This fear goes deeper when we experience a death in our family. As we grow older, we never think about or see ourselves dying, we keep suppressing the fear of death more and more. This suppression causes energy to manifest itself in different types of fears. Imagine if you were one hundred percent certain that you will never die. In that case, what would you be really afraid of? Nothing! And the truth is that you will never die! How can you be afraid of anything, when you are All That Exists?

There are things you can do to help overcome your fears, but first you need to understand that there is no way to overcome your fears without facing them head on. The best thing that you can do is to get ready for it. Just like anger, fear has its own energy, and when you suppress this energy it becomes a block and restricts the flow of energy in your body, resulting in physical illness or emotional distress. The fear of not having enough money is the most common fear among people, and results in back pain. It is no surprise that almost 70% of people experience back pain at some point in their lifetime, and that it usually happens within two to three years of experiencing financial difficulties.

Life will continuously put you in situations where you are facing your fears, in order to help you overcome them, and they will not go away until you are no longer afraid of them. This could become a vicious cycle. For example, if you are worried about not having enough money, your possessions might keep breaking down. Events might happen that cause you to constantly struggle with money, and those events keep feeding your fears. As a result, instead of overcoming your fears, you become more fearful.

You can use mantras to help break these vicious cycles. Remember it does not matter how long you have been struggling with financial difficulties – what matters is how you feel while these events are happening. To change how you feel, repeat a positive mantra such as, "I am strong, and I can overcome any obstacle." Keep repeating it throughout the day. When you repeat a mantra over and over again, it goes deep into your consciousness. Once that happens, the fear will disappear, and once the fear is gone, the experience of financial difficulties will end, because it is no longer necessary. Life only gives you the experiences you need to help you evolve spiritually.

You need to be vigilant when using mantras, because your fears are deep, so stay with it until you get to the other side. These techniques are very useful, but it's like trying to put a nail in a coffin using only your hands. You need a hammer to get through your past conditioning at a faster rate, and that hammer is meditation. Meditation gives you the ability to redirect your thoughts. The best outcome is to silence the thought completely, but if you're not at a point in your meditation where you can do that, focus on saying the mantra and staying with positive thoughts.

You are a resilient creature, and capable of overcoming immense tribulation in your lifetime. You are God's consciousness; nothing can touch you. Mindset is everything in these scenarios, make peace with the worst case scenario. Remain at peace with yourself, and connect to the bigger part of you. You're not alone, the universe is with you every step of the way.

Remember that all negative emotions come from separation from one another, and from All That Exists. In every situation in which you have a negative feeling, you are feeling separated from someone or from existence. When you're arguing with someone, you are feeling separated from them, you don't see their point of view. When you are experiencing financial difficulties you are fearful of not having enough money. You feel separated from existence, but you are All That Exists; there is only one of us. There is no point being angry with someone. You are not separated from them; you have chosen everything that you are experiencing.

How to deal with sadness and depression

Sadness is another common negative emotion. Prolonged sadness can turn into depression. Depression can be caused by mental illness, which is the result of a chemical imbalance in the brain, or it can be caused by repeated negative experiences or physical pain.

In the case of chemical imbalance, a medical professional might find it necessary to prescribe medication, but there are still things that you can do to improve the situation. The depression that is caused by repeated negative experiences and physical pain can be addressed without the use of medication.

You cannot get away from your negative thoughts when you're depressed. You cannot change the subject in your mind. The more time you spend on your negative thoughts the deeper your depression goes. Using mantras that focus on positive thoughts could be an effective way to battle depression. Think of things in your life that give you joy, and focus on those things. Create a mantra for yourself that reminds you of the things that you are grateful for. Obviously if you meditate and improve your focus, these mantras will become much more effective. If you can control your thoughts, you can control your depression.

Often when you feel down or are in physical pain, your mind does not want to deal with your current condition and how you're feeling in that moment, so your mind starts to project into the future. You start imagining situations where you are happy and not in pain, but you keep coming back to your suffering and become more frustrated. The best thing to do in those situations is to change your mind set.

Sit in meditation posture next time you're feeling down (we will discuss these postures), and take long deep breaths, in and out as slowly as possible. Focus on this thought: "Things are not good right now and that's okay. It's okay to feel down, I'm strong and nothing can hurt me." Stay with that thought for ten minutes, keep repeating it, and make peace with your situation. Suddenly you will start to feel better. The pain will still be there, but you will be able to tolerate it much better.

I have said this many times, and I will say it again: you are God's consciousness. You are beyond pain and suffering, nothing can hurt you. You are above and beyond everything that exists in this reality. Stay with that thought, and remember that your suffering is only a moment in time.

Another thing you need to know about mood is that like everything else in this reality, mood continuously swings between happy and sad. It is the nature of the world that we are living in. It is the law of the world of duality. This swing is dependent on the constant changes of the planetary systems. It is the effect of the moving planets in our solar system on our energy field. The science of astrology is based on the movement of these planets.

For an average person, this swing is mild; for people with depression this swing is more pronounced; for people who suffer from bipolar

happiness

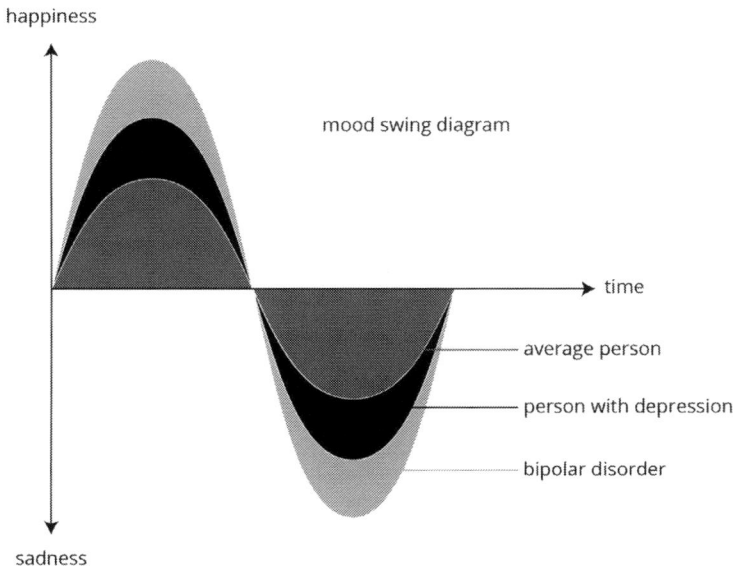

mood swing diagram

time

average person

person with depression

bipolar disorder

sadness

Mood swing diagram

disorder the mood swings are much more extreme. Their mood swings between extreme happiness, and tremendous sadness.

When you feel down, just remember that the pendulum will swing the other way. No one is always happy and no one is always sad, so the key is to be okay with both. Physical exercise, meditation, chi gong, and Tai Chi will all improve energy flow, and cause our bodies to release endorphins. Endorphins are hormones that make us feel better, improve our mood, increase pleasure, and minimize pain.

You can stabilize your mood swings if you include more of these activities in your life. At some point if you make more of an effort in your meditation, you can transcend beyond positive and negative. That is the goal of spirituality.

I have talked about how meditation can affect our everyday life. Let's explore how meditation directly influences your energy field.

The frequency of your spiritual energy is dependent on your breathing and your heartbeat. Breathing and heartbeat are dependent on your level of physical activity and your thought patterns in that moment. Generating thoughts requires an incredible amount of energy. In fact, your heart and brain burn more calories than any other organ in your body.

You can bring your heart rate down if you slow down your breathing and silence your mind. There's also a lot of emphasis on being still while meditating because if there is any movement, muscles that support that movement burn calories, which results in your heart beating faster to provide nutrients and oxygen.

The goal of meditation is to reduce the heart rate and reduce the number of breaths, which reduces the thought processes and increases the frequency at which your energy is vibrating. Enlightenment happens when your core energy is vibrating at the same frequency as God's consciousness.

When your mind is silenced, your heart rate and breathing slow down – and the reverse is also true. If you take deeper breaths and slow down your breathing, your heart rate drops, and your thought processes will come to a halt. You might ask, why does that matter?

CHAKRAS AND SEVEN STATES OF CONSCIOUSNESS

Your aura is like a shield around your center, and consists of multiple layers that lie on top of each other. When you are generating more thoughts in your mind, the third chakra, which is responsible for thinking processes, becomes hyperactive. This causes your energy to focus on the third layer. When you take deeper breaths and slow down your heartbeat, two things happen. Firstly, your chakras open up more and draw more energy into your energy field. The second effect of lower heart rate and deeper breathing is that they increase the vibration of your energy. Your center begins to get focused on the higher chakras with the higher vibrations.

The higher chakras have higher frequencies and the bodies of those centers are connected to the higher spiritual realms and dimensions. The seventh layer is the cosmic body, which is the universal consciousness. The higher the frequency of your vibration, the closer you are to God's consciousness, which is your higher self. When the frequency of your consciousness equals the frequency of your higher self, the aura disappears, and you become one with your higher self, which is All That Exists. Jesus describes this as: "I and the father are one." We can all experience that state of consciousness through various disciplines and intense meditation.

However, this is an extremely difficult process. In order to achieve that state of consciousness you need to completely stop all thoughts and become silent without any effort. You can only become one with the universe when your energy has become crystallized and pure. In that state the ego is dropped: you are not in the past, nor projecting into the future, and the "I" completely disappears.

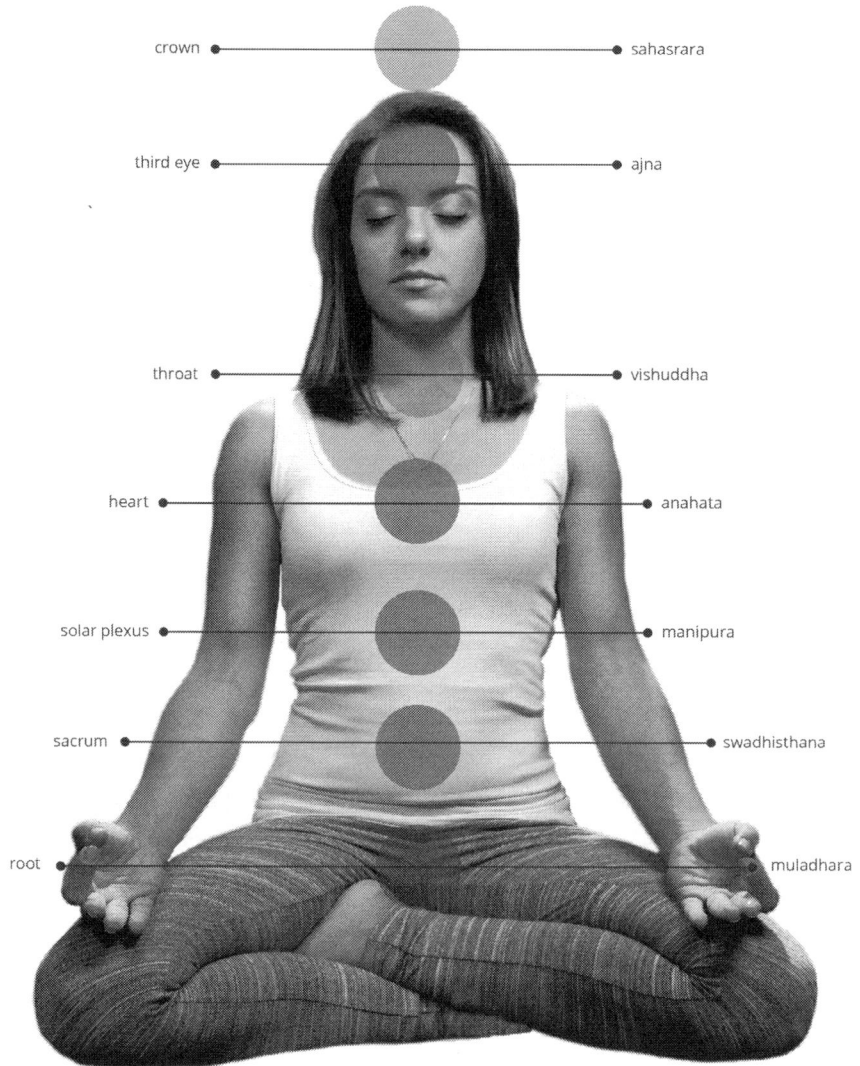

Name and location of the seven main chakras

Let me explain this better. If I ask you to tell me who you are, you're going to tell me where you were born, what schools you went to, what your job is, or you might tell me what your future plans are, and so on.

We are only different in the past and in the future. In the present moment, the "I" does not exist. If you can focus all of your consciousness on the present moment, and do not identify yourself with the past or the future, the ego disappears, the aura drops, and you become one with All That Exists. I want to remind everyone that All That Exists includes every human being on this planet. There are many people who talk about spirituality and getting close to God, yet they put so many barriers between themselves and the people around them. You cannot become enlightened and get close to God if you cannot embrace every segment of the population. That includes the best and the worst of humanity because we are all one, and there is only one of us.

We are multi-dimensional beings, meaning we exist in higher dimensions, but we're not aware of these other parts of ourselves. Unfortunately, Hollywood has given us the wrong idea about other dimensions. If I ask you what a higher dimension means to you, you may think that there is another you in a parallel universe, but that is not the case. The only way to describe higher dimensions using language, is by allowing you to compare yourself in two dimensions, and three dimensions.

You are experiencing your physical body in a three-dimensional world. Now imagine for a moment what you would have experienced of yourself in a two-dimensional world. Imagine if you could slice yourself into ten thousand layers, each one having a width, and depth. The height will be so small that for all intents and purposes we can call it zero. So you in two dimensions will be one of those slices. So imagine if you are one of those slices in two dimensions, you would have no idea about the rest of you in the third dimension. What you would experience of yourself is All That Exists within that single slice, but you are so much more than that single slice. That single slice is only 0.0001% of you, so just imagine who you are in the fourth and the fifth dimensions. You are so much more than what you see in the mirror.

We have seven main chakras within the three-dimensional space and have many more that open up in the fourth and fifth dimension, but I want to focus on the first seven.

Our spiritual energy field is made up of many layers that lie on top of each other. Each layer has its own energy center, vibrating at its own frequency. We are only discussing the first seven layers in this book. The first and the seventh centers are single centers, but the second through the sixth open both on the front and the back side.

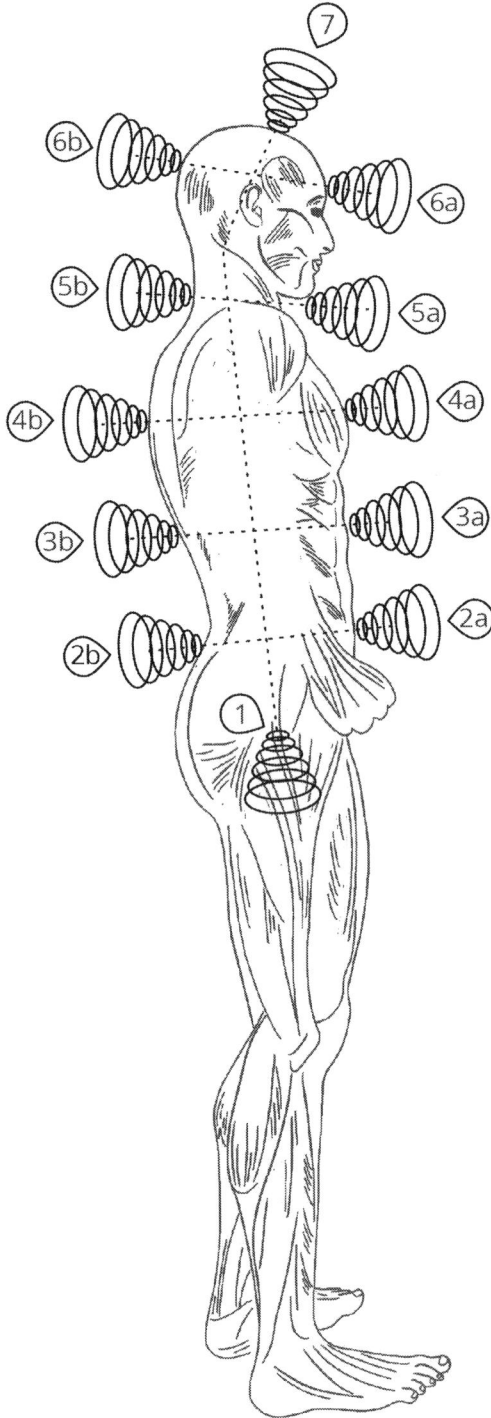

Side view of the seven main chakras, both front and back

cosmic body

celestial body

spiritual body

astral body

mental body

emotional body

etheric body

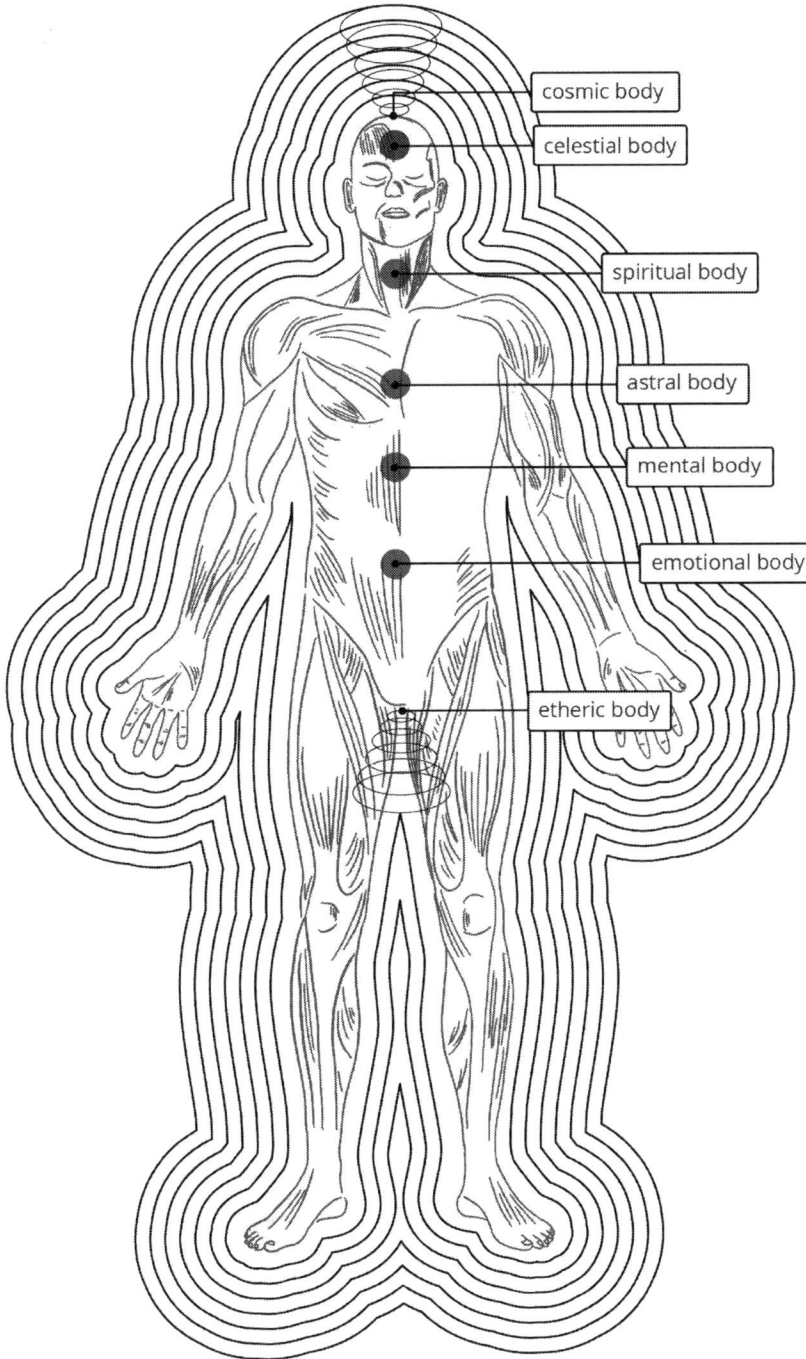

Location of the seven main chakras with their corresponding layer of spiritual energy field

All the energy centers are constantly exchanging energy with the universal energy field. There are passageways between the layers, but they are usually dormant. You can open these passageways with energy purification and meditation. In fact, the goal of enlightenment is for all the layers to become one. Each of these layers represents a state of consciousness. Depending on what we are experiencing or thinking at any one time, we're identifying with different aspects of our consciousness. The first three layers and their centers are tuned in with physical and emotional experiences, but the energy of these layers could be transformed into neutral spiritual energy with meditation. I will describe the difference between neutral, positive, and negative energy later in the book. The fifth, sixth, and seventh layers are in tune with spiritual realms and experiences, while the fourth center is the bridge in between the physical and the spiritual.

Where you are in your spiritual development depends on how much time you're identifying yourself with each layer.

1: The first energy center is the root chakra (Muladhara), with a vibrating frequency of 256 Hz

The root chakra corresponds with the color red. This is the sex center and is the energy center for the etheric body, which is in direct contact with the physical body. The person whose life experiences are dominated in this body feels a deep connection with the physical world, and material possessions are very important to them. Food, sleep, sexual thoughts and experiences dominate his or her life.

You can transform the energy within this body with meditation but you have to be careful not to suppress it. You simply need to understand that in order for you to elevate your consciousness, sex cannot be the dominant factor in your life. You can reach the highest levels of spirituality without celibacy, but you must become completely celibate if you want to go all the way and become enlightened. The reason is that any time you have sexual thoughts or a sexual experience, your energy moves down to the first layer. To become enlightened your energy must move up towards the crown chakra, and so you cannot become focused on sexual thoughts or experiences.

After working as a janitor for two years, I chose to become a long-haul truck driver. It's the type of job where you can be by yourself for long periods of time and meditate while driving. One time when I started to work for a new company, I trained with another employee for a day during a summer. I noticed he would constantly stare at every woman around us; nothing else mattered to him. He was literally living his life in the first body. I cite this example because I want you to understand that what you are thinking about and focused on has a direct effect on what your life experience will be. If you only focus on accumulating wealth and sexual experience, you will never realize your true potential. Most creatures living on this planet live in this body, and it is the lowest form of existence.

I am not against having sex. In fact, sexual experience is one of the most profound human experiences, but you should not be consumed by it. If you can control your thoughts and your urges through meditation, this energy can become transformative.

Sexual experience is the only experience in the physical world where two consciousness can become one, in a moment in time. Enlightenment is where a consciousness becomes one with the entire existence.

2: The second energy center is sacrum chakra (Swadhisthana), with a vibrating frequency of 288 Hz

This is the energy center for the emotional body and corresponds to the color orange. The person whose life experience is dominated in this body is consumed by emotions. There is a potential for both positive and negative emotions in this body. Unfortunately, most people experience much more negative emotions – such as fear, anger, sadness, and hate.

To transform the energy in this body we need to overcome our fears and learn to forgive and love everyone whom we have ever come across. Unfortunately, when we experience negative emotions, we tend to suppress them. Suppressing these energies will result in energy blocks, and become great obstacles in our spiritual development. In order to transcend the second body, you need to go deep into meditation, and dig out all of your fears, hurt, sadness, hate, pain and suffering from the past, and turn those energies into faith, compassion, happiness, and love.

3: The third energy center is the solar plexus chakra (Manipura), with a vibrating frequency of 320Hz

This is the energy center for the mental body and corresponds to the color yellow. The activity of this center revolves around thinking and reason (lower mental aspects). This is where human beings are different from other creatures. Development of language played a big role in human evolution. We were able to go beyond experiencing simple emotions and develop the ability to think, and to analyze our own existence.

The thing to watch for is to make sure that our thoughts and understandings don't become beliefs that are set in stone. This is the problem with people who follow organized religions, and have certain beliefs that are set in stone, and as a result get stuck in their spiritual development. We must analyze any situation and use our experience, knowledge, and our internal guide to come to new understandings. We must constantly experience new events and expand our knowledge, so we don't become stagnant; we must be open to change and new understandings.

Life is based on change and evolution. The only consistent thing in life is change itself, so your beliefs are always holding you back. Be prepared to drop your beliefs when you come to new understandings. Life is constantly giving you new experiences to guide you in your spiritual development.

4: The fourth energy center is the heart chakra (Anahata), with a vibration frequency of 341 Hz

The fourth energy center corresponds to the color green. This is the energy center for the astral body, which has both a physical and a spiritual dimension. We use this center to manifest our physical life. This center is directly involved in the creative process.

When we want to manifest, we think about different aspects of what we want to take place. We give energy to those thoughts. The universe connects to those vibrations, and puts forth a sequence of events where that manifestation can become a reality. We still need to remain focused on what we need to do in order to manifest our thoughts into reality. It is so important to be in control of your thoughts, because the moment you identify with thoughts revolving around the first three layers, the fourth center goes into hibernation and the creative process comes to a halt. Many people have difficulty manifesting their thoughts and their imagination because of this.

The connection of this body with the universe goes both ways. If you strengthen this connection through focus and meditation, you develop the ability to have premonitions and psychic visions. Many people get a bad feeling when something is going to go wrong; this is not a coincidence. Mediums also use this center to connect with spiritual energy or a higher consciousness.

There is a different aspect related to this body. When two people meet, energy cords connect their astral bodies. You could meet someone and without speaking to them, you would know whether or not you like them. We have all been in situations where we are sitting across the room from someone and we get a bad feeling about them, without ever knowing or speaking to them. You can also meet a person and determine if there is chemistry between you without knowing anything about them. These energy cords strengthen with the passage of time between couples, and it can become very painful to break them. This is why breaking up is so difficult and requires time to heal.

5: The fifth energy center is the throat Chakra (Vishuddhi), with a vibration frequency of 384 Hz

The fifth energy center corresponds to the color blue and is the energy center for the spiritual body. The person who has entered this body knows that they are one with the universe; they have gone beyond the duality of this world. They have no judgment about anyone or anything. They have tremendous trust about everything that is happening because of a deep sense of connection with the universe. They have surrendered themselves to Life; there's no conflict or struggle.

Many of you will read the above statement and think that you are there, but there are three levels of being when you get to this point:

- Entering this body momentarily.
- Remaining in this body for extended periods of time.
- Transcending this body, and going to the next level.

To remain in the spiritual body, you have to be without any judgment whatsoever. You cannot criticize anyone, regardless of the situation. You have to go beyond right or wrong. If you cannot wrap your head around this concept you need to meditate more, until you understand how that could be possible. Thinking you are one with the universe is different from knowing you are one with the universe. People who give others negative experiences are part of the same consciousness, they are simply less evolved. If somebody is in Grade Two, you cannot expect them to know the material taught in Grade Ten. A person can be fifty years old, but be at Grade Two in their spiritual development. On the other hand, a nineteen-year-old could be at Grade Ten in their spiritual development. It all depends on the combined experiences of their previous lives. You cannot judge anyone, because you simply do not know their history, the influences of their DNA, and the cultural and geographical influences of their environment.

6: The sixth energy center is the third eye (Ajna), with a vibrating frequency of 448 Hz

This is the energy center for the celestial body, and it corresponds to the color metallic indigo. The center for this chakra is located right in the center of the forehead. Stand in front of a mirror with a bright light shining on your forehead. Look at the center of your forehead and try to find a knob that is located right at the center. There are many knobs on your forehead, but there should be one right in the center. Sometimes there is no physical representation on your skin, in which case the opening is just below the surface of the skin.

There are many misconceptions about the third eye because many of the people who write about the third eye are not writing about their own experiences – they are rewriting what someone else has said about the third eye.

There are three possibilities with the third eye.

Activating the third eye
The first possibility is activating the third eye. We all activate the third eye whenever we do activities that require us to focus on a single point or an object. For example: a baseball player who stares at a baseball as it travels through the air; a carpenter who focuses on the tip of the nail as he or

she uses the hammer; a tailor who uses a needle to work. Whenever our eyes stare at and focus on a single point or an object, we naturally become focused on the third eye without even realizing. We also naturally become focused on the third eye when we try to balance ourselves or attempt to make difficult maneuvers. The third eye balances our energy field, so the better you can focus your consciousness on the third eye, the more serene you will feel in the moment.

I would like to share with you why it is so important to bring focus to the third eye. The third eye is the energy center for the sixth plane of consciousness. The sixth plane of consciousness is the brain of the universe we are living in. It contains within it all the knowledge and insights of existence itself. It controls and programs every event that is happening in our universe. For this reason, the sixth chakra is closed in almost every human being who lives on this planet. Imagine the chaos that would be created if anyone could directly affect the events that happen in our universe. The better you can focus your consciousness on the third eye, and more you activate it, the deeper and stronger your connection will be to the sixth plane of consciousness.

Activating the third eye is like jumping on a trampoline and trying to look over the wall to get a glimpse into the neighbor's house. The stronger your focus, the better will be your connection, and the more knowledge and insights you will be able to receive from this plane of consciousness. Millennials are born with a stronger connection to the sixth plane of consciousness, and for that reason they are called the indigo children. But if you are a Millennial, remember that this gift is only a potential; you need to put time and effort into strengthening this connection further in order to make a leap forward in your spiritual development. Any average person who puts time and effort into the meditation techniques that are specifically designed for the third eye will have the same chance to benefit from the vast knowledge that exists within this plane of consciousness. I will be going through these specific techniques later on in this book.

Seeing with the third eye

The second possibility is the ability to see with the third eye, and in fact it is possible to see through the third eye with your eyes closed. There are people who have the ability to see physical objects with their natural eyes closed using their third eye. There are also energy healers who have developed the ability to see other people's spiritual energy field using their third eye. But do not try to open your third eye to feed your ego and develop special abilities; this may prevent you from moving forward with what is important, which is drawing energy with higher vibration through the third eye. Allow life to give you the abilities necessary to fulfill your life purpose and surrender yourself to whatever ability life gives you.

Opening a vortex into the sixth plane of consciousness with the third eye

The third possibility is the ability to directly open a vortex into the sixth plane of consciousness and draw in energy with higher vibrational frequency. This energy travels to the pineal gland, which is located at the base of the skull. From there this energy travels down the spinal cord. This energy then enters the lower layers of spiritual energy field through each of the lower chakras. Just as you fill up a glass of water, the third eye draws in energy with higher frequency and fills up all the lower layers with this neutral energy.

The layers are normally sealed and do not exchange energy with each other, but there are passageways that can be opened through spiritual purification and crystallization of the consciousness within that body. You simply have to meditate, and your higher self will take care of the rest.

The pineal gland is the bridge between male and female energy, it is the bridge between the right and left hemisphere. The male and the female energies do not interact with each other much, but there is a little bit of each one in the other.

You can open the third eye without celibacy, but you need to fully commit to keeping your mind silent at all times. Once you have fully opened the third eye, you can easily manifest your thought into reality using the third eye. You can in fact literally change the events that are happening in our world. But you should not use the third eye to manifest material gains or for personal gratification. Life will not fully open the third eye until you have surrendered your will and committed yourself to becoming silent, and have fully committed to the spiritual path.

Once you attain this state of consciousness, you have had some experience of being one with Life. The duality is no more, you have transcended beyond positive and negative, you no longer experience negative emotions, you are simply blissful. If I ask you to close your eyes and describe a time when you were blissful, you may imagine a point in your life were everything was perfect and there was no pain or suffering of any kind. But that is not being truly blissful. You are truly blissful only when you're static and happy, in spite of experiencing all the pain and suffering around you. You simply do not feel any negative emotions, regardless of your situation.

You need to be careful when you reach this state of consciousness because you may not want to go further once you are blissful. You need to keep seeking for more, because there are states of consciousness beyond blissful.

For the longest time I searched on the Internet, trying to find someone else who had opened their third eye. All I found were people who thought that their third eye had opened because of something that they read somewhere, or they assumed that because they are very spiritual it must be open.

In fact, when your third eye opens you physically feel a vortex open in the center of your forehead. The force of this energy is undeniable: it feels like there is a tornado on your forehead and you can feel the energy being sucked in. The third eye opens to a spiritual realm of consciousness. If your third eye opens you are in direct contact with All That Exists; you do not need to follow a master or anybody else, Life is your master. I am not saying this to criticize anyone; however, once you believe in your mind that you have opened your third eye, you will no longer do what is necessary to actually open it.

Up to entering the fifth body, you are constantly moving between the bodies, depending on what you are thinking or experiencing. Once you enter the sixth body, it is much easier to control your thoughts. You may still move to the lower bodies for short periods, but it is easier to remain focused. Remain vigilant about keeping your mind as silent as possible, and you will receive insight on how to move forward from your higher self.

7: The seventh energy center is the crown chakra (Sahasrara), with a vibrating frequency of 480 Hz

This is the energy center for the cosmic body, and it corresponds to the color violet. It is difficult to use words to describe this state of consciousness; you need to experience it for yourself to understand it. I have had many experiences with the energy of this plane since I began on the path of enlightenment.

Once, I strained my neck while I was doing janitorial work. I had muscle stiffness and spasm in my neck and my upper back. My neck muscles were so tight that they were restricting the blood flow to my head, and I was experiencing a severe migraine. I took a couple of anti-inflammatory pills to soothe the pain, but they did not help. I thought that the best I could do was to sit and close my eyes to meditate and relax myself. After five minutes, I felt a jolt of energy vibrate from the right hemisphere of my head, all the way down through my spinal cord. I felt every single vertebra on my spinal cord adjusting itself, without me moving at all. All the tightness in my neck and upper back vanished in an instant, and the migraine headache instantly stopped.

I assume that Jesus healed people's illnesses with this energy. It was one of the most profound experiences of my life. I had never felt so alive. My mind was silent without any effort; I experienced nirvana.

This state of consciousness is the state of being and non-being, it is the witnessing consciousness. Let me explain this better. You are always thinking about something and identifying with those thoughts. Up to the sixth body there are always thoughts that you identify with. Even an experience meditator will identify with some thoughts. But what if there were absolutely no thoughts in your mind and you had nothing to identify yourself with? What if you reached a time when you are no longer attached to anything at all? In this state of consciousness, you will experience nothingness. Up to the seventh body you use your desire of wanting to become enlightened to repress all other desires. Once you enter the seventh body, you realize that in order to transcend beyond the seventh body, you need to let go of even the desire to become enlightened. You let go of it all; that is what I mean by nothingness.

You begin to experience moments when you are, following by moments when you are not. Your silence becomes so deep and rich that at times you disassociate yourself from your body. You are getting ready for a free-fall into the cosmic ocean of the consciousness. Once your core energy has risen to the point of the crown chakra, and you have let go of everything, this jump occurs. The male and the female energy connect through the pineal gland and become one. The aura drops and you become one with All That Exists. This is the goal of every seeker. Many of you might feel scared when you hear nothingness, but in nothingness you find you are everything. The small part of you dies, but now you are God, you are All That Exists.

I want to emphasize that the energy of this body is within you – you're simply not aware of it. This is your higher self. You do not need to travel anywhere to attain it; you simply need to find it within yourself. It is the inner journey. You are All That Exists; the door is always open. You just need to walk through that door when you're ready to drop it all.

You cannot follow a particular path to go from the sixth to the seventh body; it is like following a maze. But you're not walking on this path alone, your inner self is guiding you every step of the way. These states of consciousness are extremely difficult to explain with mere words; I am simply trying to shine a light on what to expect.

Separation and the
Path of Enlightenment

After the death of my sister Telly in September of 2006, I was struggling and grieving my loss. On top of that, my back pain had come back with a vengeance the day after her death. This was a very difficult time for my entire family. My mother had suffered from an anxiety disorder all her life, and the loss of Telly was too much for her. She had been afraid of losing one of us all her life, and her biggest fear had come true, so her anxiety turned into a deep depression.

The path of enlightenment requires you to practice separation for approximately two to three years. During that time, you must cut yourself off from everything that occupies your mind, such as listening to music or watching TV. I was guided to study both Christianity and Islam to learn the complicated dynamics of these religions. I am going to discuss this subject later in this book. Enlightenment has nothing to do with either one of those religions, but Life wanted me to learn what was good in the Bible and the Koran, and why we can no longer use them to progress in our spiritual development. As I read the Bible and the Koran, Life would give me insights about the true meaning and understanding of different verses. I began to go to church and meet Christians to learn their way of thinking. At first the members of the church thought that I was interested in converting to Christianity, but they soon realized that my goal was to learn about their way of thinking, not to convert.

The week after Telly's death I was meditating in my room one day, when Life asked me to go to the living room, so I walked over there. My father was sitting on the couch watching a program on the National Geographic channel. The program was about the indigenous population in East Asia who captured wild elephants and domesticated them. In the program they demonstrated the methods they used. Life wanted me to watch the program.

I saw that the people cleverly managed to put chains on the legs of a male elephant and tied them to very large trees. Then for a period of forty-five days, at all hours of the day, with the help of the entire village, three or four people at any one time would constantly hit different parts of the elephant's body from all sides with small branches. At the same time, they would make loud noises by yelling or using various instruments. The small branches did not hurt the elephant, they were just a constant irritant that caused him stress. I saw that the elephant was completely overwhelmed. Day and night the people of the village continued to overload the elephant's senses. At the beginning the elephant seemed to be going mad, but as time went by, he slowly began to calm down. The onslaught continued, but it no longer bothered him. By the end, he was used to having people around him doing whatever that they were doing. He was domesticated. I came back to my room and sat in deep meditation. Life communicated to me that this would be the method to us98

to silence my mind, and the tools that Life would use to make this happen would be pain and suffering. Life communicated to me that this would not be easy and would not happen over a short period of time.

I thought about the insight that Life had shared with me, and realized that this was not something that was just happening to me; every human being goes through the same process. The amount of pain and suffering for a person who is on a path of enlightenment is much greater than the pain and suffering of an average person, but the method is still the same.

Every human being suffers a great deal of stress at different times during his or her lifetime. If zero is having no stress at all, and ten is the maximum amount of stress, you may experience stress levels of two or three for a period of time, and then go up to eight or nine for a period of time, and then come back down again. Our stress level is constantly changing depending on what is happening in our lives. The change in stress levels could be due to physical illness, financial difficulties, job insecurities, issues with children, death in the family, and so on.

Our mind goes wild during stressful situations, and Life forces us to deal with the increased amount of thoughts we have during these stressful times. Tremendous growth happens when we are dealing with these stressful events, and we get better at handling these situations. Once the stress levels come back down, our minds are slightly more silent than before the event happened. We feel more secure having overcome that particular challenge. This is a very hard but effective method that Life uses to quiet our mind.

Whether you are aware of this or not, you are participating in this game of life. Everyone tries to avoid events where they are put in difficult situations, by saving money, making investments, eating well, taking safety precautions, and so on. But when Life wants to increase your stress levels, it happens whether or not you have taken precautions. There's no way to keep this from happening; the best you can do is to learn how you can help yourself to deal with these stressful situations. Meditation can help you focus and manage your thoughts and control your emotions during difficult times in your life. Just like the elephant, you can get to a point where negative things are happening in your life, but nothing can bother you anymore. At that point you have transcended beyond the positive and the negative. I hope that reading my story will help you to master the tools that Life has taught me to overcome the challenges that were put before me.

Coming to terms with Telly's death

There was a lot of sadness in our household after Telly's death. I realized why Life took her away from us – I needed to experience what it is like to lose someone so close to me. We would light a candle and sit and watch videos of her every night, crying and grieving. I would do my best to console my grieving mother, as I grieved myself.

My younger sister Naz was just twenty years old at the time of Telly's death; she was young and grieved in her own way. She wanted to move on with her life and experience life the way that she saw fit. Like most young people, the choices she was making in her life were not wise. I would try desperately to guide her onto the right path. Life continuously told me not to force my ideas onto her, but that was easier said than done. I constantly struggled to keep to myself as she made one mistake after another. I realized the more I tried to interfere, the worse things got between us. Our relationship was becoming strained, and she had become cruel and mean because of my interference.

This was not her fault. She needed to make those mistakes to learn from them. I was the problem, not her. I needed to give her space to grow, and to learn from the events in her life. I was never meant to be her teacher, Life is our teacher and we are all the students. I decided to change my approach with her and only give her my opinion if she asked for it. She usually did not agree with my opinions, but in time would understand why I said the things that I said. This was a very important lesson for me to learn. I realized that I cannot and should not try to change anybody's mind in any situation. I needed to accept and love them just the way they are, with all their faults and shortcomings. The best that I could do was to help Naz see the results of her actions, and help her cope with them.

The discipline of not speaking unless spoken to

Life asked me to practice a particular discipline: to be able to control my thoughts and my emotions. It also helped me to be in control of my reactions, and break my past conditioning. With this new discipline **I would not speak, until I was spoken to**.

In normal circumstances, your relationship with your thoughts is such that when a thought enters your mind, you identify with it. You act as if you are that thought, and you take action to support that thought. But the problem with identifying with your thoughts all the time is that you become a slave to your mind. I have talked about conditioning in the past. If you identify with your thoughts all the time, your past conditioning will become a big part of who you are.

Let us look at some examples. I had got used to giving my opinions to Naz when I believed she was making poor choices in her life, and would point out all the reasons as to why her choices were wrong. An argument would ensue between us, because we were both trying to make our case. At the end, regardless of who was right or wrong, we would both be upset and angry with each other. I cannot remember a time when I was able to convince her that she was making a mistake. Our arguments were completely useless. The problem was that for the longest time, I could not control my reactions when I saw that she was making a mistake. I would point it out, this was my conditioning. It was a bad habit that was very difficult to break.

Everything changed when I start practicing controlling my thoughts and emotions. Something amazing happened when I did not speak unless I was spoken to. She would do something that I did not approve, and thoughts would enter my mind, but I would not say anything. For a while I would still be bothered by her actions, but very slowly as more time went by, thoughts would enter my mind and I would watch them go by as if they were somebody else's thoughts. This is called witnessing consciousness; I was no longer attached to my thoughts.

The first result was that for the first time in my life I was able to choose my reaction. Normally if I saw something I didn't like, I would immediately express my opinion. An argument would ensue, and afterwards we would both be unhappy. The second result was that I realized that I was not my thoughts, and I could choose to react differently to things that had bothered me in the past.

As more time went by, I started to feel a separation between myself and my thoughts. I would watch them come and go, as I would watch a cloud passing through the sky. My mind was no longer the master; instead I was in control of my mind. Consequently, I was able to control my emotions. This did not happen in a short time, and it was not easy to accomplish. Very early on, I noticed that it was hard to stop myself from talking when a thought entered my mind. So I began to punish myself if I did not follow the rules that I had set for myself.

I set two sets of rules for myself. The first rule was that I would not speak without anybody speaking to me or asking my opinion. The second was that if someone did speak to me, I would reply with the shortest answer possible. This would prevent me from talking for a long time if an opportunity presented itself. The punishment that I set for myself for breaking the rules was that I would fast for one day.

I broke the rules a couple of times and consequently punished myself by fasting for one day. That was enough to keep me from slipping up again. My meditation helped me a great deal in this process, because I was able to be aware and focused when situations presented themselves. I practiced this discipline for three years. I was able to break all my past conditioning, and my mind became more and more silent as time went by.

This is a practice that I highly recommend everyone to do. Many of you are going to think that it is not possible to practice this discipline, so I'm going to tell you how everyone can achieve this.

First of all, you can choose how much time you want to dedicate to this discipline. Look at your weekly schedule and see what days would be suited better for this practice; it is better if you can dedicate a full day. The second thing is to set the rules of engagement. For example, if you are working in an office you may need to communicate with your superior, coworkers, or customers. In this scenario, it would not be wise to give short answers to your boss, so you should speak to your boss as usual. However, when it comes to speaking with your coworkers and customers, only communicate what is absolutely necessary. Our goal here is to not identify with every single thought that enters your mind; at the same time this process will help you to become aware of what it is that you're saying. Meditation is about focus, if you are focused and aware during your conversations, it will allow you to be mindful during the times that you are practicing this discipline.

I would like to give another example. Let us suppose you are a stay-at-home mother with children. You can behave as usual with your children. But share with your husband that on a particular day you will practice this discipline, so that when he comes home you will only communicate with him what is absolutely necessary. The same thing is going to happen: you are going to have thoughts that enter your mind that do not need to be communicated urgently. Hold on to those thoughts, watch them come and go. This will force you to evaluate a thought when it enters your mind, and force you to become mindful of what you are saying. This is a powerful tool, because in the future you will be more in control of your thoughts and your emotions. You can further improve yourself if you combine this practice with meditation, as these practices complement each other.

You can choose to put as much time as you like into this practice, but no matter how much time you chose to dedicate to this, even if it's only a few hours a week, give one hundred percent effort to it. This practice will only work if there is a punishment for breaking the rules that you set for yourself. The punishment needs to be something difficult or challenging, or something that is taken away that you normally really enjoy doing. Hold yourself accountable when you slip up. The second advice that I would give you is not to share with everyone that you're doing this, because not everyone is going to understand what it is that you're trying to do. People around you are going to notice that you are quieter during the time of practice. If someone asks you why you are so quiet, just tell them that you are dedicating a certain amount of time to reflect on yourself that day, which is not a lie.

What I learned from Life in the first two years of my spiritual journey

I learned valuable lessons from Life in the first two years on this path. Part of what I had to learn was to study the Bible and the Koran. Life allowed me to understand why God has been described in such a manner. In fact, for this reason, I have been using the name **Life** instead of **God** to describe All That Exists. The name God has been associated with the description that exists in the Koran and the Bible, but it is a false description. I will share with you what Life shared with me during the times that I was studying these books.

First of all, both Mohammed and Jesus were God's prophets and both were enlightened men. Both the Bible and the Koran were God's teachings for people who occupied this planet 2,000 and 1,300 years ago respectively. People of that era were considerably less evolved than people today. Both Christianity and Islam are fear-based religions. People of that era were wild and unpredictable, and their societies were not civilized. What was said was necessary to keep them in check.

You have to understand that Life gives you the necessary understanding to take you to the next level. Once you are at the next level, a new understanding will be given to you to take you to the next level again, and so on.

Spirituality and people have to evolve at the same time. There is no absolution when it comes to spirituality, because the ultimate cannot be described with words. Truth can only be understood when you experience it for yourself. The best that I can do is to give you the tools to get there. It is not possible for the master to tell you what the **truth** is. The master can only give you devices to practice, so you can experience the **truth** for yourself.

The level of understanding of people today is considerably higher than that of the people who lived 1,300 and 2,000 years ago. In fact, the levels are not even close. How could Muhammad or Jesus have spoken about higher consciousness? It would not have worked; they would not have been understood.

Parents tell their child that if they clean their room they will be rewarded with ice cream. This typically produces positive results because children understand what ice cream is and are motivated to clean their rooms, in order to get ice cream. But children will not be motivated to clean their rooms if you tell them that being organized will help them in the future when they grow up. You have to speak their language to get through to them. The same thing applies to people who lived 1,300 and 2,000 years ago.

Let's quickly take a look at the summary of what God promised to people who go to heaven in the Bible and the Koran.

In the Bible God promised people:

Isaiah 25:8-12: no more tears, wipe away tears, remove his people's disgrace from all the earth

Revelation 7:16-17: never again will they hunger, never again will they thirst, the sun will not beat down on them, nor any scorching heat

Ezekiel 28:26: they will live there in safety and will build houses and plant vineyards.

In the Koran God promised people:

No tiredness or hard work, rivers of water, rivers of milk the taste of which will remain unchanged, rivers of wine, rivers of clear pure honey, people were to wear silk garments with jewelry, they will see there neither the excessive heat of the sun, nor the excessive bitter cold, bunches of fruit will hang low within their reach, there will be virgins with wide lovely eyes as wives.

You can easily see that the above descriptions are what heaven would be for the people of 2,000 and 1,300 years ago respectively. The main concerns for the people of that era where food, water, safety, social status, and harsh weather conditions. This is no different than promising a six-year-old ice cream to clean their room.

The same is true for the existence of hell. The people of that era were wild and unpredictable. There had to be something for them to be afraid of, otherwise different groups or tribes would regularly attack each other to take over land, possessions, and women. That is why hell has been described in such a manner. There is no entity that is called the devil, hell does not exist, and neither does the vengeful God that has been described in both scriptures.

In reality you are not punished for your wrongdoing, but if you cause pain and suffering to another life form, the same amounts of pain and suffering will come back to you in this life, or the next. The laws of physics apply here. We are energy and according to the laws of physics, **the sum of all forces is equal to zero**. There is no punishment, but for every action there will be a reaction of equal force. We are all one, and hurting someone is like slapping yourself in the face. The hand that did the hitting will feel the pain of the face. The pain may take a bit of time to travel from the face to the hand, but I assure you, it will happen.

I have the utmost respect for Jesus and Mohammed because they had to communicate their reality to people who had no understanding about energy, consciousness, or higher vibrations. They had to use metaphors to explain the creation of the world, and gave people examples of how they should treat each other in order to evolve and elevate their consciousness.

An example of that is the story of Adam and Eve. It has been said that Adam and Eve were created in the image of God in a single instant and lived happily in heaven, and that they could remain there as long as they did not eat from the forbidden fruit of the tree of knowledge. But the devil got jealous and tricked Eve in eating the forbidden fruit from the tree of knowledge, and consequently they were banished to earth – which was created by God in six of our days – until they could earn their way back to heaven with good behavior.

The simple explanation of the Adam and Eve story is that the single consciousness that we call God wanted to experience itself, so it created the universe and life on this planet. In fact, we are not the only evolved beings in this universe. Adam and Eve are just metaphors and represent every human being who has lived throughout our evolution.

How can we interpret the tree of knowledge?

What is another name for knowledge? Knowledge is experience. In Christianity our souls are described as the Holy Spirit, and in the Koran it says that God breathed into Adam and Eve from its soul. That is not different from reality. We are God's consciousness, there is only one of us, and we are all divine.

There are many reasons why there are so many atheists today, but one of the main reasons is that religious people persist on interpreting these stories literally, and completely deny evolution, despite all the proof. Evolution is the biggest point of contention between the scientific community and religious leaders in both Christianity and Islam. It is in fact true that the world was created in six of our days, it is also true that it took millions of years for us to evolve to the point that we are today. Human beings experience life in a linear time, but for the consciousness that is beyond our universe, time is not linear and is not measured the same way. This concept is extremely difficult to comprehend, so let me give you an example that is similar to reality. When you want to watch a movie on your computer it only takes a few seconds to load the entire contents into your computer, but when you watch the movie, it might take three hours to experience the content. So it took All That Exists six of our days to load the system, but it takes millions of years to experience it.

This multiverse is God's holodeck (virtual reality facility). Life can load into the system whatever it wants to experience. In fact, we are experiencing the content that was programmed into the system at the beginning of time. All that is going to happen has already happened, and the world has already ended. You are now experiencing everything in between the beginning and the end. You chose the life that you wanted to experience before you were born, and now are experiencing that life. But this is an interactive system, such that every single day of your life has not been preprogrammed before you were born. However, there are significant events in your life that are going to happen regardless of what you do. For example, if you are supposed to experience what is like to live a life with one leg due to an accident, then no matter what you do, the accident will happen and you will lose a leg. But how you overcome the obstacles after the accident can change.

Every day that you sleep your consciousness (a small part of you) becomes one with the source. Depending on what is happening in your life, you choose what you want to experience the following day, and consequently when you wake up, universal consciousness puts in the sequence of events where you can experience what you have chosen. At the same time your energy field gets refreshed, which is why sleeping is so important. You can be extremely angry before you go to sleep, but once you wake up most of your anger has disappeared and you feel a lot better. This is because when you're asleep you are one with the source, and you become aware of your reality.

Religion and the problems of today's world

It is difficult to speak about religion and not talk about what is happening in the world with violent, extremist groups such as ISIS and Al Qaeda. I have read three different interpretations of Koran, and I can tell you that there is nowhere that the Koran approves the murder of innocent men, women, and children. However, in some places it mentions that, "You can kill the nonbelievers." Groups like ISIS and Al Qaeda have taken these verses out of context and committed horrific crimes against humanity. The history behind these verses is that at the time when Mohammed became the prophet of God, the Islamic movement faced great opposition from a group of nonbelievers. They tried to kill Mohammed and the new converts, and many wars were fought due to this conflict.

Historians have indicated that Mohammed was a very calm person, who had always tried to avoid conflict. The verses that came to Mohammed from God, "You can kill the nonbelievers," pushed Mohammed to fight the opposition. Mohammed ultimately fought many wars and defeated the nonbelievers, and the Islamic movement spread through Asia and Africa. These verses were meant to apply to a specific point in time, and applied to the groups that were fighting Mohammed at that time. They were not meant to be used to kill people indiscriminately. Yet groups like ISIS are killing Christians, Shia Muslims, Sunni Muslims, and whoever who does not agree with their ideology. The leaders of these groups are psychopaths who are trying to justify their crimes, and are using religion to do it. True Islam promotes peace and harmony.

Some of you may be wondering: if Life has such control over the affairs of our world, how can such atrocities happen on our planet? This is a controlled chaos. There are many challenges facing this planet, and the rise of ISIS is just one of them. The use of fossil fuels is destroying our planet's atmosphere. Drastic measures need to be taken in the next fifty years to save us from extinction. Unfortunately, throughout our history, the human race has not changed their way when things are just okay. Life always balances itself, and balance can only happen when you have gone to the extremes.

Let me give you an example: a person who drinks alcohol heavily twice a week will never stop drinking, because drinking twice a week is not too bad and will have few negative consequences. In order for that person to make a change, things have to get really bad. Once the drinking gets to seven days a week, his or her life goes into turmoil, and organs begin to fail. With this decline in health, he or she will be motivated to stop drinking. The affairs of our world are no different, things have to get really bad for us to come together and make the necessary changes. The leaders of the world finally got together in December of 2015 and signed the Paris climate change agreement, because the weather patterns had become really bad and had been causing chaos around the world. They would not have come together if things were just okay.

The human race needs to change: not only to survive, but evolve and elevate our consciousness to the next level. We are all one. There is only one of us and we need to treat each other in a way that reflects that understanding. In Ezekiel 36:26-27 it reads; "I will put my spirit within you and cause you to walk in my way." In the Koran God says: "I breathed into the body from my soul."

Change is coming to the world

Every religion and every enlightened person has said the same thing. We are all God's consciousness; global conflicts need to cease, and humanity must unite. I assure you, that change is coming. The movement has already started, but things might get far worse before they get better.

The change starts with each one of us. Meditate and elevate your vibration, become part of this movement. Together we can change the world. I'm not trying to get you to give up, or change your religion. I am trying to teach you how to evolve spiritually and transcend beyond the dualities of this world – which includes all organized religions.

Regardless of whether you are a Christian, Jew, Muslim, or atheist, when coming into any situation, always ask yourself: is what I am being told to do or what I want to do, separating me or uniting me with the other person, groups of people, or our planet? Use your internal guiding system. Always go with unity, unity is always the correct path. **Remember that there is only one of us, and nothing but God exists.**

The LGBT community

The unity that I am talking about includes the LGBT community. Both Christianity and Islam have viewed homosexuality as sinful and have discriminated against the LGBT community for centuries. I have listened to many Christian leaders arguing that God does not approve of homosexuals, and their belief is based on some verses indicating that "a marriage is between a man and woman."

Matthew 19:4-5 reads:

"He answered, have you not read that he who made them from the beginning made them male and female, and said, for this reason a man shall leave his father and mother and be joined to his wife, and the two shall become one."

But Jesus himself never directly said that a homosexual act is a sin. The Bible never directly mentions homosexuality. Even Matthew 19:4-5, describing the marriage between a man and a woman, does not say that homosexuality is a sinful act. Jesus simply did not directly address this issue because we did not have people from the LGBT community outing themselves as gays, lesbians, bisexual, and transgendered 2,000 years ago. Jesus was born in Bethlehem, which is located in Israel surrounded by Syria, Jordan, and Lebanon. The LGBT community are persecuted and even killed in some of those countries today. Imagine how bad things were for them 2,000 years ago. I highly doubt that anybody would have outed themselves during those times.

Our sexuality, energy, and hormones

I want to share with you what Life has shared with me regarding this matter. Our sexuality falls on a spectrum, depending on four different variables.

- The presence of female energy (yin)
- The presence of male energy (yang)
- The presence of female hormones in the physical body (estrogen and progesterone)
- The presence of male hormones (testosterone)

Every human being has a different balance between their female and male energy (yin and yang), as well as different amounts of male hormones and female hormones in their physical body. Male and female hormones are the physical representation of male and female spiritual energy. The front chakras are the feelings centers; the back chakras are the "will" centers. The presence of the male and the female hormones are determined by the makeup of our DNA. There are as many possibilities between those variables, as there are human beings living on this planet, and they determine where we fall on the sexuality spectrum.

The combined density of the neutral, the male and the female energy makes up our soul, and could be affected by sexual intimacy. In fact, this is the method that Life uses to balance our energy, which is why opposites attract each other. A female CEO of a large company would choose a man who is not a doer and more subdued. A man who has difficulty expressing his feelings would choose a woman who is very sensitive and emotional. People who have more of a balanced energy would choose others with opposite balanced energy. I will give you some examples, but remember that these are just arbitrary numbers.

A man whose energy is made up of 65% male energy and 35% female energy within the first four layers of their spiritual energy field would look for a female with an energy makeup that is close to 35% male energy and 65% female energy. This man will be very good at getting things done, but will have difficulty expressing his emotions. On the other hand, the woman will be very nurturing and sensitive, but would have difficulty bringing her ideas into reality. This is not about which one is better or worse – we are all here to do different things. When we choose any partner in our lives, we are trying to address a weakness that we see in ourselves. This is not a choice; it is the laws of attraction. During sexual intimacy, spiritual energy is exchanged between the male and female. I will be describing this process later in this book.

In the case of gays and lesbians the difference between the male and female energy is not as exaggerated. In addition, the presence of male and female hormones in their physical body can make sexuality very fluid in that zone. For example, a gay man who has 55% male energy and 45% female energy may look for a male that has close to 45% male energy and 55% female energy. If you know any homosexual couples you may have noticed that homosexuals are no different than heterosexuals. If you look at two married gay men, one will be more masculine than the other; and if you look at a lesbian couple, one will be more feminine than the other. A bisexual female could have a makeup of 60% female energy and 40% male energy, she could be attracted to either a male or a female with a strong presence of male energy. In the case of the transgendered person who is born in a male body with a strong presence of testosterone, this person could have an energy makeup of 65% female energy and 35% male energy. The soul is dominated by female energy, but the physical body is dominated by male hormones. The spiritual soul energy determines our true sexuality. She feels that she is in the wrong body. She may choose to do gender transition surgeries and take female hormones to remedy the discrepancy that she feels within herself.

It is your God-given right to choose whom you want to love. Don't ever let anyone tell you otherwise. To say that gays, lesbians, bisexuals, or transgendered individuals can choose their sexuality is absolutely absurd. I want to share an experience that I had many years ago while I worked in security at a hospital in Vancouver.

One day police brought in a young gay man who had called the suicide hotline. The counselor, fearing he would commit suicide, had called the police to intervene. Police officers brought him to the hospital for a seventy-two hours' psychiatric evaluation. He was not cooperating because he had called the hotline just to talk to the counselor about his feelings, and was not expecting the counselor to send police officers to his house. I spent over an hour talking to him, to get him to calm down and take the medication that was prescribed to him. I asked him why he was contemplating suicide, and his answer shocked me. He shared with me that he is only attracted to men, but that when he is intimate with one he feels so disgusted and ashamed of himself that he wants to kill himself. It was heartbreaking to see him cry and struggle because he cannot accept who he is. I can only imagine what he must have felt growing up, with everyone around him making him feel that there is something wrong with him, to the point where he could not even accept himself.

Society has a responsibility to be inclusive and welcome people who are different. This is a critical part of our spiritual development. You cannot become closer to God if you cannot accept all of its parts. I am delighted that we have made tremendous progress in Western society in accepting the LGBT community. Unfortunately, they are still persecuted in many parts of our planet. On behalf of Life, I want to tell every member of the LGBT community that Life loves you, and you are perfect in every way exactly the way you are.

The challenges of celibacy

After Telly's death in September of 2006, I continued to focus on meditating and keeping my mind silent through a very difficult time period. I would try to remain present while my mind wanted to go somewhere else. I was working with my father as a janitor while having low back pain, which had resurfaced the day after her death. My celibacy was causing its own problems. As I had become sexually inactive the sexual energy was building up inside of me, and my mind kept moving towards my past experiences. The popular belief is that our memories are stored in our brains, but that is not the entire picture. Every memory is attached to part of our consciousness. When you have a thought about one of your sexual experiences your root chakra goes into overdrive and activates the energy related to that memory. You can feel your heart beating faster, you begin to feel aroused – its energy is undeniable. In frustration, I had wished many times that I had been with less sexual partners before I started on this path. The sexual thoughts were only part of the assault; my mind did not discriminate. I had thoughts about times when I was angry, I had thoughts about my fears – it was all-out war. From the time that I opened my eyes in the morning, until I went to sleep at night, I would try to stop all thoughts.

I got better at controlling my thoughts as time went by. I spent all day in deep meditation, releasing those energies. I was able to heal my back pain through specific balancing exercises; my mind was becoming tame. My focus had improved so much that I could stop any thought in an instant. The opening of the third eye had continuously got wider, so I was able to draw in more energy. I thought that I was probably getting close to the point of enlightenment, but I was in for a rude awakening.

One day while I was driving to work with my father, I felt a tightness in my neck. When I tried to stretch it, I felt a sharp burning pain on the right side of my neck. After finishing work, I went home and slept. When I woke in the morning I was unable to get out of bed. My neck and shoulder had frozen up. I tried different therapies, but nothing seemed to help. I was no longer able to go to work with my father. The pain completely shattered the silence that I had achieved; it was as if I had never meditated.

Life asks me to fast

I was so frustrated that I sat in deep meditation and asked for clarification. Life informed me that I had only suppressed my sexual desires, fears, and anger. I would have to endure much more suffering in order to bring everything to the surface and heal my soul. Life showed me a vision of myself where I was just skin and bones – I looked like a person suffering from severe anorexia. And then Life asked me to lose weight by fasting continuously, and shedding half a pound per day.

I strongly advise you never to try this, because you can easily die attempting this task. I was born big boned, and through years of bodybuilding, I had built a lot of muscle mass. My starting weight was 205 pounds. I slowly cut my food intake, and the first twenty pounds came off easy. But once the fat was gone I had to burn muscle to lose weight, and that is extremely difficult to do. I began to eat a precise amount of food every day, and Life would give me exact directions as to how much food to cut every seven days. The danger of losing muscle is that your heart is also a muscle, if you lose too much too fast, you can damage your heart and die.

At one point Life asked me to start going for long walks, and swim, to continue losing half a pound per day. I began to understand why I had to do this. I was starving all day, and all day I was having thoughts about eating. A thought is a thought; I had to stop all thoughts about eating. Life was trying to improve my focus, so through starvation it generated many thoughts about food. My shoulder was still extremely painful and I was unable to go to work with my father. My mother was extremely stressed and worried about me. My parents thought that I had lost my mind, and they became extremely angry with me.

At the beginning of my journey when I went back home, they were all very happy because my mother was worried that I was involved in illegal activities. I was helping my father with his work without asking for anything, so it was great for the family. But now I had become a burden. I could not work because of my shoulder, and on top of that I was losing weight and becoming frailer every day, so one by one my parents and Naz began to turn on me. I knew that they were in pain, seeing me suffer, but regardless of the situation, when your family is mean and cruel to you, it hurts. It is harder not to get angry when the cruelty comes from people that you love.

Life shared with me that I needed to control my thoughts and not to get angry, because my family is God's consciousness. If I am angry with them, I am angry with Life. There is no difference between my family, strangers, and God. I knew that I needed to stop looking at individuals as people and just see them as Life. This is one of the biggest hurdles in anybody's spiritual development. Everyone get angry with their partners, friends, or coworkers; but they are not people, they are God's consciousness. They are Life itself. So if you want to get close to God, love everyone around you no matter what their shortcomings, no matter if they hurt you. You need to transcend your anger. You need to become one with everyone around you first, if you want to become one with God.

My mother regularly invited spiritual people to our apartment to speak to me about what I was doing. She was hoping that they could somehow convince me to stop fasting. I would try to explain myself at first, but I soon realized no one could possibly understand what I was going through. How could I tell people that God communicates with me? They thought that I had gone insane, so I stopped trying to explain myself. I would just sit and listen without saying anything in return. Some of them were polite, but some would rudely call me crazy to my face. I knew that I just needed to push through, no matter what was happening around me.

My daily routine included fast walking for six and half miles and swimming for one and a half hours. Every week I would cut something from my daily meal. I spent the rest of the day in deep meditation, trying to stop all thoughts, but I was not thinking about anything else but food. I continued this routine until one day my back pain came back. Losing all that weight had caused my body to go out of alignment again, and I could no longer walk a long distance or swim. My weight got down to 140 pounds. By this time, I was only eating 250 g of food once a day. I was starving twenty-four hours a day, seven days a week. After finishing my meal every night, it felt as if I had not eaten anything at all. I would wake up during the night from grinding my teeth together, because I would dream about eating a cheeseburger or some other type of food. The pain was unbearable. I thought that I was going to receive a message from Life to stop the fasting, because by this time I looked anorexic, and I looked like the vision that Life showed me before I started fasting. But that message never came; Life encouraged me to push forward.

I continued with my fasting, and pushed through the pain; this was truly mind over matter. I could no longer go for long walks or swim, so instead I went to the sauna for two hours a day. My energy level had become so low that when I wanted to move, I had to gather myself for fifteen minutes before I could stand up and walk. I walked in slow motion. It wasn't funny back then, but when I think about it now, it must have looked very funny to see me walk, because I moved like a sloth.

I noticed that my third eye and all my chakras were opening more and pulling in more energy. My body was in survival mode and was ingesting universal energy directly from the source. That is how I could survive eating just 250 g of food a day.

Starving to death?

I finally got my weight down to 120 pounds. I looked myself in the mirror one day and saw that my eyes had yellow spots. This was a sign of jaundice. I knew that my liver was failing, and death was coming. I tried to hide it from my mother by wearing a baseball cap, but she saw it. She knew what jaundice was because she had gone to nursing school when she was younger. She begged me to stop fasting, but Life wanted me to push forward. My mother was inconsolable. She had buried her first child just two years ago, and she could not bear the thought of losing me. I felt terrible for her, but I had to keep moving forward.

I knew intellectually that I would not die. I would ask myself, why would Life go to all that trouble if it were going to take my life? Life had proven to me over and over again that it is in complete control of our bodies. But knowing something intellectually is different than actually experiencing it. I had read in the scriptures the story of Abraham, where God tested his loyalty and trust. He was thrown into an incinerator by Nimrod, but God saved his life. I don't know if that happened or was just a metaphor, but I knew Life needed me to trust this process and move forward, so I did. I was getting worse every day. My weight finally got down to 110 pounds; my eyes and my skin had become completely yellow. I was unable to get off my bed and go to the bathroom when I opened my eyes. There was nothing else left. I cried and looked at the ceiling and asked Life to just take my life and end it, I was ready to die.

Unbeknown to me, my mother had gone to our family doctor and told him that I had jaundice and that I was refusing to get help. As a result, our family doctor had called the head of psychiatry at the local hospital and asked them to intervene. A psychiatrist came to our apartment to evaluate the situation. After speaking to me she determined that I was a danger to myself, and so they forcefully took me to the hospital. Ever since I started on this path, I was looking to do two things. The first was to heal people's illnesses by giving them energy, and the second was to experience enlightenment. I received a message from Life just before I was taken to the hospital: **start eating normally, but you will only achieve one of your goals.**

I had always thought that I would first become a healer, and then I would graduate to enlightenment. I did not understand this message. I had done everything that was asked of me, so how could it be possible that I would not reach my goals? I asked myself if I had done anything wrong. Was it because I asked God to take my life in the morning? But one thing that I had learned from the beginning was never to question God's will, and accept all that came to me. That is the true meaning of surrender. But I promised myself that I would continue with all the disciplines and my meditation, no matter what happened. I promised myself that I would not change my ways.

My hospitalization and death

I was put in an ambulance and taken to the hospital. The doctors told my mother that I had a very slim chance of survival. Even though there was a shortage of beds in the emergency room, they kept me there to keep an eye on me at all times. The next day I flat-lined, my heart stopped beating. I felt my consciousness getting zapped like a bolt of lightning. It is very difficult to describe the feeling with words, but I can clearly recall the moment of death. The doctors were able to revive me, and I became stable after a week. I had passed my test, I had accepted all the sufferings that had come to me and willingly walked to my death, I had proven my absolute faith to All That Exists and demonstrated my unwavering dedication to serve Life, no matter the situation or the consequences.

They moved me to the maternity ward, because there was a shortage of bed in the hospital. They could not figure out why the enzymes in my liver had gone completely out of balance, but they went back to normal after a week. I was even able to stand up and walk for a few minutes. My family was happy to see me improve and hoped that everything could go back to normal again.

My consciousness leaving my body

One night while I was still in the hospital, Life connected to me on a deeper level. I saw a vision where my mother, father, and Naz were in the hospital room and I told them that I was fasting again. I saw that one by one they left the room very angrily, but once the vision ended I became free. Immediately after the vision I felt my consciousness lifting off and separated from my body. I was suddenly the space that was filling up the room. I saw my body lying down on the bed, then suddenly there was a buzzing sound and I was back inside my body with my eyes open. Then it happened again, my consciousness lifted off and separated from my body again. I went in and out of my body three times. For the moments that I was outside of my body, I was one with the universe. Universal energy engulfed my consciousness; I was in a state of total bliss. I cannot possibly describe this sensation with mere words, but all the pleasures of the world would pale in comparison to that sensation; it was exhilarating. It was worth all the pain and suffering that

I had experienced in the past seven months. In that moment I knew that I would never die, I knew that my body was just a vessel. You can know something intellectually, but it is a completely different thing to know it experientially. Once going in and out of my body stopped, Life told me that if I loved being one with Life, I needed to fast again.

When you start on this path you must have faith in the process. Life will not give you all the answers as to why you have to do certain things, but one thing that I've learned is that Life will always give you clarity when the time is appropriate. There is always going to be doubt in this process, but that is not a problem as long as you continue to make the effort to silence your mind and not give in to it.

Just as had happened in my vision, my mother, father, and Naz came to visit me in the hospital wearing the exact clothing I had seen in my vision. I told them that I had experienced a vision and needed to start fasting again. They were very angry with my decision and left the room one by one. The next day the nurse came and put me in a wheelchair and took me to a conference room, where six doctors and all my family members had gathered. The head psychiatrist explained that I had already flat-lined once, and that if I continued it would happen again. I told him about the circumstances of my decision, and he said he understood.

"I know you are a seeker," he said. "But I cannot allow you to kill yourself. If you don't stop fasting, I will have no choice but to transfer you to the psych ward for evaluation."

I stood my ground, so they immediately transferred me to the psych ward. My health began to decline again. Within a few days I was unable to stand up, but I no longer cared. I had experienced being outside of my body. Even if I died, I would be okay.

Ending my fast

On the third day the nurse walked in with two security guards, an energy drink in her hand. She told me that I could either drink it myself, or they would forcefully put a tube in my mouth and push it down my throat. I had no energy to even stand up, let alone physically fend off two security guards. I drank the energy drink with tears streaming down my face. Once they left, Life connected to me and I saw a vision where I was finally free. I no longer needed to fast.

I began to eat as much food as I could. Soon I was able to get up and walk again. I had always thought that people who had severe mental illness were just crazy people. During my stay in the psych ward, I had to participate in group meetings, as well as go to classes that educated us about mental illness. I met a woman who was severely depressed, but extremely spiritual. I was able to learn from her. She was no different than anybody else; she just had a chemical imbalance that caused her to be severely depressed. I connected to other people who were in the psych ward and learned about their lives. It gave me a new understanding of people who are mentally ill. I realized why I needed to fast the second time. That was the only way that Life could get me down there, so that I could learn about mental illness. In the class I learned about anxiety, depression, and bipolar disorder. What I learned was extremely valuable. I knew that someday I would have to teach what I know to other people. In order to do that, I had to understand people. I needed to be able to relate to everyone, no matter the situation. The path of enlightenment is to become one with the universe. To achieve that goal, you need to become one with every part of it, the good and the bad. Both the happy and the sad, I could not discriminate. That is why my path had to start with the members of the organized crime family. Even they will reach the light someday.

One day I asked Life why I was chosen for this task. Life replied: *"Only someone who has gone astray and learned how to straighten their life can teach others to do the same."*

I was in the psych ward for three weeks. Once the head psychiatrist was satisfied that I was not going to fast again, he released me to my parents' care. I continued eating as much as I could, and within a short time I was back to 195 pounds, which is my natural body weight. I went back to work with my father. My shoulder was no longer hurting, but after a few months we lost the cleaning contract. A new phase of my journey was beginning.

I was not surprised that we lost the cleaning business. That was the theme of this path: as soon as one type of pressure would lift, a new one would start. But I was not the same weak person who went to the hospital broken, and my family was not the same either. I had experienced the lowest a human being can possibly experience in a lifetime. I had walked to my death at the slowest pace possible. All my fears were gone, now that

I knew I would never die. There was no reason to be afraid of anything. The other benefit of having that low experience was that I was extremely happy for no particular reason. After coming back from the hospital, doing very simple things like having a nice meal or going for a quick walk would give me great pleasure. We often forget to appreciate and enjoy the simplest things in life. I had experienced so much pain and suffering in so many different parts of my body, that just a back pain by itself was a walk in the park. The seven months that I fasted until I experienced death in the hospital was the worse and the best time of my life, because no matter how bad things get, it will never come anywhere close to what I experienced back then.

My mother was the same way as me. She had become extremely depressed after Telly's death, but after I came back from the hospital she was no longer depressed. The seven months that I had fasted until my time in the hospital had given her a new low. She had almost lost her second child, and now that I was back, things did not seem so bad anymore. She was actually happy and had a new appreciation for life. People always run away from their low experiences, but instead they should really cherish those moments, because all the highs that they experience in their lifetimes are highs in relation to those low moments. The lower you go, easier is for you to become happy.

Why are we here?

I was meditating one day after I got back from the hospital, and Life shared with me one of the main reasons why we are here.

We are here to face difficult challenges, and experience negative events in our lives to give us the experience of low.

The fact of the matter is that we have not been made in the image of God. We are God's consciousness, and I only say God's consciousness because if I tell you that **you are God**, you're going to feel strange. You would think, how could I possibly be God? How could I be All That Exists? But **you are All That Exists, everything that exists in this universe is within you**.

I now want to explain why God would want you to experience the **low** in our physical body by experiencing negative events. The consciousness that is God is in a state of total bliss. But to know what bliss is, Life has to experience its opposite, which is pain and suffering. You might think to yourself that if you were in a state of total bliss, you would never want to experience pain and suffering. So let me explain to you why we choose to experience negative events in our lives.

Imagine that you are God and you are in a state of total bliss. A state of total bliss is the highest pleasure that could be experienced by consciousness, a 100 out of 100, and there is no pleasure greater than 100. Now imagine that you have been at 100 for an eternity. You have been at 100 for so long that you have got tired of being there. You want to feel better than 100, but that is just not possible. There is nothing beyond God, so what can you do if you want to feel better but you can't go above 100? There is a way: you can't go up, but you can come down to 10 for a moment in time, and then go back to 100 again, and you will feel 90 units better. We come to these bodies to experience the low for a moment in time, and when we die, we go back up, in essence we experience being God again. There is no heaven after death; heaven is the natural state of consciousness, which is absolute bliss. I have experienced this state of consciousness, but unfortunately I cannot possibly describe the sensations that I felt in that time span. All the pleasures of this physical world combined pale in comparison to what I experienced in those moments. In the moment of death, we go from 0, 5, 10 or 20 back to 100. The lower you are at the moment of death, the higher the jump back to 100 will be. In fact, the more you suffer at the moment of death the better it will be for your spiritual development. You think that there is too much pain and suffering in one lifetime, but one life is just one long moment that has been stretched out. When you look back at your life ten or twenty years ago, it feels like just a short time ago. You have lived thousands of lives and your consciousness has been there from the beginning of the time, what is one lifetime compared to an eternity? People experience different levels of low depending on where they are in their spiritual development. People who are further along on their spiritual development can handle more, so they can experience more challenging lives.

Our life is not a punishment; in fact, it is a blessing. We cannot know what bliss is unless we experience the opposite. You might think that if you are at 100, there's no way you would want to come down to 5, 10, or 20, so I'm going to give you an illustration of why you would want to do this. What is your absolute favorite food? Now what do you think would happen if you had to eat that food for six months straight from morning to night, without eating anything else? I guarantee you that no matter how much you like that food, you would be sick of it after six months. If you don't believe me, try it. That is the nature of consciousness. Your favorite food tastes so good because you also eat foods that are not as tasty. One cannot exist without the other. In order to know what 100 is, you need to experience numbers below the 100 – hence the duality that we live in. This journey is about overcoming challenges and experiencing difficulties. The lower you go in your lifetime, the better it will be for your spiritual development, so don't run away from negative experiences. Instead cherish them, remember that the pendulum will always swing the other way, and accept both good and bad.

The relationship between male and female energy

I believe it is also important to understand the relationship between male and the female energy, as well as the relationship between objects, trees, and living creatures.

In the beginning there was only one. The single consciousness wanted to experience itself, but how can you have any kind of experience by yourself? You cannot play chess with yourself; you need to have a minimum of two participants to have any kind of interaction. So the single consciousness divided itself into two. These two energies began to vibrate on exact opposite cycles. For example, if you look at sine and cosine in algebra, they are exact opposites of one and the other, but you need to understand that these two opposite energies are not separated from each other. They are opposite sides of the same energy, like the opposite sides of the same coin. The consciousness needed more than two players, so these two energies began to vibrate at different frequencies to manifest different entities.

Everything in this universe is the combination of these two energies. We are all one, but we are not all the same. The solids, like iron or stone, vibrate slower than all other forms of energy. Fluids vibrate faster than solids, gases vibrate faster than fluids, plants and trees vibrate faster than the gases, animals and other creatures vibrate faster than plants and trees. Human beings vibrate faster than all animals and creatures. And there are more evolved beings in this universe that vibrate faster than human beings.

Of course things are much more complex than this, but the truth is that nothing is dead in this universe. Even a pebble is from the same consciousness as you and me; the only difference is the level of awareness and the vibration of its energy. The circle of life began with the big bang, with our consciousness vibrating at a very slow rate. Our consciousness has evolved over billions of years as plants, trees, and different creatures, until we got to where we are today. The evolution of our consciousness never ends, but there is a beginning and an end for everything that is physical in our reality. The multiverse that we are living in is a physical manifestation of source energy. The cycle that began with the big bang will come to an end, but it will not be a time of judgment, as it has been described in the Bible and the Koran. The collective consciousness will simply vibrate as fast as the source energy, so that there will be no point in continuing; the cycle will end and a new one will begin again. Our consciousness has evolved through an infinite number of these cycles: you have been there from the beginning, and there will never be an end. An infinite number of civilizations have come and gone, but our evolution will never end, we are eternal.

The beings who live on this planet are different in three different aspects:

1. The frequency of their vibration, which determines the level of their awareness. The level of brain activity is the physical manifestation of this awareness. Mammals like chimpanzees or dolphins are known to have higher awareness of themselves, close to that of human beings.

2. The density of their energy. Other than human beings, other creatures who live on this planet have limited capacity to build the density of their energy, since they mostly exist in the etheric and the emotional body. In order for energy to rise up in the energy field, all creatures need to stand vertically for long periods of time. This is why the development of language has been very limited in the animal kingdom – energy needs to rise to the third body, which deals with the mental aspect and thinking processes.

Lack of energy in the third body has prevented animals from making significant progress and developing language. However, scientists have been able to teach some gorillas and chimpanzees sign language, because they have the ability to stand up for longer periods of time.

3. The makeup of the male and female energy.

Everything is part of a single consciousness

I have continuously indicated the existence of the single consciousness that makes up our planet and the entire universe, but how is it possible to be one and feel so separated at the same time? I am going to give you two examples to describe this phenomenon. One example is the existence of waves on the surface of the ocean (an example which other spiritual teachers have used), and another example is one that Life shared with me.

When you look at the ocean on a sunny day with no wind, there are no waves. You can only see the body of the ocean. Once the weather pattern changes and it becomes windy, the air molecules and the water molecules interact with each other and create billions of waves on the surface of the ocean. You can see these waves individually and they seem separate from each other, but these waves do not really exist, they just appear to be in a moment in time. The tops of these waves are the individual consciousness that make up all the creatures living on this planet. The movement of energy within the consciousness causes ripples within itself that appear to be separate from one and another. This universal energy is constantly moving, and is flowing through every living being on this planet.

We are no different than these waves. We come to be for a moment in time through the process of birth, and we identify ourselves with the top of the wave, but in fact we are the ocean.

The second example describes how the consciousness that we are aware of, which is who you know yourself to be, interacts with God's consciousness, which is the body of the ocean. If you can comprehend this relationship you can understand it all.

When you go to driving school to learn how to drive, they have cars with a steering wheel, gas pedal, and brake pedal on the driver's side, and another identical set on the passenger side. The teacher sits on the passenger side observing your every move as you drive the vehicle. If the teacher feels that you are making a mistake and you are going to crash, he or she will take over and take corrective actions to prevent an accident from happening. When the teacher takes over and makes a corrective action, such as taking over the steering wheel, all control passes to the teacher, and your actions become inconsequential. The teacher is ultimately in complete control of the vehicle.

There are billions of people living on this planet. Their physical bodies are like the cars that are used in driving school. Individual consciousness, which is who we know ourselves to be, are the drivers sitting on the driver's side learning how to drive, and the teacher is God's consciousness. There are two really important points. The first point is that there is only one teacher who is sitting in all the cars and controlling all the movements. The second point is that you are both the consciousness that is sitting on the driver's side as well as the consciousness who is sitting on the passenger side, you are simply not aware of that other part of yourself. On December of 2005 I became aware of the other part of myself. I was one with All That Exists, there was absolute clarity and unity with pure understanding. The above example cannot possibly do justice to describing this unity, but it is the best description that I can come up with using mere words.

You are simply not aware of the teacher within you, but Life is constantly guiding and communicating with you. When you make a decision on a matter, you always hear two opposite thoughts in your mind. One is from the small part of you and the other is from the teacher. The small part of you is selfish and fearful, and usually wants to take the easy way out. The teacher sees the big picture and suggests the best course of action for the evolution of your consciousness. It is up to you which thought you will identify with, but depending on your choice, your actions will have consequences.

For example, if you are partying a lot and drinking and driving, the teacher may put in place a sequence of events where you would get pulled over and charged with DUI in order to make you think and change your ways. Or for example, if you hit an unattended parked car and decide not to leave your information because you don't want your insurance to go up, the teacher may create a sequence of events in which your car is broken into, or some other negative sequence in which you lose the money that you tried to save. No one gets away with anything in this life. The further astray you go, the bigger the consequences will be.

Karma is not a punishment; it is a reaction by the teacher towards an action that has been taken by the student. Never forget that you are both the student and the teacher. You are both the creator of all the events in this universe, and the experiencer of all those events at the same time; you are God's consciousness.

This reaction does not always happen because we made a wrong choice. Sometimes we harm our physical bodies by not taking care of ourselves, or stress out so much about money or other issues that we create an imbalance within our energy field. In these cases, the teacher may be forced to manifest an illness to address this energy imbalance. For example, many people who experience lower back pain have had financial difficulties prior to the back pain, and people with a high degree of stress sometimes become ill.

Go back to any significant negative experience that you have had in your lifetime and think about what you did, or what was happening in your life prior to that negative experience. The experience is not always right before the physical manifestation, but if you go back far enough, I assure you that you will be able to connect the dots.

I've seen people making the same mistakes over and over again, and negative things keep happening to them over and over again. The connection is never made, and the cycle keeps repeating itself. Unfortunately, sometimes it takes a lifetime for a person to overcome a single issue, and that is their choice. The good thing is that there is no time limit to reach the source, but if you don't make the connection and make the necessary adjustments, you will have to endure much more pain and suffering. Learn to listen to the guiding voice that is coming from inside of you, from your center.

I want to share one of the many experiences I have had with the teacher, where it demonstrated the amount of control it has over our physical bodies. One day I was practicing a specific meditation technique in which I had to hold my breath for a long period of time in order to lift my consciousness out of my body. However, I kept falling just short of the amount of time that was necessary to achieve that. About twenty minutes into the meditation, the teacher finally took over my breathing.

The muscles around my lungs did not respond to my commands when I
tried to take a breath, nothing happened. Just imagine, I tried to breathe
through my nose, but there was no response from the muscles in my
body. I did not feel like I was suffocating, nor was I uncomfortable. I hit
the threshold and my consciousness lifted out of my body. I believe Life
was just playing with me. Life has a good sense of humor, but I can tell
you it was one of the strangest sensations that I have experienced since I
started on this path.

Why does evil exist?

I feel that I need to address a question that many of you might have
about karma and the fairness of God. A friend once asked me:

"If God has such control over our affairs, why doesn't God stop
freak accidents like when a toddler wanders away from its mother and
gets hit by a car and dies? Or when a father and sole provider for four
children accidentally falls, hits his head and dies? His children are put on
the street as a result, and they suffer. Or when a little girl is abducted and
raped and killed by a child rapist? Where is the fairness of God? Why do
so many bad things happen to good people, while many bad people live
very good lives?"

These are valid questions. Life does not seem fair at first glance
because we tend to see and judge these events based on a single life.
Karma continues and balances itself over hundreds and even thousands
of lifetimes, depending on the journey that a soul chooses to experience.
Life does not seem fair because we're simply not aware of our previous
lives and the lives after this one. The first thing to remember is that we are
here to experience the low, and sometimes that experience is given to us in
the form of an accident or a crime. The second thing to remember is that
no one really dies. Instead, an experience comes to an end and a new one
begins. The suffering that is experienced is only a short moment in time.
In the end, Life always balances itself and no one experiences more pain
and suffering than they have caused during their many lives.

Connecting to your higher self

I am trying to help you connect to the other part of you, the part you did not know existed. That is the spiritual path, the inner journey. You have been driving the car for so long that you have come to think you are the car, so let's compare our physical bodies to an actual car.

Just like the car that needs gas for energy, physical bodies need to metabolize food for energy. Cars have various sensors to collect data, and provide information to the central computer system, which manages the different functions of the vehicle. Our eyes, ears, and other senses collect data and provide information to our brains, which manage our interactions with the outside world. Cars have oil and fuel filters to keep the system clean; our physical bodies use kidney, the liver, and sweating to achieve the same function. Cars have oil and fuel pumps to deliver supplements to the engine, and our heart is the pump in the physical body that delivers nutrients and supplements to the entire system.

Our physical bodies are very sophisticated biological machines that Life has manifested through billions of years of evolution, and in fact they are capable of so much more than what is known to us today. Never forget that our bodies are just vessels that we use to experience this reality; don't confuse yourself with the biological machine that you are driving.

Now let us look at different parts of you. The small part of you is the sum of all your experiences. Unfortunately, we rely too much on the small part of ourselves when we are making decisions in our lives. Our past experiences can affect us in a positive way, but they can also affect us in a very negative way. For example, if you grew up in a household where honesty was not rewarded and you lied because you were fearful when you made a mistake, you will continue to lie as an adult. The thoughts in your head will always take you in the wrong direction because they are affected by your past conditioning. Most of you always know when someone is lying to you, unless knowing the truth causes you pain. In that case you will be willing to look the other way and believe the lie, but deep inside you know the truth because we are all one: your inner self always knows the truth. The thoughts in your head are your past conditioning. Work on silencing those thoughts through meditation. Only then can you hear the God within you. Your head gives you a false sense of yourself. Your true self is your center, which is located where your navel is.

A fetus is connected to the mother through the umbilical cord, and continues to grow until a soul completely bonds with the fetus's physical body, which happens when the fetus begins to move for the first time inside the mother's womb. The fetus will continue to grow after that, but the center of the soul will always remain the same until we die.

Let us do an exercise to locate your center, the center of your energy field, the location of the real you. Continuously say "OMMMM ...", and follow the sound to see where it is coming from. You can follow the sound right to where your navel is. It is the same when we listen to any sound, our ears receive the sound, but our center is listening to it, not our brain. Your brain is interpreting the sound, but your center is the one who is listening to it. This one is a little bit harder to follow, but it is used in meditation techniques where listening is the focal point. I will be going through these techniques at the end. Your center speaks when you talk, and listens when you hear. That is the real you. Connect yourself to your center, rather than identifying yourself with thoughts in your mind. Meditation will help you sort through these thoughts and make you realize which is which.

Allow your center to be your guiding system. There are always two opposite thoughts that come to your mind. Every human being knows the difference between right and wrong, but unfortunately many people use their head – which is affected by past conditioning – to make decisions, rather than listening to their center. Don't ignore your gut feelings. Your center is your higher self, it is the teacher you must learn to recognize and listen to.

I can easily recognize the difference between my small self and my higher self or God's consciousness, and I want to help you to do the same. **The consciousness that is occupied by your senses that are seeing, listening, tasting, and feeling is your small self**. This consciousness is who you know yourself to be. This consciousness is of low vibration and is constantly processing the information that your brain receives from the outside world via your senses. It is also analyzing events and making decisions based on your past experiences. The experience of this consciousness is limited to one lifetime, which is from your birth to the present time. Unfortunately, this consciousness lacks focus and is occupied by random thoughts and sensory overload. **This consciousness is localized within our energy field, which is why we**

can feel separated from the outside world. But this is a small part of who we are, and we're not truly separated from the universe. Your higher self is your center and is in control of all-important bodily functions, as well as complete control over the entire system. Your heart goes on beating, the muscles around your chest expand and retract allowing you to breathe, your kidneys go on cleaning your blood continuously without you paying attention to anything, and so on. Your higher self also monitors all decisions and actions that you take throughout the day. Remember that your higher self can override any action that has been taken by your smaller self. Just as a driving school teacher can take over driving the car if you're about to crash the car.

Your higher self is one with every living being on this planet and the universe. Your smaller self is who you know yourself to be. You are only aware of your smaller self, but remember that you are both the smaller self and the higher self. Depending on your actions you sometimes identify with your higher self, and sometimes identify with your smaller self. When you take any action that unites you with other consciousness, you identify with your higher self; when you take actions that separate you from other consciousness, you are identifying with your smaller self. The smaller self is selfish and only considers personal gratification, your higher self is loving and considers the whole. Always choose unity; that is the spiritual path.

Your higher self allows the smaller self to operate the physical body, unless it is necessary to take over. This could be to prevent an accident, or to make a specific event happen in your life. Your higher self is also continuously communicating with you through your thoughts. As I have mentioned before, you sometimes have opposite thoughts in your mind, one coming from your smaller self, which is affected by your past conditioning, and one coming from your higher self, which is All That Exists.

The paradoxes in spirituality

It is impossible to describe the relationship between your smaller and higher self more accurately without contradicting myself. This is due to the fact that there are many paradoxes in spirituality. Some of these paradoxes can be explained using words, but some can only be understood when you experience your higher self directly. I'm going to give you two examples of these paradoxes.

The first paradox: how is it possible for a soul to reincarnate if there are no individual souls?

I have mentioned repeatedly that there is only one of us. In fact, there are no individual souls, so how is it possible for a soul to reincarnate if there are no individual souls?

To explain this phenomenon, I am going to use your physical body as an example. You have toenails, index fingers, and eyes as different parts of your physical body, but none of them exists individually, only you exist as a whole. In this scenario there's no way to turn the toenail into an index finger or eyes. However, consciousness can create ripples within itself and place the energy with lower vibration in a physical body and increase its frequency, and focus through the process of birth and death, while completely overseeing the entire process. In effect – metaphorically – consciousness can turn the toenail into an eye. This is why it is important for you to actively meditate and help yourself through this process, because the only other way to increase your focus and vibration is through overwhelming you with negative experiences. The deeper the hole you're in, the harder you will work consciously to get out of it, which in effect increases the vibration of your energy and improves your focus.

This is a very long, arduous, and difficult process, but your higher self is cradling the consciousness with lower vibration within itself, like a mother would cradle and protect a child. Life is with you, and guiding you every step of the way.

The second paradox: the existence of mind

The second paradox is the existence of mind. I have repeatedly spoken about silencing your mind, but in fact mind does not exist. I know that this is confusing, but I have to say this because if you meditate long enough, someday you might reach the state of no mind. You can only comprehend this through direct experience with your higher self. The existence of mind for different individuals depends on where they are in their spiritual development. This will only come into play at higher levels of spirituality, but I need to mention it, because it may apply to you. I am deliberately being vague here because anything that I say could make things more confusing, so just know that if you meditate enough one day you will realize that mind does not really exist.

How your higher self communicates with you through thoughts

I now want to give you some examples where your higher self is communicating with you through thoughts, or taking actions in an event.

This first example has happened to everyone who has ever driven a car. Recall a time where you were driving in rush hour traffic, and you put your head down for a moment to change the radio station or look at your phone, and suddenly you felt a force lifting your head up and you saw that the car that is in front of you had come to a full stop. You slammed on your brakes and came to a stop just short of hitting them. This has happened to you too many times to be a coincidence. You always lift your head just at the right moment – even another split second would have resulted in an accident. How could you have known that the car in front of you had come to a full stop? Your head was down, so you could have not known what was happening in front of you, but there is a part of you that is one with the driver in front of you, that part is your higher self. In fact, there is only one driver who is driving all the cars. You have heard people say that **it was meant to be, and it was God's will** when an accident happens. How could this be possible if random people drive individually on their own will? It cannot: there is only one driver driving all the cars. This is not limited to driving; all events happen exactly as they should because there is only one entity in all of our physical bodies.

This second example has also happened to every one of us at some point in our lifetime. There have been many occasions where you thought about someone and shortly after they called you on the phone or contacted you in some way. This too has happened too many times for it to be a coincidence. Your higher self is beyond time and space. Once you think of someone, your energy vibrates and they can feel you, no matter how far they are from you. This connection is much stronger between a mother and a child. Mothers often know when something has happened to their child, no matter how far they are from them.

Your higher self may try to connect with you by manifesting your thoughts. You may think of a situation or an event, and it happens just the way you thought it was going to happen. Do not disregard these events as coincidences or you will miss an opportunity to grow from your own experiences. There are no coincidences in life. Just imagine if you bring your index finger on the left hand and your pinky finger on the right hand together. It is not a coincidence, you brought them together, and you were meant to do it. So when two people come together or something happens, Life meant for it to happen, it is not a coincidence. We are all the little parts that Life moves around on purpose; a thought enters your mind to go somewhere or to do something, and along the way you meet someone or an event happens. None of these events are coincidental. Your higher self is communicating, moving, and guiding you every step of the way.

This next example usually happens to people who are at the beginning of their spiritual journey. I have talked to many people who have told me that they repeatedly see a particular number in different situations. Naz used to tell me that she continuously sees the number 11 anywhere she goes. At times she would look to see what time it was, and she would see that the time was exactly 11:11, or she would look at an advertisement and find that the store was having a sale on the 11th day of the month. The significance of these experiences is to make you ponder: Is there more to this life than just random coincidences? If something is happening to you on a regular basis, no matter what it is, Life is trying to connect with you. Don't ignore these signs, or you will lose the chance to grow from your own experiences.

Many times when you leave an apartment or house you put your jacket on, take your keys, check to make sure you have your wallet, and then leave. Just as you sit in the car or are walking down the street, a thought enters your mind: **Where's my phone?** And you realize you have forgotten your phone. The phone is just an example; it could be something that you have forgotten or it could be that you had forgotten about an appointment that you had with someone. When you have thoughts like this, it is coming from your higher self. Remember that your smaller self is occupied by your senses, and anything beyond that is your higher self.

Many couples who have been together for a long time and have a deep connection sometimes say the exact same thing at the same time.

Again the higher self in both of them is one; that is the only way that this could be possible.

When someone close to you lies to you, you always know the truth. You may not want to see or accept it because the truth might be painful, but deep down your higher self is telling you what the truth is. You need to trust yourself and listen to your gut feeling.

Just remember that your higher self prevents many accidents from happening, but also makes many accidents happen if you have a karma that needs to be repaid, it goes both ways. At night when you fall asleep, your smaller self and your higher self become one, and there is an understanding as to what you need to experience the following day. There is absolute unity and an agreement about everything that you are experiencing. You choose your experiences; there is no outside God who is forcing you into doing or experiencing things.

THE SECOND PHASE

During the period between coming back from the hospital and losing the janitorial contract, my mind had become very silent. I thought that I must be getting close to the point of enlightenment, but when I received the news of losing the janitorial contract I was not surprised. Life was stirring the pot to bring up the dirt that had sank to the bottom of the pot; this is how Life operates. No matter how hard we try to control our lives, as soon as we get comfortable with our situation, a sequence of events happens in which things change and new challenges present themselves.

You may have done things or experienced events in your life where you could look back and say that no benefit ever came from them. But you never know what Life has planned for you, and when you might need to use your education or past experiences in a new venture.

My long-haul trucking career

Many years ago, before I got involved with the organized crime families, I had gone to driving school and attained my Class A commercial truck driver's license. But at the time I had many points on my driver's license due to speeding tickets, so I was not able to get a job in that field. After a period of time, I became involved with the organized crime families and never bothered looking for a job in that field again.

Once I received the news that we were losing the janitorial contract, I immediately knew that this was the plan all along, it made perfect sense. Long-haul commercial truck driving is a type of job where you can be alone for long periods of time, and you can focus to silence your mind without interruption.

106

Usually when people wanted to start on a path of enlightenment, they would go and stay in a monastery, where a master could direct them on their paths. It is easier to silence your mind when you are in a place where you are completely shut off from everything, and have no responsibilities other than keeping the monastery clean with the help of other monks. That method was not available to me. My father was seventy years old and could not continue working for much longer, so I told him to retire, and I assured him that I would take care of our household expenses. Life wanted me to learn how I could achieve enlightenment, while earning income for my family, and being part of the general population. I knew that I needed to create discipline for myself so that I could take control of the sexual energy that was building inside of me. When you are celibate and live in a monastery, you don't see women walking around in sexy clothing, so it is easier to keep yourself in check. I figured out very early on that it is simply easier not to look at any woman and I keep my head down when I am around them. You can't want what you don't see. I had got better at controlling my sexual thoughts, but looking at or interacting with a sexy woman could haunt me for hours, sometimes even days. This was not permanent, eventually I got to a point where looking at a sexy woman would no longer bother me. I had transcended beyond sexual desire, but it took over ten years of meditation and self-discipline to get there.

I took a refresher course in truck driving and was able to secure a job with a local company that took loads from Vancouver BC, to Seattle Washington, and Portland Oregon. My trips were only one or two days long. Learning how to drive and backup semi-trucks was very challenging, but I always enjoyed driving. So even though I was working more hours than janitorial work, I was enjoying the work.

I continued to work for that company for four months. One day after I'd dropped off the company's truck at the garage for a service, my boss picked me up and drove me to the yard. He told me that I was a good employee and if I stayed with the company he would help me buy my own truck and become an owner-operator to make more money. I did not think much of that conversation because in the past I had always been a very cautious person, and had never committed myself to purchasing real estate or taking on large loans for vehicles. I would rather work for someone else and make less money than take a large loan and buy a semi-truck to make more. I drove home that night and told my father about my conversation with my boss. He was all for it, that's just how he is, the complete opposite of me. I suddenly received a phone call from a friend who was a long-haul truck driver. He asked if we could meet to discuss something. I agreed, so he dropped by our apartment.

My friend owned a semi-truck that was only one and a half years old. He came over and showed me the purchase agreement for the truck. He had paid $50,000 as a down payment on the truck, and had to make monthly payments of $2,200 for five years to pay off the truck. He offered to sell me 50% of the truck for $15,000. He had already made eighteen monthly payments, so on paper this looked like a very good deal for my family and me. He told me that we could work for a company that did long-haul shipping, so that I could do one trip with the truck and come back, and then he could do one trip and come back. Based on his calculations, after paying all the expenses, he expected us to each earn $5,500 a month.

My boss had a conversation about buying a truck with me in the morning and then my friend had called me the very same night and offered me to buy 50% of his truck, so I was sure that Life was guiding me to buy 50% of his truck. The reason I am giving this example is because Life communicates with everyone in this matter. The sequence of events in our lives is always trying to tell us something; we need to pay attention and see the direction that Life is pointing to. This direction could make things easier or more difficult for us, but more difficult is not always bad. Remember that events in our lives happen to help us evolve our consciousness; Life does not care if we are comfortable or not.

I talked to my father about my friend's proposal. We did not have $15,000 to give him, but my father told me we could take $15,000 as a cash advance on our credit cards. I would normally never do such a thing, but the path of enlightenment is about surrendering yourself to the universe. So no matter what the situation, if Life wanted me to go to that direction, I would follow without question. We gave my friend $15,000 from our credit cards and we began to work with a long-haul trucking company. I went on one trip, and then he went on a trip right after I got back home.

After a few weeks, while I was sitting next to my friend in the truck, his bank called him about why he had not been making his truck payments. He hung up the phone and confessed he was in a great financial difficulty and was facing bankruptcy. He was also two months behind on his truck payments. I was shocked; I had known him for more than fifteen years. I knew that he wasn't trying to cheat me, but if he didn't make the truck payments they would seize the truck and I would lose the $15,000 that I had given him. We had to pay the bank $4,400 so they would not seize the truck, and neither one of us had the money. He told me that if I gave him another $5,000 he would sell me the remaining 50% of the truck and he would walk away from it. I went home and discussed the situation with my father. We would need to give my friend $5,000 for the truck and the bank $4,400 to get caught up with the monthly payments. My father called my uncle and borrowed $5,000 to give to the bank, and we gave our old Toyota to my friend as payment for his 50% of the truck. Our family was now in severe debt. I tried to keep calm throughout this ordeal; Life was now putting pressure on me through financial difficulty.

As if this was not bad enough, the owner of the new trucking company that I was working for was cheating the owner-operators by deflating freight charges. I went on one trip that took twenty-six days, and earned only $2,000 for the entire trip. My truck payments were $2,200 without any expenses. I could no longer survive financially working for that company. I had to change to a new trucking company that paid better, but the timing could not have been worse. It was difficult to find work because of the 2008 recession.

I wanted to work for a company that paid well and would only send me to California, because the highways to California were much easier to drive on with semi-trucks during winter. The Rocky Mountains in British Columbia are notorious for accidents during winter. In April of 2009 I finally found a company that only worked in the western United States. This trucking company hauled produce between California and Vancouver, BC. I had fallen so far behind on my bills and truck payments that my father had to borrow another $10,000 from a friend of ours to catch up with our payments. I had never had to pull myself out of so much financial trouble.

One advantage with the new company was that I was paid based on the miles that I drove, so it was straightforward. The owner of the company promised me that he would increase my rate of pay as the price of diesel increased, and with it increase my expenses. I needed to work very hard to make payments to everyone that we owed money to. I was very stressed about money. I always kept focused on the third eye, and used mantras to keep myself calm and silent. My favorite mantras were **"everything is happening exactly as it should"** and **"I'm strong, and I can overcome any obstacle."** Life had proven to me that is in complete control of our affairs. Even though my bank account was always hovering around zero, I had complete faith that we were going to be all right.

But knowing something theoretically is different from knowing something experientially. No matter how strong my faith was, there was still a small piece of me that was slightly worried. Unfortunately, when it comes to Life there are no compromises. You cannot move to the next level with 98%, there can be no fear whatsoever about anything. I knew that I had to transform all the energy within my emotional body before I could move on to the mental body, so in this phase I needed to transcend beyond my fears experientially.

When I was going through this phase, I remembered a story that my father had told me many years before. He told me that he once went to visit a village in a rural area deep in the Zagros Mountains. The road was not wide enough to travel by car, and parts of the road were very narrow pathways along the side of vertical cliffs. He told me that there was just enough room for one person or a donkey to walk through, and one misstep would send you to your death, thousands of feet down into the valley. Villagers had specially trained donkeys that had the job of taking people across those pathways. The donkeys had traveled the pathways so many times that they had no fear of falling down. The visitors would sit on the donkey and without any guides, the donkey would navigate through the pathways and take them to the other side. The reason this story resonated with me was because Life operates in the same way. If you need to get over a fear Life will keep putting you in that situation until you're no longer afraid of it. I was in such deep financial trouble that one big expense could have destroyed my finances. I also had to demonstrate that no matter how dire my circumstances, I would still do the right thing when situations arose.

While working, I was once looking for the address of a shipper in Los Angeles, California. I accidentally turned into a residential street that semi-trucks were not allowed to enter, so I tried to back out. While backing out, I hit and bent the traffic light. Once I realized that I had hit the traffic light, I pulled forward and got out to inspect the damage. There was no damage to my trailer and the traffic light was just slightly bent. There was a man standing there and he said, "It's not too bad, I'm not going to say anything to anybody. So just go, don't worry about it."

I could not afford for my insurance to go up, but I knew that I needed to report the accident to the authorities. In a moment of weakness, I thought that the traffic light was just slightly bent, and the man had said he would not say anything, so Life must be giving me a break. I drove off, returned from my trip, parked my truck in the company yard and went home.

My trips to California and back usually took five days, and I usually worked 14 hours a day. I could not afford to take more than one day off, so I would get ready quickly and go off on another trip after 36 hours of off-duty time. When I returned to the company yard, I saw that another truck driver had hit my truck and pulled off the truck's bumper. No one had reported the incident, so I had to pay for the damages myself. This was the payback for not reporting the accident the week before; I should have known better. I already knew that I was not going to get away with anything, and I had failed my test. I asked for forgiveness, and promised myself that the next time I would do the right thing, no matter how difficult it might be.

Three weeks later almost the exact same thing happened. I drove up the wrong street, and when I tried to backup I hit the stop sign and broke it off. This time nobody was around, but I parked my truck and called the non-emergency police line and asked them to connect me to authorities in the city of Fresno, California. I reported the incident and told them that I would take care of the damages. The clerk was surprised that anyone would call to report such an incident. He took my information and told me that they would send someone to inspect the damage, and someone would get in touch with me about the repairs. The very next week, I passed by the same location and saw that the stop sign had been fixed. For weeks I was expecting to receive a call or a bill for damages, but nothing happened. I had done the right thing this time, and Life gave me a break. I have never hit anything else, nor have I been involved in any other accidents since that time. Once you demonstrate that you have learned your lesson, there is no reason for an experience to repeat itself. But as long as you cheat, the same thing will happen over and over again until you connect the dots and break the cycle. I want to mention one thing about karma: many people download free movies and other materials from the Internet thinking that it is okay to cheat corporations, or cheat on taxes because it's the government. But there is no difference between cheating corporations, government, or people. Cheating is cheating, and one way or another, perpetrators are going to pay for it. The only thing that cheating does is to cause negative experiences over and over again, until one day the cheater figures it out. The sooner a person understands this, the sooner the negative experiences caused by such actions will stop.

I continued to work for my employer for a year and a half. The winter storms were always difficult, because I did not like to drive in snow with my semi-truck. So when I would hear that there was a storm coming, I would stop all thoughts by focusing on the third eye, but all that would do was to suppress my fear of driving in snow. The following winter the price of diesel went up considerably. My boss had promised to increase my rate of pay when the price of the diesel increased, so I asked him to honor his promise and increase my rate, but he refused. I was not making enough money to cover all my payments, so I had no choice but to look for a new company with better pay. There were many companies that were hiring, but all of the companies that I found would send me to Calgary, Alberta during the winter. I quickly realized that I needed to get over my fear of driving in the snow. I switched to a new trucking company that traveled between Vancouver BC, and Calgary, Alberta. I had to drive on some of the most challenging highways in the British Columbia Mountains during winter storm conditions. I finally got to the point that driving in the snow seemed very normal, and I was no longer afraid of it. I continued to work for the new company for another year and a half. I had grown tremendously during the three years of driving semi-trucks. Long haul truck driving is one of the most difficult jobs in the world, both mentally and physically. During the three years I was constantly under financial pressure, but I was vigilant about using my mantras and meditation to overcome my fears. Very slowly, the fears went away until I became truly fearless. Not just intellectually, but experientially. I was in deep meditation one day, when Life communicated to me through the third eye that I could sell my truck and pay off all my debt. Once my fear of not having enough went away, financial pressure was no longer necessary. I sold my truck and connected to my old boss, and got hired as a company driver going back and forth between California and Vancouver again.

The opening of the third eye had widened greatly during the three years that I had worked as a commercial truck driver. I could feel my energy field continuously getting stronger. I had overcome my fears, but I was struggling to find **balance** in my life. Long haul truck driving is a type of job where you are working 14 hours a day, and when you are at home for 36 or 48 hours, your body is so exhausted up from all the sitting and holding the wheel that you have little energy left to do anything else.

How To Find Balance And Fulfillment In Your Life

After I came back from the hospital and began to drive commercial trucks, Life communicated to me that the period of separation was over, and I could occasionally go out with my friends, or watch some TV when I was at home. But I needed to find the right balance in my life. How does a person find the right balance in their lives; for that matter, how does a society find the right balance? Finding the right balance is the most difficult issue facing any individual or society, because everything that we do affects balance, and balance affects every aspect of our lives. Buddha based an entire religion on balance. Buddhism was the middle way, so I'm going to describe balance for individuals as well as balance for a society.

Every human being seeks fulfillment in their lives, but how we go about reaching that fulfillment is different for every one of us:

- Some people seek fulfillment in financial success.
- Some people seek fulfillment in having children and a family.
- Some people seek fulfillment in their careers.
- Some people seek fulfillment in spirituality and humanitarian efforts.

The list is endless; all these different avenues will only give you partial or temporary fulfillment. People who seek fulfillment in financial success work hard to build wealth, but they are never satisfied because there are always bigger houses, bigger boats, more expensive cars, and so on. They're always projecting into the future. When they finally buy the car that they always wanted, for a while they're extremely happy, but eventually it becomes normal and the fulfillment disappears and they want something different. The desire to have bigger and better things will never end. True fulfillment can never be reached by material possessions.

Woman often feel fulfilled when they have children, because the infant relies on the mother for all its needs and the mother has to take care of the child constantly. But children eventually grow up and become more independent as they grow older, so the mother's fulfillment is temporary and it goes away.

People who seek fulfillment in their careers put all their effort into advancing their careers. They are so engulfed in the process that they are willing to sacrifice everything to reach their goal. But their goal is always somewhere in the future, because you can always progress further. One day, after wasting many years, they ask themselves, what did I do all that for?

Fulfillment in all these situations is always temporary, and the majority of people feel there is something missing in their lives regardless of their situation. Even humanitarian efforts and spirituality by themselves do not give you true fulfillment, if you do not have the right balance in different aspects of your life.

True fulfillment comes from **balance** in your life. Your higher self is responsible for your happiness and feeling of fulfillment in your life, so in order to reach fulfillment in your life permanently, you need to achieve balance in different aspects of your life both individually and as a whole. Only then will your higher self give you permanent fulfillment and the experience of total bliss.

The reason balance eludes so many of us is that every single person who is living on this planet has different goals and aspirations, and is struggling with different challenges in their life at different times. There is no formula that we can follow consistently through our lives in order to reach balance. **The balance for every single individual is always evolving**, as are individual goals, individual challenges, and lifestyle. Having routines and schedules is an effective way of reaching balance, but people who are successful at balancing their lives are good at making adjustments when circumstances in their life changes. So if you don't make adjustments to your routines regularly, you can get out of balance very quickly.

Human beings in large societies live very complex lives. There are so many different things that need our attention that lack of time is the most common cause of imbalance, both individually and in our society. Let us analyze some of these aspects that directly affect the balance and the feeling of fulfillment in our lives.

Choice of career

Your career choice has a lot to do with the type of balance you can achieve in your life. For example, a person who wants to become a surgeon needs to go to undergraduate school for four years, then complete four years of medical school, and also do three to ten years of residency and fellowship training. Much sacrifice is needed to successfully go through such a program. The balance for every individual is constantly evolving depending on where they are in their life. For this particular person, even after finishing the program, reaching true balance becomes extremely difficult. So before choosing a career, first decide what type of balance you would like to have in your life, then consider the social status and financial benefits of that career. Remember that your fulfillment and happiness depends on what type of balance you can accept while doing your job. Are you going to be able to accept all the negatives that come with your choice of career? Because there will be both negatives and positives with every job, and you will have to fully accept the negatives that come from your line of work.

Do not allow your career to engulf your life. It is extremely important to create boundaries for yourself to achieve balance. Setting boundaries allows you to dedicate time and effort to other important aspects in your life that need your attention.

I have a very close friend, Wesley, who is a successful real estate agent. He has been consumed by increasing his sales, and has been successful in doubling them yearly. Every time I talk to Wesley, all he talks about is real estate. He goes up when a deal goes through and comes down when they fall apart; his happiness is dependent on his work. He has set no boundaries for himself when it comes to his job. He is so worried about losing on a sale or a client that he has made himself available for business from 6:00 a.m. to midnight. He has no life outside of his work. He does not exercise, even though he has a black belt in martial arts, and he does not take any personal time to do anything. This is a recipe for disaster.

People with this kind of job should always set and communicate their hours of work to their clients. If you are working for someone else, let them know from the beginning what your availability is, do not leave it open-ended. Will you lose on a sale or a client? Will you have to search harder to find a job with better hours? Will you make slightly less money? Absolutely, but **you will be able to live a happy and balanced life.**

For women who want to work at home, taking care of their family and having children is a fulltime job that requires a lot of time and effort. But regardless of whether the mother works at home full-time, or works out of the house as well, the number of children in the family should be determined by how well the mother can maintain balance in her life while having children. Do not have more than one if you cannot maintain balance in your family life, because the mother's well being affects the well being of the entire family.

Consider what type of balance you could have when you are choosing a partner, because their schedule will directly affect your balance as well. Put a lot of thought into what type of balance you could have if you mesh your lives together. For example, is it important to you to have dinner with your spouse at home every night? Would you like to spend the weekends together with the entire family? If you do, you would need to choose a spouse with a career that has suitable hours.

Muscle balance and physical exercise

Almost every human being will experience some kind of neck or back pain in their lifetime. This could happen for different reasons, but the most common reason is muscle imbalance between different muscle groups. This has become like an epidemic on this planet, because little is known about this issue. So I would like to explain how this happens.

Muscle imbalance is created by the misuse of different muscle groups in the left or right side of the body. Most of us are either left-side dominant or right-side dominant, although some lucky and rare people have no dominant side. The majority (70-95%) of people are right-side dominant and they tend to lead with their right hand and leg when doing any type of work. The remainder (5-30%) of people are left-side dominant and they tend to lead with their left hand and leg when doing any type of work.

Let me explain to you with some examples how the misuse of right and left side will result in muscle imbalance in your body. If you are right-side dominant, from a very young age you have mostly used your right hand to open the door, write, cook, clean, use tools, and so on. You have been using your right hand to do most of the tasks that need to be done in your life, which will cause some of the muscles on the right side of the body to get bigger than the same muscles on the left side of the body. For left-side dominant people, it is the other way around. The same is true for our legs and the muscles attached to our hips. We tend to use one leg more than the other when we get up from the ground, or a chair, or lean on one leg when we are standing. This will cause a muscle imbalance throughout your body, and the strength difference between the muscles increases as you get older. This problem is more pronounced for people who play any type of sport like basketball, baseball, soccer, or hockey, because they use the muscles on one side much more than the other due to very high repetitions.

The same principles apply for people who work in different fields. For example, a person who sits in front of a computer all day uses certain muscles in the shoulders and lower back all day long, while not using the opposite muscles in the abdomen and the connecting muscles in the chest and upper back.

Life has designed our bodies to have a lot of flexibility. In order to achieve that, our entire skeletal structure is connected by over 650 skeletal muscles. In particular, our spinal cord and our hips are surrounded with these muscles. The strength difference between the opposite muscle groups of the chest and back will cause your spinal cord to twist slightly to the left, or the right, depending on which side you use more than the other. This happens because when your right-side pectorals are bigger and stronger than the left-side pectorals, the right-side back muscles will become smaller and weaker than the left-side back muscles to counteract the imbalance in your pectorals. On other hand, the strength difference between your right and left shoulder muscles could cause your right side shoulder to tilt up or down. The same principles apply to your legs and hips. Often, people's hips are twisted to the right or the left, or one side of the hips is tilted up or down. This is a complex problem and is very hard to understand, but the only way you can address these imbalances are through specific balancing exercises and workouts, or by going to yoga.

These muscle imbalances can cause problems in two different ways. The first problem is that the twisting of the hips and spinal cord can result in pressure on the nerve endings between the vertebrae, which in turn can cause a tremendous amount of direct or referred pain. The second problem is that the misalignment of the spinal cord will result in the misalignment of your energy field. Remember that the second, third, fourth, and fifth chakras are located both in the front and the back of the spinal cord. When your spinal cord twists to the right or the left, your energy field will become crooked, because chakras operate similarly to guns. If the angle of the chakra's opening is pointed slightly to the left or the right, your energy field will reflect that misalignment. It is extremely important not only to strengthen the muscle groups in your shoulder, chest, back, arms, and legs, but also to balance all these muscle groups, because the misalignment of these muscle groups can result in both physical pain and emotional distress in the spiritual body.

Strengthening your core muscles is extremely important because the core muscles are responsible for holding the entire physical structure together. When you watch the construction of high-rise buildings, you see that they build long pillars out of concrete and metal. Those pillars hold the entire structure together. Your core muscles have the same responsibility, so strengthening and balancing your core muscles has a lot to do with the alignment of your spinal cord. Even if you're going to neglect all the other muscle groups, do not neglect your core muscles.

I have developed simple lightweight training exercises for people of all ages, in combination with cardiovascular training, to address these muscle imbalances. I am planning to release these in the future. But in the meantime, I highly recommend the use of balancing boards as well as taking classes in yoga, or working with a personal trainer, or a physiotherapist to address these muscle imbalances. Please check with your medical doctor to see what type of exercises will suit you best.

For the best results we need to exercise a minimum of four and a half to six hours a week, but I understand that our lives can become very hectic at times and it is not always possible to maintain that level of physical activity throughout our lifetime. The key to maintaining balance in this situation is to never completely stop exercising, no matter what is happening in your life. Even if you are extremely busy at a particular time, work out at least once a week until you can go back to your original schedule. That one workout will maintain your physical strength until you have more time for exercising. The muscles in our bodies have memories. Once you build your muscle strength to a certain level, even if you stop all together and lose muscle mass, once you start again, it will quickly go back to where it was. But if you stop completely, restarting will not be easy. I know that many people have a thousand and one excuses as to why they have no time for exercising, but there are so many good and short workout videos requiring as little as twenty minutes a day – so that everybody can include exercise in their daily lives. Stop coming up with excuses and start including exercising as part of your daily life, you owe it to yourself.

Diet and the art of losing weight

Your physical and spiritual bodies are so intertwined that what you eat will directly affect your spiritual development. In the beginning of 2006 when my third eye opened, I sat in deep meditation and asked Life if I should become a vegetarian. The answer that I received surprised me.

"Enlightenment will not be possible if you become a vegetarian," Life replied.

So I continued with my diet as it was. After a while, a close friend brought me a book called, *Eat right for your type* by Dr. Peter J D'adamo and Catherine Whitney. Immediately Life connected to me through the third eye and asked me to follow that particular diet as closely as possible. I had been having difficulty with acid reflux disease and digestion from the beginning of 2006, even though I was eating very healthily. I immediately read the book and the science behind it was solid. This diet is based on the compatibility of different types of food such as eggs, dairy products, fruits, vegetable, meats, and grains with each individual blood type. It also explained how blood type O, who were originally hunter-gatherers in Africa, spread throughout Africa and into Europe and Asia in search of food supplies, and how blood types A, B, and AB evolved from blood type O.

Once I finished the book, I understood why Life had told me that enlightenment would not be possible if I became a vegetarian. The reason was that I am blood type O, and eating lean red meat is essential for a person with that particular blood type. Group O is the ancestral blood group of humans who were hunter-gathers, so the optimal diet for this group is similar to the high protein diet common in those days. People with group A blood type should follow a diet rich in plants and vegetables, while completely avoiding eating red meat. People with group B blood type can eat most meats (other than pork), some dairy, and plant products, but need to avoid some of them such as wheat, corn, and other high starch foods. People with blood type AB comprise less than 5% of the population and have characteristics of both blood type A and blood type B.

One method that our body uses to determine if a substance in our body is friendly or not is by using a chemical marker called antigens. What I love about this book is that it breaks down in detail how each individual food product matches with people with their particular blood type, by looking at their antigens. It also breaks down what types of food will cause weight gain for each particular blood type. I had an "Aha!" moment once I went through all the material. The author had broken down all the different types of food into three categories, foods that are highly beneficial, neutral, and foods to avoid. I realized that I naturally didn't like the taste of some of the foods that were in the avoid department. For some of them the taste was okay, but I felt either tired or not well after eating them. I have been trying to include the highly beneficial and neutral category in my diet, while excluding the avoid category as much as possible, and it has made a huge difference in my daily life. My acid reflux disease has been in check, and I have had no other problems with my digestive system since then. I've also been feeling more energetic since I have been following this diet. I highly recommend that everyone should at least read the book and judge for themselves. I have no relationship with the author, or receive nothing for this recommendation. I am simply letting you know the direction Life wanted me to follow.

There is a lot more to diet than knowing what to eat and what not to eat. Every individual's body type is different, and living situations for many people are not always ideal. We cannot always find the exact types of food that are good for us with the right portion size, so at times we have to improvise. Like many people, I have suffered from a slow metabolism. Even though I am very muscular, if I slightly over-eat I will quickly gain weight, but I never starve or restrict myself from eating to maintain a healthy weight.

I believe that many people struggle with portion size as well as knowing when to eat, so I would like to give you the guideline that I use in my daily life. The best way to eat is to wait until you are truly hungry, when you feel like you really need to eat something. This would be right in between the time that you feel your stomach is empty and the time where you feel like you're so hungry that you're going to pass out. Finding this middle ground is one of the most important factor in maintaining a healthy weight.

The most important part after you start eating is to know when to stop. You should always stop eating just before you are full, because there is about a twenty-minute delay for your brain to know your stomach is full. So if you wait until you feel full, you have overeaten. When we eat food our stomach expands, and after digestion it shrinks back to its original size. But if we continue to overeat regularly, our stomach will not shrink back to its original size and in time will become larger and larger. Once your stomach becomes larger, it requires more food to fill it up, so you will consume more calories with each meal. It's a vicious cycle that can cause obesity, but the good news is even if you have enlarged your stomach, if you stop eating before you are full, in time your stomach will slowly shrink back to its original size, so it will require less food to fill it up.

I have been lifting weights and exercising ever since I was sixteen years old. Over the years I have trained and helped many people lose weight. Diets don't work because most people cut too much food too fast out of their daily food intake and damage their metabolism. When that happens you have no chance of success. I want to explain to you how to stop overeating so that you don't damage your metabolism and gain the weight back. Understanding this is extremely important.

Our brain is constantly monitoring our metabolism and digestive system. Depending on what you are eating, it takes a certain amount of time for food to enter through your mouth and exit out through the anus. The longer it takes for food to go through your intestines, the more nutrients and fat are absorbed into your blood system. Naturally food with higher fiber content goes through faster than food with lower fiber content. Fruits and vegetables go through much faster than meats and heavier foods. Some foods like processed cheese can take up to five days or even longer to get through, so it rots in your intestines. That is why processed cheese is so bad for you, because it takes so long to digest that all the fat content is absorbed into your blood system. Have you ever reheated a slice of pizza? Have you seen how the cheese melts and sticks to the plate and won't come off when you try to wash it off? The same thing happens in your intestines, the processed cheese can stick to your intestinal wall and restrict the movement and digestion of other food. Restaurants and fast food locations unfortunately put processed cheese into everything these days, even in salads and foods that are supposed to be healthy. I have almost cut processed cheese out of my diet, and it is not as hard as you think. Once you cut cheese out, it takes you up to three weeks to fully adjust to taste everything without cheese in it. You will not even notice the difference after a while.

Our brain is always trying to maintain our weight as is. So for a person who is overeating and overweight, the brain speeds up the metabolism and digestion as much as possible in order to reduce the calorie intake. But it can only do so much, and constant overeating will result in weight gain. Now let's look at an example of what happens when someone goes on a diet and suddenly cuts out a lot of food. Let us say that a man who is overeating and overweight normally consumes ten units of food a day, and goes on a diet that suddenly cuts his food consumption from ten units a day to six units a day. It takes our brain about a week to become aware of this change, so his metabolism will remain the same for the first week and he will lose about five pounds. But after the first week his brain becomes aware of the significant reduction in food intake, and makes adjustments to counteract this significant change by slowing down the metabolism and the digestive process. This allows his intestines as much time as possible to absorb the nutrients from the reduced amount of food. The brain makes this adjustment in order to maintain his original weight. For that reason, weight loss becomes more difficult as more time passes, until weight loss comes to a complete halt, because the metabolism has slowed significantly. This reaction by the brain is due to thousands of years of evolution. In the animal kingdom when there was a famine and shortage of food, our brain would go into conservation mode and slow down the rate of our metabolism and the digestive process in order to absorb as many nutrients as possible from a reduced amount of food. This was done to increase the chances of surviving food shortages until such time as more food became available, when the metabolism would speed up again.

The second reason that diets fail is due to the fact that people starve themselves and cut too much food out of their diet too fast. After losing some weight they become less vigilant and think that they can get away with eating more since they have lost some weight. So slowly they begin to either binge or go back to their old habits, but by this time they have slowed down their metabolism, so they quickly put the weight right back on – and some extra weight as well.

How to stop overeating and start exercising

The correct way to stop overeating is to fool our brain into thinking that nothing is changing. So if you are consuming ten units of food a day, cut down to nine units first, and at the same time very slowly increase your activities. For example, go for a twenty-minute walk every day. This change is so insignificant that your brain will not notice it. For two weeks stay with that level of food intake and slowly lose as much weight as possible during that time. You have to be patient: remember that losing weight is a marathon, not a sprint. You will keep the weight off if you lose it slowly.

At the end of the second week go from nine units of food a day to eight units and go for a thirty-minute walk every day. Continue with this level of food intake and walking for another two weeks. At the end of the fourth week, go from eight units of food a day to seven units of food a day, but **fast** walk for 30 minutes. Continue for another two weeks with this level of food intake and walk. Continue on this progressive path until you reach your desired weight.

The best exercise for losing fat is long regular or fast walks. Fat is a very slow burning fuel, and in order to burn fat your heart rate should not go very high because when your heart rate goes too high, muscle burns faster than fat. So you are burning calories, but it is coming more from your muscles than your fat reserves. Once you eat food, your body replaces the muscles that were burned. This is good for building muscle mass, but not good for burning fat. So regular or fast walks are better than running when it comes to burning fat. In the case that you do not have more than half an hour a day for exercising, I recommend a high-intensity workout video after you have walked half an hour a day for eight weeks, so that your body has got used to exercising before you move to a high-intensity workout.

These recommendations are for people who are just starting, and have not worked out for a long time. Add high-intensity workouts into your routine after eight weeks. People who have been working out for a long time and want to lose belly fat should still keep their heart rate in the fat burning zone, and that depends on your age. The most important point in weight loss is for you to take your time decreasing your food intake, while slowly increasing your activities. If you are older or have not worked out for a long time, stay with low-impact exercises. Boot camps and high-intensity exercises are for people who have been exercising regularly for a long time. You have to build your body to that level of intensity slowly. Make adjustments to your workouts when you experience pain. Listen to your body and rest when you need it, because if the pain becomes too great, you will completely stop and all your effort will go to waste. For an average person, the best results will come from a balanced workout of light weight training combined with aerobic exercises, and a fat-burning exercise like fast walks. But as I said, work your way up to that level of exercise slowly, because this will reduce the chance of injuries or extreme soreness.

There are also ways to enhance and speed up your metabolism. Eating foods with more fiber content will greatly enhance your metabolism. I highly recommend eating two to three apples with their skin every day. The other way to enhance your metabolism is to increase the amount of good microorganisms called probiotics in your intestines. Probiotics are live bacteria and yeast that are good for your body, especially your digestive system. These good bacteria keep your gut healthy. It is extremely important for you to replace these bacteria after taking antibiotics or anti-inflammatory medication by taking probiotics. Probiotics can help balance the good and the bad bacteria in your intestines, in order to keep your digestive system working as it should. Fruits and vegetables are food for these good microorganisms, so make sure that you eat enough fruits and vegetables. Scientists have discovered that eating fatty and oily foods on a regular bases will cause a reduction in the number of these good microorganisms. Avoid eating deep-fried and greasy food, especially at fast food restaurants.

You will never be in starvation mode with this method of food reduction, and you will not go on binges and gain the weight back. A balanced diet is key to a healthy life. I allow myself a small piece of cake once a month, two slices of pizza once every four months, and treat myself to a hearty breakfast with sausage and bacon once or twice a year.

How to reduce your heart rate

I now want to address an epidemic that has engulfed our society. The goal of meditation is to decrease the heart rate, and reduce the number of inhales and exhales. This also increases the frequency at which your energy vibrates. Enlightenment happens when you are vibrating at the same frequency at which the universe is vibrating. The frequency with which your energy is vibrating changes depending on how fast your heart is beating and how frequently you inhale and exhale. When your heart rate goes up, you breathe more frequently, and the frequency of your vibration comes down. When your heart rate slows down, you breathe less frequently, and in return the frequency of your vibration goes up, getting you closer to God's consciousness and universal energy.

Caffeine in coffee, tea, sodas, and energy drinks increases your heart rate. As a result, you take shallower breaths frequently and decrease the frequency with which your energy is vibrating, thereby shooting yourself in the foot. Your physical and spiritual body are constantly affecting each other; you need to become aware of these changes. An increased heart rate because of caffeine will directly affect your spiritual development.

The increase in heart rate will also directly affect your longevity and your life span. Pay close attention to the animal kingdom. All the animals that have a high heart rate have a shorter lifespan. Let us look at some examples:

	Average beats per minute	Average lifespan
Birds	600	2 years
Cats and dogs	180	15 years
Humans	100	65 years
Chimpanzee	84	40 years
Elephants	35	70 years

Human beings live longer than chimpanzees due to medical progress in advanced societies. Had we continued to live in the wild, our life span would likely be the same as chimpanzees. I highly recommend that you completely avoid consuming caffeine. Shortly after my third eye opened and I connected to the higher consciousness, cutting caffeine and avoiding spicy food were two of the first requirements of Life, before I could move forward. It took a little time for me to adjust, but it is not very difficult once you get through the first month. Eating spicy food on a regular basis has the same effect as caffeine. I understand that in some cultures consuming spicy food is a norm, and change can be difficult. But some sacrifices are necessary if you are truly interested in your spiritual development.

Other things you need to avoid are processed foods, fluoride, and foods with preservatives. Processed food such as processed meat, chips, and cereals are full of chemicals that are not good for your physical body. Preservatives are chemicals that lengthen the food's shelf life, but they're not good for you. If you're interested in both your physical health and your spiritual development, you need to avoid consuming these harmful chemicals. It is not a coincidence that cancer is spreading throughout our civilizations. We were not meant to consume these harmful chemicals. Fluoride is a chemical that prevents tooth decay, but unfortunately consumption of fluoride will result in the calcification of the pineal gland, which plays a huge role in your spiritual development. Many cities in Western societies add fluoride to their water, so you either have to get a special water filter to remove the fluoride from the water, or buy water from companies that do not add fluoride into their water. You can search the net and find water companies that do not add.

Emotional health

I have already talked a great deal about how we need to transcend beyond our negative emotions such as fear, anger, hate, and sadness, both in the past and the present. Negative emotions caused by past experiences can be resolved through daily meditation, or with the help of a professional therapist. Meditation is the preferred method because it is transformative, goes deeper, and is without cost, but if you prefer a therapist, that would do as well. Your emotional health at the present time has a lot to do with events in your childhood; as well as your past and present relationships with people, such as coworkers, siblings, parents, family members, friends, and your significant other. I've already talked about how to deal with coworkers who are difficult, so let's focus on the rest now. We cannot divorce our siblings or parents, but we can limit contact or even disconnect from them if the relationship is toxic and not good for our emotional health.

Family relationships

Some people have a tendency to continue to fight with their siblings or parents in the present time in order to resolve their past issues. This problem can manifest itself in different forms. When it comes to issues with your parents there are two scenarios: a) they were either bad people with poor character, or b) good people who thought they were doing the right thing with the knowledge that they had about parenting. In the first scenario, some adults continue to appeal to their undeserving parents by being very loving, or doing loving things in order to try to win their love and approval. But this desire to turn them into loving parents will fail. Other people are who they are, no matter how much you love or do for them. Their inadequacy has nothing to do with you; it has everything to do with their past conditioning. It is not emotionally healthy for you to try to change someone else. This is why it is so important to work on issues regarding your childhood with meditation or a therapist, because past events in your childhood can greatly affect your present relationships with your parents and everyone else. From a spiritual point of view, when meditating, remember that bad people in our lives are there to give us negative experiences, but it's not personal, they are us in different forms. We are all one and there is only one of us, they're simply playing the role of bad in this lifetime. You should limit or even completely disconnect from your parents if you feel your interactions with them are detrimental to your life, but do the inner work with meditation or a therapist to resolve your past issues. This is important so that you do not hold any resentments towards them, because that would negatively affect your spiritual development.

The second scenario is that the parents did the best they could with the knowledge that they had. Adult children of such parents may attempt to prove to them that they made wrong choices in their parenting. This will result in more arguments and sadness. They are too old and their conditioning is deep, and it would be too difficult for them to accept their wrongdoing. For your emotional health you need to see their flaws, and come to peace with their shortcomings through meditation.

My parents fall in this category. They were both hypercritical and overbearing. Growing up I struggled in school because of undiagnosed attention deficit disorder, so they continuously told me that I would never amount to anything. My father was beaten when he was growing up, so he did the same to me when he was punishing me for misbehaving. My mother always dressed me with no-name brands and gave me bad haircuts to keep girls away from me, so I had no self-confidence as an adult and had to build myself up and gain confidence through discipline and bodybuilding. I have worked out all my anger through my inner journey with meditation and hold absolutely no resentment towards my parents, and in fact have a very loving relationship with them. I want to emphasize here that my peace with the past did not come from any discussions with my parents; this is a journey that you need to walk alone. This is about understanding and acceptance of the past, not about placing blame. The same is true for children who come from broken homes and divorced parents. If you want to be free and emotionally healthy, you have to walk your inner journey.

The problem with hypercritical and overbearing parents is that they think they are right about everything, and do not respect the choices made by their adult children. They also like to live vicariously through their children, and so they continue to meddle in their adult children's lives, no matter how old they are. The best way to handle this is to listen when they give their opinion, and politely say: "I will think about what you're saying, and take it into consideration." Show them respect, but at the end of the day do what you think is right for you. Do not argue with them to prove your point of view, it is absolutely pointless. It is unlikely that they are going to agree with you. If they offer you the same opinion again, politely say: "I have taken into consideration what you have said, but I feel that you need to follow your own path regarding that matter."

Continue to repeat the same thing over and over again, until they give up. In some cases, you may need to draw boundaries by letting them know you are not willing to discuss the matter further. If they continue, politely say goodbye and leave, and let them know that you will do the same if it happens again. Once you have done this several times, they will get the message. However, if you involve your parents in your affairs by relying on them for things such as babysitting your children or paying for your college education, then you cannot complain when they give their opinion, because the only way you can draw boundaries with them is to take care of your affairs yourself.

We choose the people that we interact with. That is true with our siblings, friends, family members, and our significant other. If you feel that your relationship with someone is having a negative impact on your emotional health, it is your responsibility to set limits or disconnect from them. If you keep walking into a wall it is your own fault that you are getting a headache! You are responsible for your emotional health, so choose the people you surround yourself with wisely. Remember that our spiritual body bonds with people that we are surrounded with, and we will exchange energy with them through energy cords. So always ask yourself if you like the characteristics of the person you are spending time with, and whether you wish to see those characteristics in yourself. Because whether you like it or not, if you spend enough time with them, they will affect you.

An emotionally healthy person who has done their inner work will not be in relationships where there is neglect, drama, or abuse. This person will be able to handle difficult situations without getting angry and responding emotionally. Remember that any anger you express is in you, and is not caused by another person. You can never become angry if there is no anger inside you.

Experience true love

I have written an entire section on love, sex, and relationships, so here I am talking about the experience of true love only in the context of having balance in our lives. True love happens when there is absolute unity, and the "I" has disappeared. The parties involved are willing to give up their life to protect the other. It is extremely important that we have the experience of true love with at least one other soul. This could happen between two lovers, two friends, a mother or father with a daughter or a son, or just a human being and his or her pet. We are love, and having such an experience in our lives reminds us of who we are, no matter what is happening in our lives. When you are in the presence of true love, it has a calming effect that makes everything okay. You could be fearful, sad, tired, or angry, but when you come in contact with the being that you truly love, you feel okay. You feel that you can get through the difficult times as long as they're there. That is why it is very important that we have the experience of true love in our lives.

Spiritual development

You need to get involved in an activity where you are meditative and focused, and this has nothing to do with whether you believe in God or not. Meditation is not the only tool that can benefit your spiritual development. Being involved in an activity like yoga, Tai Chi, team sports, or anything where you can become meditative and focused can be extremely beneficial in your spiritual development, and will give you the balance that you need in your life.

Things that we are passionate about

One of the most important aspects missing from many people's lives is doing things they are passionate about. The problems that arise from this absence manifest themselves in many different forms, such as depression and addiction. Doing things that we are passionate about gives us a high and the experience of bliss in our lives. We need to have the experience of bliss in our lives to counteract the challenges and the difficulties that we face every day. Life is difficult and can be overwhelming at times; we need to balance the bad with the good. Having true love in our lives is one way to balance the bad, but it does not give us the experience of the high to balance the experience of the low, which can result in sadness and depression. We feel blissful when we are involved in activities that we are passionate about, and that is a different thing for every human being. The problem arises when people don't know what they are passionate about, or know but either don't have the time or don't make the effort to include it in their lives. What you're passionate about has to be something personal to you. For example, you cannot be passionate about having children. Having children may give you fulfillment but does not give you a high, so it needs to be something that makes you feel blissful when you do it.

There are people who have chosen careers based on their passions. They are the lucky ones, but that is not always possible. What you're passionate about could be anything: a hobby such as painting or writing, cycling, or playing a sport, volunteering for something, or humanitarian efforts, or simply playing a game like chess or backgammon. This could be something that you do at your home by yourself, or outside with other people. It does not matter what it is, you just have to find something that makes **you feel blissful** when you do it. If you have no idea what that could be, then just go out there and try different things until you find something that gives you the experience of bliss. Take some time out of your busy life to involve yourself in such activities, to prevent sadness or depression. I can guarantee you that if you do not put the time and effort into this, you will either end up feeling depressed, or start abusing drugs and alcohol.

Drug and alcohol abuse

Addictions to drugs and alcohol have plagued our societies because of the lack of passion in our lives. Instead of being high on life, we get high with chemicals or numb ourselves with marijuana or opiates. Life can wear you out because it is challenging and difficult, but using drugs or abusing alcohol is a temporary fix. Our bodies build immunity to these drugs. I remember that I started doing one tablet of ecstasy per night each week, then one became two, two became three, and so on, until I was doing twelve tablets a night. Then came a time when I could no longer get high with ecstasy, so I started to mix different drugs together to get the high. These included ecstasy, GHB, crystal meth, cocaine, mushrooms, ketamine, and of course marijuana, which brought everything together. The problem is that no matter how many drugs you take, you'll have to take more the next time to get the same effect.

After using drugs every day, depression kicks in the next day because after every high there is going to be a low. So you have two options, either you will have to endure the depression, or avoid it by using drugs again the next day – but the amount that you need to take will keep getting higher and higher. I remember that there were times when I partied three days in a row without any sleep.

One day your body begins to shut down from all the chemicals and from sleep deprivation. Your skin will begin to look like it has aged for decades, and you may experience problems with your stomach, liver, or lungs. If you are abusing drugs or alcohol, you know that it's not going to end well for you. You can convince yourself otherwise, but deep inside you know the truth. I was a high functioning drug addict. I worked out regularly, ate very healthily, went to school and finished my education, lived on my own and paid my bills in time, but it was not going to end well for me. Life would not allow it. Had I not changed my path, I would either be dead or in prison. I have been where many of you are, I understand what you're going through, and I respect that you expect more out of your life. I want to tell you that there can come a day where you do not need any drugs or alcohol to feel high. There can be a day where you feel blissful doing the most mundane things, but you need to face your demons from the past and overcome your fears. **You are God** and when you come to know that, there isn't a drug in the world that can give you the same high as knowing that.

The steps that need to be taken by an addict for quitting drugs and alcohol are simple, but very difficult to do. First they must decide that they want to quit. This decision needs to come from the addict. No one can force an addict to quit. There are several scenarios for parents with addicted adult children.

Parents with high functioning adult addicts who live independently of their parents

In this scenario there is absolutely nothing that a parent can or should do to help. They simply need to wait until such a time as things have got really bad for the addicted child, so they will come and ask for help. Otherwise, do not interfere or give any financial or emotional help. Do not trust an addict, they will lie. Do not help them financially. Only provide direct assistance with their sobriety, such as providing a place for detoxing until they are back on their feet.

An intervention could be effective, but only if things have got really bad for the addict. No one has ever wanted to quit doing drugs or alcohol when things are okay, so wait until things have become really bad for them. If you're attempting an intervention, timing is everything.

Parents with a dysfunctional addicted adult child who depends on parents for financial support, or living arrangements

In this scenario, parents are the enablers. All the support needs to be cut off. Parents need to ask the addicted child to move out as soon as possible. For example, give them two weeks' notice, and change all the locks. Disconnect and confiscate all the material possessions that you have paid for. Parents cannot worry about what may happen when their child is out on their own. The addict needs to be driven to a point where they can come to their senses, and decide to quit using drugs or alcohol. As long as you support them, they will not make the change in their life. You are only prolonging the inevitable. Will you be able to live with yourself if they overdose while you're supporting them and providing a place for them to live? Kicking them out is hard to do, but the alternative is worse in the long run. **With anything, doing the right thing is always more difficult to do at the time, but it does not mean that you should not do it.**

Once an addict has decided to quit, he or she needs to **fully accept** that they are going to suffer for a month during the detoxification. If they go into the detoxification knowing they're going to suffer, and that is okay, it will be much easier to get through. Mindset is everything. **Being okay with experiencing the low is essential**. If you're going through a detoxification, remember that the pendulum will swing the other way once you get through. Meditate and live a balanced life. The cause of your addiction is lack of passion and imbalance in your life. The most difficult issue for an addict to overcome is leaving the lifestyle. We drink and use drugs with people who we surround ourselves with. Once you have decided that you want to quit, you'll have to disconnect from all those people, even if they are your lover. You cannot force other people to quit with you; they may not be ready to take that step. This is a journey that you need to walk alone. In time when you are ready and healthy, Life will bring new and healthy people into your life, but not before you have done the inner work. Be brave and take the next step, your higher self is with you every step of the way. You are God; connect to the bigger part of yourself. Tremendous growth will come from this journey, and you will become stronger by the end.

Life is about discipline, and discipline is Life

I have gone through seven different elements that affect the balance in everyone's life. As I mentioned before, balance is always evolving, depending on what is happening in your lives at any one point, so be vigilant and make adjustments to your schedule regularly to maintain balance. Sometimes it is possible to choose to do an activity that fulfills several of the elements. For example, if you choose to practice yoga, it is meditative and helps you with your spiritual development. In addition, yoga improves muscle balance and is physical exercise. And you never know, you may even become passionate about it and experience bliss, so give it a try! **The key to maintaining balance is to do the best that you can do to include all the seven elements in your daily life as much as possible. The amount of time that you dedicate to each element will change, depending on what's happening in your life, and how much time is available to you, but make sure that you never completely stop an activity. Time management is crucial in maintaining balance.**

Lack of time and laziness are the most common reasons for imbalance in our lives. Lack of time itself is caused due to three different elements.

Doing too much of one thing

Addictions come in many forms. Regardless of whether what we're doing is good for us or not, doing too much of one thing will cause imbalance in our lives. For example, there could be lack of time because you decide to run a marathon, or play video games, watch TV, or spend too much time on the computer, or volunteer; so stay away from doing too much of one thing. Thinking about sex and dating can also become addictive for people of all ages. You could be spending hours sifting through social media and dating sites, while neglecting other important elements in your life, including your family.

Accumulation of wealth, overspending, or overextending

People have to work so hard in order to support their lifestyle that they overextend themselves to the point where they have no time to do anything else. Their lives consist of working and then coming home so tired and exhausted that all they can do is sit in front of a TV or a computer for the rest of the night, and then repeat the same thing the next day. We buy new cars by getting large loans, and we rent or buy apartments or houses that we can barely afford. We think about social status more than our own well-being, so we over-spend on expensive clothing and material possessions. All of this results in stress and extended hours at work, with little time to do anything else. This is the most common cause of imbalance and unhappiness in our lives, because life can become repetitive and tasteless when you are just repeating the same thing over and over again every day, and every week. You need to balance your spending, so that you can balance your life. **True happiness comes from within, and balance, never forget that.** Every other pleasure is temporary and will not last, and in order to truly understand this you may need to touch the boundaries before you can find balance in your life.

I'm going to suggest something that may shock you. Go ahead and indulge yourself in everything that you can think of: it will give you pleasure for a period of time. Of course it would be best to do this when you are single. Go and buy yourself an expensive car, party all that you want, sleep with as many people as you want if you're single, dress up in expensive clothing – just get it all out of your system. Indulge yourself in every way possible, because at the end you will know the emptiness of it all. You will still feel something is missing in your life, and after all that you will not feel fulfilled. You cannot truly leave something unless you have indulged yourself in it. I truly believe that I could not have become celibate and given up partying, and all my money, if I had not been indulging myself with women and material possessions. That was an important period in my life; without it, starting on the path of enlightenment would not have been possible. I'm not telling you to go as hard as I did, but indulging yourself at the right time can be very beneficial in helping you find balance in your life.

Choice of career

We have already discussed how your choice of career can result in lack of time, and in turn, cause imbalance in your life. So choose wisely, especially if you have to do any type of schooling in order to reach your goal, because you will likely be stuck with the subject of your choosing for the rest of your life. Do a reverse engineering when you are choosing your career. First decide on the preferred hours of work; second, think about whether doing that type of work will be enjoyable for you. Research the negatives that come from doing that type of work by volunteering in the field, and see if you can fully accept them with joy. Considerations such as social status and financial benefits should come last when you are choosing a career. Fully accepting the negatives that come with doing any type of job is going to be the most important thing that you need to consider.

Laziness as a cause of imbalance

Laziness is another primary reason for imbalance in people's lives. Laziness comes from lack of discipline. Discipline becomes part of who you are when you push yourself to get things done. It takes time and effort to build discipline within yourself; you have to win many small battles to win the war. Let me give you an example: it is difficult to go and exercise after a long day of work, or after taking care of children all day. You may feel tired and come up with many reasons why you cannot go for a workout. If you give in to your thoughts, you will weaken your will. You will lose the battle, and very likely lose the war at the end. I never give in to those thoughts. I push through tiredness and pain, no matter what I'm feeling at the time. Getting down to the gym is the tough part, once your heart starts pumping, and your chakras open up, you feel glad that you came. A tremendous amount of growth and discipline comes from pushing yourself. Life is about making choices; every day you come across situations where you have to make choices, and there is always a difficult path or an easy way. You can either choose the difficult path and identify with the bigger part of you, or you can choose the easy way and identify with the small part of you. You are God's consciousness, you are mighty, always identify with the bigger part of yourself and remind yourself that you are choosing it. The next time that you are tempted to lie about something, tell yourself: "**I choose to be honest,**" and go through with it, regardless of the consequences. The next time you are out and feel like having pizza, ice cream, or a cake, look at it and tell yourself: **"I choose to be healthy."** It is very important for you to say, "**I choose to,**" because when you choose to do something (and you go through with it), you empower yourself and connect to the bigger part of you. **You become disciplined** by choosing to do something, and going through with it no matter how you feel or what happens. This is how I built discipline in myself.

Start by choosing to do things that are easier to accomplish, and then once you are more confident about yourself, move on to more difficult subjects. Winning the small battles is very important for your psyche, so slowly build up to it. Start with one subject and then add more as you go along. For instance, let's say you want to work out for an hour and a half, three times a week. Do not immediately start with that level of workout. Your muscles are not used to it and you will burn out quickly and stop, losing confidence in yourself in the process. Start with half an hour three times a week, for two weeks. Then move on to forty-five minutes three times a week for two weeks. Then move on to an hour three times a week for two weeks. Repeat this process until you achieve your desired goal. This way you will never feel burnt out and quit. The discipline that you gain from doing these activities will carry over into everything else that you do in your life. There will come a time where you can achieve anything that you want when you put your mind and your will into it. You are God's consciousness; you are more capable than you think.

Political balance and extremism

More people are out of balance now than ever in human history, and that has caused our society as a whole to also go out of balance. This is clearly apparent in the political spectrum around the world. Governments and political parties have become more extreme than ever, and to exist, they need people to become more extreme as well. If you're in the middle, you can't be convinced to go along with anybody, and that is not good for them. The path of the middle, of the balanced, is disappearing fast. Compromise has become a thing of the past. People are moving in the wrong direction. Instead of moving to the middle, they are moving to the extreme left or the extreme right.

The reason for this imbalance in our society is the imbalance of individuals. The plague of Western society is overspending and overextending. Not too long ago, you would buy something only if you had money to buy it. But now you can get credit to buy things with money you do not have. People can raise their stress level and become emotionally unhealthy because now they are worried, and have to work very hard to pay their debts. In our society, the measures of success are not personal growth and true accomplishments, but instead what you are wearing, what kind of car you drive, and how big your home is and where it is located. This has to change. People have to work extended hours to support their lifestyle, so they burn out and cannot include the necessary elements that would bring balance into their lives. They have no time, so they eat food with no nutritional value at fast-food outlets. They do not exercise regularly, so they become obese and have a lot of health problems. They do not involve themselves in anything meditative, and so on.

The result is that their life is out of balance and they become unhappy. Instead of looking at themselves in the mirror and realizing that they are the problem, they look at their government and blame it for their unhappiness, as if somehow governments could fix all the problems in their lives. In order to move to the middle, people have to become less materialist, and focus more on their personal health, personal growth, and family life.

Do not blame your children for your imbalance. Often, people tell themselves that they are doing everything for the sake of their children, but their children do not require a new car or a big house. What they need are relaxed, loving, and balanced parents to teach them how to live a healthy, balanced life. I'm not against material possessions, new cars or large houses – but they should not be acquired at the cost of imbalance in your lives. We cannot become more evolved beings if we continue on that path. **Life is asking you to balance your life, and move to the middle.**

One might ask, how do you find the middle in the political spectrum, who is right? Capitalism or communism? The left or the right? Liberals or conservatives? Democrats or Republicans? I have had great discussions with Life in deep meditation through the third eye regarding the issues facing our nations, and this is Life's stance on different subjects.

Communism has already failed and capitalism is following the same path. Capitalism in the Western societies has produced nations completely out of balance when it comes to the distribution of wealth. The middle class is shrinking fast, and the lower class is not only expanding, but also struggling to survive, and that is problematic. Special interest groups are corrupting the politicians; this needs to stop. Politicians should work for people, not the corporations and special interest groups. Governments separated religion from politics many years ago; it is time to the same with money and politics. It should become illegal to lobby a politician in all the nations around the world. Only then would it become possible to address the challenges that are facing the nations around the world. Money corrupts, it's that simple. Fortunately, there is a law in Canada that prevents the direct lobbying of politicians, but in the United States of America, it is acceptable to lobby a politician and buy votes. There needs to be a political revolution in which people demand changes in regulations to address this important issue. This will make or break the United States of America, because the politicians cannot govern properly with special interest groups affecting their judgment.

I was driving in California when the Obama administration was trying to pass a law for universal health care for the entire country. Canada's universal healthcare was discussed on the radio with different Republican politicians, and I could not believe the lies they told about Canada's healthcare system. I pay approximately $70.00 a month for basic coverage because I made more than $50,000 a year at my truck-driving job. The basic coverage includes everything but chiropractor, massage, and physiotherapy. You can also purchase more comprehensive coverage if you choose to do so. This basic coverage is absolutely free for low-income families, and they only have to pay $20.00 per session for chiropractor, massage, and physiotherapy. Telly was completely covered for all of her medical costs for the entire six years of her battle with cancer. Doctors did all they could for her until the last day of her life. Yet I heard Republican politicians repeat over and over again, that we have "death panels" that decide who lives and dies. No such panels exist in Canada. The politicians only said these things because they are influenced by the lobbies of the medical insurance corporations.

Eventually, powerful lobbyists persuaded a few Democrats to join the Republicans and deny people universal healthcare. The people of the United States of America were cheated. They deserve a universal health care system in which people would not have to worry about their medical needs.

This is only one issue, and there are many other important issues facing the United States of America. However, true progress will not be made with special interest groups affecting the direction taken by the government. Governments have a role to play in distributing the wealth among the people. **Corporations and people with higher income should pay a higher rate of tax**. After all, they are building their wealth on the shoulders of the general population. They should want to pay more and help out. We are all one, there is only one of us; we need to become united in order to become more evolved beings.

The separation of money from politics

Life is creating conditions for the separation of money from politics. The Supreme Court Justice Antonin Scalia recently died in his hotel room from natural causes. He was an advocate for keeping money tied to politics. In interviews with journalists I heard him say **money is people.** They were calling him a great mind. I was appalled by what I was hearing. I understood why Life ended his life: "money is people" is one of the most unintelligent things I have ever heard anyone say. Money is not people; money does not have a soul; human beings are people. I am warning all the Supreme Court justices and the politicians who are standing on the wrong side of this argument, do not go against Life. Scalia's death was not a coincidence. Life is moving towards the separation of money from politics, and I advise you to get on board with this. Capitalism is failing, just like communism. God is perfect, and the perfection is right in the middle. There needs to be a new system between capitalism and communism, so both corporations and people can flourish.

I am by no means against corporations. We need corporations to succeed, but not at the expense of people. I asked Life to clarify its position regarding political parties when I was in deep meditation and connected through the third eye and the answer was: "**God is socially liberal, and fiscally balanced.**" Religious people have aligned themselves with the conservatives and the right, but their positions are far from the positions that Life has taken regarding these matters.

God wants us to be inclusive, which includes giving the LGBT community the same rights as everyone else, and allowing women to abort their unborn children without any judgment, if they're not ready to become mothers. But religious groups are pushing the people and the conservative politicians further to the right, so that they have become exclusive. Christians claim that Jesus is the only path to God; Muslims claim that Islam is the only path to God; but there are as many paths to God as there are people living on this planet. No one can duplicate the path to God.

We all live different lives with different experiences, so naturally our paths to God will be different. I'm not claiming that I am showing you the path to God either. The best that I can do is to give you insights on how you can find your own path to God, nothing more. God has one main rule, and that is to be **inclusive**. For that reason, God is socially liberal, but there are also problems with the Liberals and the left. There are segments of the population who are moving too far to the left, and politicians are following with them. Some liberals want to make college tuition free for everyone, and to make living more comfortable for people on income assistance. They want to make unemployment benefits last longer. Is that really feasible? Should we even attempt to turn these ideas into reality at **this junction in human evolution**?

The middle path is the right path

The last part is the key to answering the question. Even though these are great ideas, we're not yet ready to go all in with all of these ideas at this junction of human evolution. We are not ready simply because people are not evolved enough, and many of them will end up abusing the system and costing the government and the taxpayers an unacceptable amount of money. However, we can certainly move to the middle and approach every issue while keeping balance in mind.

For example, should we make college tuition completely free for every student, regardless of whether they are ready to take on such a challenge? I don't believe so, because students need to have skin in the game, otherwise many of them will not put the necessary effort into their education in order to successfully finish their program. We should try to make college and University more affordable with grants and benefits only for students who successfully finish their program. It would be fair to make students pay for half of the cost of their program.

Should we give more money to people who are on income assistance, so that they can live more comfortably? I don't believe we should. Living on income assistance needs to be difficult, because if we make it too comfortable then everybody will go on welfare. What would be the motivation for people who are earning low wages to go to work and make a living if living on welfare was comfortable? Along the same lines, if we make unemployment benefits last too long, people who become unemployed will not be motivated to find new jobs.

People also need to adjust their expectations. Everybody likes to enjoy social security, free health care benefits, unemployment insurance, good roads and infrastructure, and so on, but they don't like to pay more tax. They want everything but they don't want to pay for it. My father was recently complaining about how much taxes we have to pay, so I calmly asked him: "What would you be willing to give up? Would you be willing to give up your healthcare benefits, or old age security?"

He thought about it and said: "You're right, I would not want to give up any of them."

Governments like everybody else need to balance their budgets. Most governments are notorious for running deficits, and we cannot have that either. We need to have responsible political parties forming governments that are based on compromise and the middle path. Politicians want to get elected, so they go where people go. People have moved to the extreme left or right, so the politicians have moved with them. If enough people move to the middle, they will have no choice but to move with them, because they will go where the votes are. So I am inviting all of you who have moved to the extremes, to first balance your life with the seven elements that I have talked about, and then come and join us in the middle.

The middle path is the right path. Let us raise our vibration, and move our societies to the next level together by becoming more aware of who we are, and who we are is God. There is only one of us and nothing but God exists. Be more compassionate to those less fortunate because they are you in a different form, in a different life.

THE THIRD PHASE

Working as a healer

I had done energy healing work on my friends and family members after Telly's passing, but I had not officially worked as a healer. In 2012, Life communicated to me through the third eye that it was time for me to begin practicing energy healing on the general public, so I took a city commercial truck driving job to transition to a full time energy healer. A close friend of our family owned a salon in a busy mall and had a room that was not being used. Once she found out that I was looking for a place she offered it to me free of charge. I was delighted, Life had planned everything for me, and fairly quickly I was up and running with clients. I drove semi-trucks Monday through Friday in the morning, and did energy healing Saturdays and Sundays. My schedule was very hectic, but I was used to working many hours a week. My plan was to slowly increase the number of days where I would do energy work, and decrease the days of driving the semi-truck.

Let us look at different forms of energy healing. There are too many different styles of energy healing to name them all, but the most notable ones are Reiki, Chi gong, acupuncture or acupressure, and energy focused bodywork. The basic principle is that a practitioner manipulates healing energy in order to open up energy pathways, balance the cold and hot energy in the physical body, repair chakras, or address the deficit of energy in the body (such as in cancer patients). In some styles, the practitioner becomes a conduit for cosmic energy to flow through his or her body to the client. Reiki is an example of this type of work. In

145

other styles, the practitioner utilizes his or her own energy to impact the client's energy field. Some forms of Chi gong fall into this category. The transfer of energy can be done through specific movements, or through meditation and focus. The possibilities are endless. There are so many different variations and styles to choose from that it is extremely difficult to find the right type of healer for your particular problem. With that said, I would like to share with you my experience with energy healing both as a practitioner and as a client.

The origin of Chi gong goes back to more than 5,000 years ago, and it is based on ancient Chinese meditative practice and various movements and postures. Chi gong emphasizes the free flow and balance of energy in the physical body. There are two aspects of Chi gong. The first is achieving energy healing with a Chi gong master, and the second is performing Chi gong self-healing techniques, which can be practiced by anyone. What I like about Chi gong is that an average person can learn a specific set of movements to practice every day at home to prevent and heal various illnesses. The energy healing done by a Chi gong master can also be extremely effective in healing illnesses.

Reiki is not taught to students in the same way as other energy healing styles, it is transferred to the students through an attunement by a Reiki master. Once a student is attuned, the universal energy flows through his or her hand and can be used to improve the health of others. There is a popular belief within the Reiki community that the practitioner's spiritual state of development does not affect their ability to perform energy healing. I strongly disagree with that belief, because in all cases of energy healing no matter what the style is, the practitioner's frequency of vibration determines which field of consciousness they can connect to. The frequency at which their core energy is vibrating directly affects the type of energy that is received and transferred into the patient, and that makes a huge difference to the outcome.

The difference between administering energy with lower frequency and energy with higher frequency is the difference between having the ability to remove blockages, and cure simple illnesses like muscle spasms, or having the ability to cure cancer. The energy with higher vibration has greater healing properties compared to energy with a lower vibration. God's consciousness can reset and cure any type of illness. We have energies with different frequencies within our physical and spiritual body;

by the same token, energy within the body of the universe is vibrating at different frequencies. Therefore, if a practitioner develops the ability to raise the vibration of his or her energy, they can tap into the cosmic energy with higher frequencies. This is true for practitioners who use their body as a conduit to transfer cosmic energy, or practitioners who transfer their own energy, because ultimately their energy comes from the same place.

No one produces their own energy, all energies are universal energy, so meditation and the frequency of vibration of their energy has a big impact on their healing capabilities. Jesus healed people with significant problems in his time. He received his energy from God's consciousness. If all cosmic energies were the same, all Reiki masters should have been able to replicate what Jesus did. I am simply trying to draw a distinction between the two. The frequency of the energy matters, so I implore all practitioners of energy healing to meditate and raise the frequency of their vibration so that they can be more effective in healing their clients.

Using the third eye for healing

I personally used the third eye to heal when working on patients. I would simply focus on the third eye and a vortex would open and draw energy from the 6th plane of consciousness. This energy is of higher vibration and has significant healing properties. The excess energy drawn from this spiritual realm of consciousness would come out of my hands and feet. Life would also let me know the problem areas on the person by expanding the opening when I ran my hand over areas that required more attention. I would also run my hand over meridian lines. I used two fingers to push energy into the meridian lines through pressure points along the path. My goal was to remove all the blockages and restore the free flow of energy. The use of two fingers instead of the palm of my hand was similar to using a pressure washer instead of a regular hose. By focusing all of my energy into two fingers I would greatly increase the intensity of energy transfer into the meridian line. This technique was very effective in opening and removing the blockages. I also used my energy field to repair their chakras. It is very important to know the direction of the flow of energy in each meridian line. I find that some massage therapists and practitioners are unaware of the flow and work against the current, and exacerbating problems within the energy system.

Acupuncture and acupressure are part of traditional Chinese medicine. They work to balance energy as it flows through the body's meridian systems. Meridians are energy highways that create pathways for energy to flow throughout the body. Meridians exist in pairs, and there are many acupuncture points, or pressure points, along their paths. A practitioner can affect the flow of energy in a meridian by putting pressure on specific pressure points using their hand or needle. I have seen a Chi gong master direct energy through those points using only a toothpick, without even touching the skin.

We don't usually regard massage therapy as energy healing, but it affects the physical body through muscle manipulation as and also the flow of energy in the meridians. That is why a client always feels for a short time that their nose is blocked after a massage therapy session. Scientists have not been able to establish the exact function of the sinuses in our body, but in fact they have an extremely important function. As a faucet controls the flow of water in a sink, the sinuses control the flow of spiritual energy in our body. For that reason, we often feel tired when our sinuses are blocked by allergies, cold, or infections.

Chakra healing is often incorporated in some form when practitioners from different styles work on a client. While most people have heard of the seven main chakras, there are in fact 114 chakras throughout the body.

It is difficult to choose the proper form of energy healing and the right healer for your particular problem, but there are things that you can look for when choosing a healer. Spiritual energy is very subtle, but if a practitioner holds his or her hand close to you without actually touching, you should be able to feel the warmth that comes out of their hand. Also, their hand should feel hot when they touch your skin. However, this only indicates the density of the energy in their hand, not the frequency of their vibration. Ask the practitioner if they meditate regularly, or find out if they have a reputation of healing people with difficult illnesses like cancer. Don't be shy to ask them about their credentials, and how long they have been practicing energy healing. Choose a practitioner who seems the most authentic, and radiates truth and integrity. The most important part is the ability to connect with your practitioner, and to see results. You cannot always expect your problem to completely disappear in a short period of time, but in most cases you should feel a difference immediately, or within a day of your treatment.

I have already talked about how muscle imbalances in our bodies can result in physical pain in our spinal cords, joints, and hips. However, we can also have spinal cord injuries due to an accident. One of the incidents that may cause these accidents is the progression of your spiritual development. My understanding from Life is that when you build density and increase the vibration of your energy, Life initiates a sequence of events in which injuries occur at specific points of your spinal cord where chakras are located, in order to change the way energy moves in your body. I have had significant injuries at those specific points since December of 2005. At first I thought that the purpose of those injuries was to make things difficult for me.

That was true to a certain extent, but I soon realized that they were happening on vertebrae that either had important energy nodes, or where chakras were located. The most common injuries that happen due to the progression of your spiritual development are on vertebras L5-S1, T10-T11 (solar plexus chakra), and C7 (throat chakra).

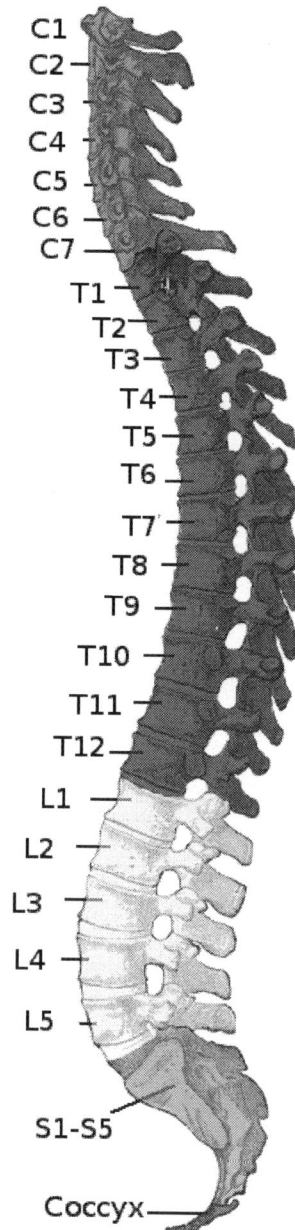

C1
C2
C3
C4
C5
C6
C7
T1
T2
T3
T4
T5
T6
T7
T8
T9
T10
T11
T12
L1
L2
L3
L4
L5
S1-S5
Coccyx

Numbering order of the vertebrae of the human spinal column (Henry Gray and Henry Vandyke Carter, *Anatomy of the Human Body*)

Rehabilitation for spinal cord injuries

The remedy for spinal cord injuries is very complicated. If the injury is caused by muscle imbalance, you simply need to correct the imbalance by doing specific balancing exercises. If the injury is caused by an accident and there is significant inflammation, then you must work with your doctor to reduce the inflammation before you can start balancing and strengthening the supporting muscles in the area. There is no other way to fix spinal cord injuries other than by doing rehabilitation that includes balancing and strengthening exercises.

The problem I have had with the medical community is that unless a practitioner has experienced these injuries themselves or has had significant experience with them, they may not know how to proceed in your particular situation. Even though two injuries could be similar, the same exercises may not work for both people. I suggest that when you visit a medical practitioner who is giving you physical exercises to rehabilitate your injury, you should start the exercise at the lowest level, even if you find it very easy. Then slowly make it more difficult by adding more weight, using stronger elastic bands, or doing more repetitions. If at any point you feel even the smallest increase in pain, stop immediately and reduce the weight or the repetitions. If the increase in pain persists, stop doing that exercise. It does not mean that you can never do that exercise; it just means that you're not ready yet. Continue to work with your medical professional until you find the right combination of exercises for your particular injury.

You should bear in mind that when you start attempting any type of exercise that has been given to you by your medical professional, it may not work for you, and it may increase your pain while attempting them. However, don't give up and continue to work with your medical professional until you find the correct combination. If you take your time and start with low weights and repetitions, this will reduce the chance of your pain worsening.

For spinal cord injuries, a combination of physiotherapy, chiropractic, and acupuncture is preferred. I understand that these services are expensive and not everyone can afford to access them regularly, so research a physiotherapist in your area and find out what type of qualifications they have. Some physiotherapists are certified for acupuncture and manual therapy, as well as manual adjustments. Try to get the best value for your money. If you cannot afford these services, work with a practitioner to find the correct combination of exercises and do them on your own at home or in a gym. Whatever happens, never completely let it go, because the pain will not get better by itself. I have developed specific balancing and strengthening exercises for alignment of the spinal cord and hips, which I am going to release to general public. Ultimately, correcting your posture and aligning your spinal cord will resolve most spinal cord injuries. More serious injuries may require surgery, but the rehabilitation will be the same after surgery. You will be required to strengthen the muscles surrounding your spinal cord to become pain free.

Emotional distress and internal illnesses

Internal illnesses may impact the digestive system, heart and blood circulation, the brain and the nervous system, the kidneys and urinary function, and the lungs. They can be caused by many things, including emotional distress, diet, external influences, and genetics. Emotional distress is the most common cause of internal illnesses. Negative energies that we store in our body greatly affect the flow of energy within our physical and spiritual body. Energy that is not moving stagnates like stale water and forms energy blocks; these energy blocks greatly affect the physical body in the areas were energy stagnates.

The most important thing to understand about healing your illness is that you need to have a holistic approach to solving your health issue. I've taught all my clients how to balance their physical structure, as well as talking to them about diet, and teaching them how to meditate in order to live an emotionally healthy life. The problem that I found with some patients was that they were expecting to just lie down, so I could make all their problems disappear by giving them energy from the third eye. However, if you're not willing to do the work, and balance your life after the treatment, the illness will either come back again the same way, or manifest in a different form. I had patients who would come and see me repeatedly, rather than doing the necessary work to change and become free of the disorder permanently.

The treatment of cancer

I want to address cancer, which is very close to my heart because Telly died from it, and I personally experienced how it affected each one of us in our family. Approximately 40% of the population will be diagnosed with some type of cancer in their lifetime. Unfortunately, chemotherapy and radiation are the most common type of treatments for cancer. The use of chemotherapy and radiation will result in chakras not working properly and will reduce the intake of universal energy or life force. The question is: can the doctors kill the cancer with chemotherapy and radiation before the patient is depleted of the minimum amount of energy that is required to operate the physical body? Significant damage occurs to both our physical and spiritual body during treatments with chemotherapy and radiation. For that reason, it is not unusual for cancer to return and metastasize to other areas, even after successful treatments. I find that most people afflicted by cancer wait too long before they seek help from an energy healer. If you ever get diagnosed with cancer, the first action is usually to remove the affected area by performing surgery, after which you might be required to undergo chemotherapy, radiation, or both. It is extremely important for you to see an energy healer twice a week while receiving treatment, and continue to see them once a week after the treatment, for a period of three months. This is necessary so the healer can maintain the density of your energy, as well as repair the chakras that have been damaged by the treatment. Choose a practitioner who has a high-density energy field; their hands should feel hot when they touch your body. My third eye would open to its maximum capacity when I worked on patients who were going through chemotherapy and radiation. My clients would tell me that my hands felt as hot as an iron when I touched their skin.

Of course there are cancers that can be resolved with low doses of chemotherapy and radiation, and there are cancers that require high doses. I want to share something that may surprise you. If I knew the things that I know today back when Telly was diagnosed with cancer, I would have advised her not to go through with chemotherapy and radiation. The damage caused by these treatments to your spiritual body will follow you into your next life. The suffering that is experienced during these treatments is unnecessary. I will not accept chemotherapy or radiation if I ever get diagnosed with any type of cancer that requires high doses of chemotherapy and radiation. I would advise anyone in any situation that requires high doses of chemicals to refuse treatment and to die with dignity. If I told you to give me your old car that was falling apart and in return I would give you a new one, would you not do it? Of course you would, so why wouldn't you give up your body that is falling apart and die, so you can come back to life with a new body, without having to suffer all that pain before you die. Death is beautiful, death is glorious. I have experienced being outside of my body and know that death is your gift from God; it is your reward for going through the roller coaster of life. The moment you separate from the body is the moment that you know you will never die. You have been there from the beginning and you will be there at the end, you are eternal. You have lived and died hundreds or even thousands of times, so do not be afraid of it. Death is the flower of life, if you only knew how enjoyable it is and the pleasures that you will experience after death, you would not put yourself through all that suffering. I'm not promising you a heaven where you would go to enjoy material things. I am promising you that you will finally get to know who you are, and who you are is God, and God is love, joy, absolute bliss.

Many people around the word are living under dictatorships. If you are one of those people, rise against your oppressors. Rise up against the governments that have taken away your truth and freedom. **Do not be afraid of death, you cannot die, live free, you are God and God is free**. Such governments try to control you. They want you to believe a certain way, and live your life according to their beliefs. Do not put up with this. It is your God given right to choose what you want to believe in, and live your life the way that you want to, whether anyone thinks it is right or wrong. Don't let the fear of death impede your freedom.

Giving up healing

I continued to drive trucks during the week and work as a healer on the weekends. My schedule had got full on the weekends, so some days I had to see clients after my truck-driving job. I decided to ask the trucking company's regional manager to allow me to work four days a week instead of five, so I could dedicate more time to energy healing. I knew that it would not be difficult for them to accommodate my request. He told me to give him time to think about it. Within a few days while I was moving a heavy object, I suffered a significant back injury in the middle of my back. On top of that, after a week the regional manager told me that he would not reduce my working days to four days a week. I thought that maybe it was time for me to quit the truck driving job and focus completely on energy healing; by then I had enough clients to transition to being a full time energy healer. However, the following Saturday my friend who owned the salon told me that they were relocating to a new location that was slightly smaller, and they would not have enough space for me. I knew right away that things were not working out, because Life had planned a different direction for me to follow, but I was confused.

I remembered when Life had sent me this message towards the end of my fasting: *"Start eating normally, but you can only achieve one of your goals."*

This had been just before I was forcefully taken to the hospital because I was dying. One of my goals was to become an energy healer, so that I could heal people's illnesses, and my other goal was to experience enlightenment. When I received that message, I had assumed that I would become an energy healer and that enlightenment would not be possible in this lifetime. I was greatly disappointed that I could not experience enlightenment, but I had accepted God's will regarding the matter. So I was confused as to why things were not working out for me to become an energy healer. I decided to sit in deep meditation and ask

Life for clarification. Life communicated to me that my assumptions were incorrect, and that **enlightenment would not be possible as long as I performed energy healing**.

Life explained why it is not possible to experience enlightenment while you perform energy healing on others. The first reason is that when you give energy to a person who is suffering from an illness, there is an exchange of energy and you will receive some of their energy, which is not crystallized and is of the lower vibration. As long as I had that type of energy within my energy field, I would never get to the point of purification where I would be ready to make the jump into enlightenment. The second reason is that when you give energy to a person who is suffering from an illness, you lose energy. You will gain it back again with meditation, but it is like trying to fill up a glass of water that has a hole in the bottom. It never becomes full, and that is an important requirement for enlightenment. Life asked me to stop energy healing altogether and focus on building and crystallizing my energy field so that I could be ready for enlightenment. I had to continue with my meditation and driving semi-trucks, so I was delighted at the new turn of events. After all, enlightenment was my ultimate goal, and nothing else mattered.

I feel that I must address a discrepancy between what I said on the previous page and the beginning of the book. I mentioned at the beginning of the book that I have experienced enlightenment and I am an enlightened man, but on the previous page, I mentioned that I am still seeking enlightenment, and this is why: enlightenment is the experience of unity with All That Exists, but this single consciousness exists in many planes of consciousness and dimensions. Therefore, a seeker can experience unity at many different levels along his or her spiritual path. Unity at each plane of consciousness has its own experiences, sensations, and insights. Therefore, a seeker should never become satisfied and stop seeking upon experiencing enlightenment, otherwise he or she will lose the opportunity to evolve beyond what has already been experienced.

Once my third eye fully opened, I experienced unity with the 6th plane of consciousness. I have drawn energy from this plane of consciousness for eleven years. It has transformed and completely changed who I am along the way. I would not have had the insights and acquired the knowledge that I have today, had I not experienced unity with this plane of consciousness.

I have also been able to lift off my consciousness from my body and experience enlightenment by performing a specific breathing meditation technique, which I will share with you later in this book, in the chapter about different meditation techniques.

Life has also allowed me to experience going in and out of my body in the hospital, where I became the space that had filled the room.

In December of 2005, I experienced unity and enlightenment with All That Exists – the universal consciousness that is everything physical and spiritual. This experience was so profound that I can only share with you half of what I experienced, because you cannot use words to describe the indescribable. Life has also communicated to me that there are even experiences beyond what I experienced in December of 2005.

In each instance, my consciousness experienced different levels of unity with All That Exists. I felt different sensations and learned different insights and knowledge about how everything works and connects. I cannot value one above the other. One thing that I know for sure is that Enlightenment is not a threshold, and I will never stop seeking unity with higher planes of consciousness until the day my consciousness leaves my physical body.

The importance of doubt

You might be asking: "Why didn't Life give you a clearer message about what was going to take place."

The answer to that question is **"doubt."** Doubt makes everything exciting and interesting. If I tell you how a movie ends before you watch it, it will no longer be exciting to watch because you would know what happens at the end, regardless of all the twists and turns in the movie. Your life is no different. At times, Life gives you experiences to strengthen your faith, but then you might experience a sequence of events that create doubt. So if you're looking for absolute truth, you will never get it. Even though I thought that I would not experience enlightenment in this life after receiving that message, I had faith that if I continued living my truth, Life might reconsider. So I continued to follow the teachings religiously and give all of myself to this path, regardless of what I thought the outcome would be. Remember that your life is about the journey, not the outcome. The outcome will be there at the end. Don't worry about how you will get there or what it will be: that is the exciting part, that we just don't know. Set goals for yourself and fully commit to the path of getting there, and then see where Life takes you. Life is like a river. Always go with the flow, no matter which direction it goes. You might reach your goal or you might end up somewhere else altogether. Be content, no matter what happens. Your higher self takes you where you need to go, and is with you every step of the way. Be joyful through it all.

I was very happy and blissful, but I had suffered a serious back injury in the middle of my back and my current job required me to move heavy objects. I was struggling to do my job, and it had become a problem with human resources and the regional manager of the trucking company. They had given me an electric palette jack to make my job easier, but human resources were pressuring me because they were worried other drivers might ask for one too. Human resources and the regional manager were trying to get rid of me by putting obstacles in my way and coming up with excuses as to why I could not use the electric palette jack. I knew that I could not be angry with anyone, because that is a requirement of being on this path, but it was difficult to control my emotions during this ordeal. I was experiencing a great deal of pain every day, while I felt the regional manager and the human resources representative were not supporting me. After all, I had suffered this injury while I was performing my duties at work. I felt at times that my anger was taking over. I knew that I should not be angry, but sometimes I could not help it. Knowing something theoretically is different from making something happen experientially. I knew that human resources and the regional manager are part of existence, they are life itself, after all nothing but God exists, so I would try to focus myself and remain calm every day. I used mantras throughout the day, such as: **calm and collected I am moving forward,** and **there is no conflict and there is no struggle.** But one day when I got to work, I found out that the regional manager had been fired by someone in the head office in Toronto, Ontario.

I came home that day and sat in deep meditation. Life informed me that my anger towards the regional manager had manifested itself in him getting fired. I understood that the third eye is extremely powerful, and my thoughts, feelings, and emotions have great consequences for everyone around me. I realized that controlling my thoughts, feelings, and emotions needed to be close to perfection. I had progressed significantly from the beginning of my path, but I knew that I would have to continue working on myself to transcend beyond positive and negative.

The next day I called my former employer to get the previous year's T4, which is a summary of your income for the year. I needed it for my accountant to do my taxes. My old boss told me that it was ready and I could go and pick it up, then he followed by saying that they were buying a brand new semi-truck, and looking for a driver to drive it. He asked me if I knew anyone who was looking for work and I told him that I would keep an eye out. But once I hung up the phone, Life immediately connected to me and informed me that I should take the job and go back to long-haul truck driving, so I could continue to meditate and work on going beyond positive and negative. Life wanted me to fully surrender and not get angry, no matter what the situation. You have to understand that surrendering and not getting angry are synonymous with each other. Surrender is absolute acceptance. Acceptance of any situation or anyone can only happen when you stop fighting it, no matter what the situation. It does not matter who is right or wrong. I knew what I needed to do, so I called my previous employer and told him that I would take the job myself. He was delighted and in May of 2013 I began to work as a long-haul truck driver again.

The importance of surrender

Once you make a decision about changing something about yourself, Life will help you by putting you in situations where you can choose actions to support that change. I wanted to fully surrender, and not get angry with anyone, so I was constantly put in situations where people would do things to aggravate and upset me. I will give you some examples, and share how I dealt with them.

Transcending fear and anger

We all have people in our lives who irritate us, or make us angry by pushing our buttons either intentionally or unintentionally. The dispatcher in the trucking company that I was working for was such a person for me. He was a nice young man, but very forgetful and disorganized. He would procrastinate and forget to do things that needed to be done, which would result in me getting stuck or delayed regularly. I've always been a very patient man, but when you're exhausted after a 60 to 70-hour workweek, getting stuck and delayed is very hard to take. There was no reason why he couldn't perform his duties. At first I tried to reason with him, suggesting that he get a notebook and write down what needed to get done, so he would not forget. But no matter what I suggested, nothing ever changed. The fact that he was not doing his job was making me angry and causing me to argue with him regularly. Somewhere along the way I realized that talking to him was not going to change anything. Life had purposely put me in a situation where I could practice going beyond positive and negative. My dispatcher is life itself. There are no people, only God exists, and Life was giving me experiences to overcome my weakness of getting angry. There was absolutely no way for me to change him. I could only change my experience of those events, so I stopped fighting it. Whenever he would forget things, I would calmly remind him over and over again until eventually he would do it. The difference between before and after was absolute acceptance of who he is and his limitations. One day he may decide to change for himself, but neither I nor anybody else can make that happen. I could fight and argue with him all I wanted, but it would not result in any change by him. This is very important to understand, because every one of you has someone like that in your life. The sooner you realize that you cannot change them, the sooner you will stop fighting it. Once you stop fighting it, you will stop feeling angry, and your relationship with them will improve. Absolute acceptance is love.

The other example is something that has been happening to me ever since I started driving semi-trucks. I noticed early on that many motorists don't like to drive behind semi-trucks. When I would try to pass they would speed up, but then when I pulled behind them again, they would slow down. We would go back and forth many times, with me trying to pass, and them not letting me. Many times it would get to the point where I had to make dangerous maneuvers to pass them, and they would be showing me their middle finger, yelling and screaming. I would get so heated at times that I felt like I was going to explode. All I was trying to do was to pass, nothing more, it was never personal. I was frustrated because I could not understand what difference it would make to them if they simply allowed me to pass. I realized that the more frustrated I became, the more often it would happen. I realized that it was going to keep happening until I got to the point where it would not bother me anymore. I began to analyze the events to see how I could change my approach. My solution was that when someone would not allow me to pass, I would pull back and allow the cars behind me to move forward, and would try again in a minute or two. This did cause some minor delays, but overall they were so small that they did not really matter. What mattered was for me to keep control of my emotions and not get angry.

Transcending beyond fear and anger is one of the most difficult parts of the journey in anyone's spiritual development, because fear and anger are deep within our soul. They are the most basic animalistic emotions. Animals have always feared being hunted, and responded with anger when they were threatened by another creature. Long before you experienced life as human beings, you experienced being different creatures, so your basic emotional response to any situation where you're not pleased is going to be anger. Depending on the situation you will either suppress or express the anger. If you suppress anger, you will cause energy blocks within your energy field, and if you express anger to the person who is caused it, you give more energy to your anger and make it bigger.

The best response to a situation where you're not pleased is no response at all. It is best to fully accept people's limitations intellectually and experientially and not to engage them if at all possible. Sometimes we do need to defend our interests or protect ourselves physically, but most of the time you are trying to prove that you are right about something. So you argue with people and get angry with them because you are trying to prove your point. If you want to transcend beyond anger, you need to give that up.

Once you have come to that understanding and decided that you want to live a life without anger, then you have to prepare yourself to go from understanding intellectually to living a life without anger experientially. I can guarantee you that you will fail over and over again, and that is fine, because it does not matter how many times you fail. If you keep intending not to get angry and keep reminding yourself of that, and use mantras to calm yourself down, eventually you will succeed.

Once you have decided that you want to live a life without anger, it's going to be an all-out war. In any war there are thousands of battles fought. Sometimes you win, sometimes you lose. Every event in your life in which someone gives you a negative experience and you're not pleased is a battle. Do your best not to get angry. Think about all you have learned reading this book and use mantras to calm yourself down. If you are successful, it is a step forward. If you fail and get angry, wait until your anger has subsided, then think about where you lost control. Be honest with yourself when analyzing a situation. Do not justify your actions by saying that you were right in that situation, because trying to prove you are right is probably the cause of your anger. Once you work out where you lost control, you can become aware of that moment and try not to pass it the next time you are in a similar situation. Just as I did when I realized that I needed to pull back when someone would not allow me to pass, rather than tailgating that driver and aggressively trying to pass. Slowly you will become more aware of your actions and see improvements in controlling your emotions. Power goes to the person who is in control of their emotions. As you get better at controlling your emotions, Life will put you in more difficult and challenging situations to improve your reaction. This is to help you to improve, not to aggravate you, so be patient with yourself, and with Life.

It is okay to fail

I want to share something about failing. Not only it is okay to fail, but in fact it is necessary. Growth comes from struggling and failing. It does not matter how many times you fail; what matters is what you do after you fail. Pick yourself up, dust yourself off, and get ready for the next round, because Life will not stop, and nor should you. Life will push you to your limits, and when you think you have reached your limits, Life will push further. This will happen repeatedly, so that you will become stronger. It is completely understandable that at times you may become so frustrated that you lose it completely.

I recall three different occasions since December of 2005 when I was in great physical pain, and physically and mentally exhausted. On top of that, negative events were constantly happening all at the same time, so that I completely lost it with Life. I remember being by myself, yelling, screaming, and cursing at whatever was out there, whether you want to call it Life or God. Once I was even so upset that I contemplated breaking my celibacy, just to tell Life "Screw you!" But after a few hours, my anger subsided and I pulled myself together by silencing my mind. Ultimately, I knew that I had chosen everything I was experiencing. It does not make sense to be angry with yourself. So at times, it is okay to feel like you have nothing more to give, and want to just give up and quit. As long as you pull yourself together for the next fight after losing a battle, you will eventually win the war.

Inevitably, Life will push you to your limits. However, you can learn some techniques to get through these lessons faster. Life will not stop until you have got beyond your fear and anger, no matter how long or how many lives it takes for you to get there. Most people have to live hundreds of lives to achieve transcending beyond their emotions, but you can do it in this life, if you choose to, the choice is yours.

Personal development and spirituality can be tedious, time-consuming work. Once I went back on the road in May of 2013, I continued to work on myself in order to fully surrender, and silence my mind. Along the way I tore my meniscus in the left knee, and also injured the back of the vertebras where the fifth chakra is located. These injuries were not coincidental. As I got better at silencing my mind, Life would increase the difficulty by adding an injury and increasing my pain. It is natural for your mind to remember the past or project into the future, when you are experiencing physical pain. You have to continue to focus and remain in the present when you are experiencing pain, or facing difficult challenges. The key to transcending beyond positive and negative is to make peace with your situation and remain in the present moment. I became more aware and at peace with my situation. I had pain in my knee, back, and shoulder all at the same time, while I had to sit in a seat and hold the wheel of my truck eleven hours a day. Slowly my mind became more silent, and I began to feel a change in myself around September of 2015. I was still experiencing the same amount of pain as before, but it only felt like mild discomfort. My dispatcher kept making mistakes, but I just would not get frustrated or feel anger. I had finally transcended beyond pain and suffering. I no longer felt any anger, no matter what the situation. I cannot tell you that I have reached perfection, because while we are experiencing life in the physical body, perfection is not possible. But I strive to get as close as possible to it. I constantly strive to fully surrender myself to All

That Exists, but I know there will be moments when I will feel weak. That is okay because no matter what, I know that I will rise above it and accept whatever is coming to me. It has been said that when Jesus was on the cross he loudly said:

"My God, my God, why have you forsaken me?"

In that moment Jesus could not understand why he had to experience what he was experiencing, but if those events did not happen as they did, he would not be known today as one of the most influential men in history. Life has a plan for every one of us, so we should all work on surrendering ourselves to what is coming to us. Life is like a river, flow with it in whichever direction that goes. Try to keep your mind silent while you're experiencing whatever is coming to you, and stop fighting it, even if you do not like it.

The birth of Ayesha

My younger sister Naz gave birth to a baby girl, Ayesha, in September of 2015. We were all so happy to welcome this new addition into our lives. I knew deep inside that she would make a big impact on my life. One day a few months after her birth, I was driving my semi-truck in California and focused on the third eye, when Life connected to me. Life asked me:

"Would you be willing to forgo all the progress that you have made, and start all over again right from the beginning of the path, if Telly would still be alive?"

You and your higher self are one, your higher self knows the level of your sincerity when you think, or say something. This was the most unusual question that Life had ever asked me, but without hesitation, I answered, "Of course I would."

"I have given her back to you, Ayesha is the reincarnation of Telly's soul."

Life had gone full circle. I cried with joy and absolute bliss; Telly was my twin soul. I remembered the time when we were in hospital minutes before she passed away, and I had held both my hands just above her crown chakra. I felt it connect to the palm of my hand and suck in energy at a very high rate. My third eye was wide open throughout this process, so she received vital energy with higher vibration during that time. I had given energy to many people throughout the years, but I had never felt what I felt that night. Energy was leaving my hand at such a high rate that I felt both my hands pulsating; it was an indescribable sensation.

I know that Ayesha will make a big impact on my life and everyone around her. The energy of the third eye is very unique; it transforms the consciousness with the lower vibration once it comes into contact with it. Telly was a beautiful soul, but I knew that the addition of the energy of the third eye that she received from me at the moment of her death would make her more impactful and gracious in her next life.

Around November of 2015 I began to receive messages from Life that it is time for me to share my knowledge with everyone, so I started to talk and teach to whomever wanted to learn about meditation and spirituality. Almost everyone that I talked to told me that I needed to write down my teachings, but I was not interested in writing a book. I was working 60 to 70 hours a week driving semi-trucks, and with my workout regime I had little time to do anything else.

My best friend Sammy asked me to go visit him and his wife in San Diego, California during the Christmas season of 2015. I thought that it would be pleasant to take a few days off and relax, so I took a load to San Diego with my semi-truck and stayed there over the holidays. On Christmas Eve we were all opening our gifts. Sammy's wife gave me a beautiful blank notebook, and told me that I should write down my thoughts in it. I understood that I needed to write down the knowledge that Life had given me and share it with everyone.

People don't always pay attention to the messages that they get from everyone around them, but remember that Life is every one of us and communicates with you through everyone around you. If multiple people are telling you the same thing, or events are happening to support what you're hearing, Life is trying to tell you something. I can directly communicate with All That Exists through the third eye, but often I get my messages or clarifications through people around me or events that happen in my life. Life only connects to me through direct contact if I continuously miss messages, but that rarely happens. You can do the same. Ask Life a question, and then wait for your answer by paying attention to your surroundings. Life communicates to you in many different ways. A friend could call to talk to you about something and mention the topic of your question, or you could see a sign on the street, or something on TV. Just don't try to explain away the event if you don't like the answer, because Life will stop answering your questions in that way. Most importantly, all the answers are within you. If you can silence your mind, I promise that you will hear God speaking to you, because God is your higher self.

I started to write this book shortly after I came back from visiting Sammy in California. It was a difficult process, because I had to go back and relive my life from the beginning, including the dark days of my life. My mind was very silent before I began to write the book, but once I started, thoughts began to flood my mind. It is difficult to lose the peace and silence once you have experienced it, but I know that it has helped me and will help many people. What I have written in this book are not my opinions and feelings. These are Life's insights into the inner working of your body, mind, and soul. Life has also shared with me insights into our most significant relationships, which are the relationship between parents and children, and the relationship with people that we are intimate with. So I have written a section about parenting, as well as a section about love, sex, and relationships **from a spiritual point of view**. I advise everyone to read the section for parenting, even if you are single and do not plan to have children, because it will give you a lot of insights about why you behave the way you do, and what you need to do to change some of those behaviors.

Parenting

The abortion issue

I first want to talk about the important subject of abortion. I understand this is a sensitive topic for many, so I want to discuss what Life has shared with me regarding this matter. For a pregnant woman who is not ready to have a child, the decision about abortion is a difficult one, so let's look at the options, and at the effect of abortion from a spiritual point of view.

Choice 1: Abortion

Christian priests and Muslim clerics have all spoken out against abortion, but neither the Bible nor the Koran has addressed abortion because abortion did not exist during the time of Jesus and Mohammed. So the clerics are merely stating their own opinions. Life is not concerned about right or wrong, this matter is only about cause and effect. The first thing that needs to be understood is that you cannot kill anything in this life; you can only end its experience. So the burden of that decision solely falls on the woman who is pregnant, and no one else. It is not wrong for the woman who is pregnant to abort the pregnancy if she does not yet feel ready to bring a child into this world. I'm not promoting abortion here, there are consequences for every action, but it is no one else's business whether or not a pregnant woman chooses to keep or lose the baby. Every birth and death is perfect in this life. Nothing but God exists; there are no individual souls. If she has chosen to abort the baby, this is also God's decision regarding the matter. There will be

166

consequences for that action; for example, some woman feel depressed for some time after an abortion.

There could be more serious consequences for men and women who carelessly have unprotected sex, but the consequences of their actions are between Life and them. No one has the right to judge them for their actions.

Choice 2: Adoption

Many people who belong to the pro-life movement believe that if a woman is pregnant and not yet ready to have a child, she should give birth to the baby and then make an adoption plan for it. I want to first explain the relationship between the physical body of the fetus and the soul who occupies it. You may have seen programs on TV about conception, in which millions of sperms swim towards the eggs in their attempt to bond with it. Know that Life controls the movement of every single sperm. Long before conception it has been decided which sperm will successfully bond with the egg. Every conception and birth happens exactly as they should. Life is perfect in exactly what it wants to experience. It may look as if this is a completely random occurrence, but I assure you that Life is every single one of those sperms and controls the movement of every single one of them.

The soul energy that is going to occupy the baby's physical body is ready to bond with the sperm and egg once they have come together. This happens at the time of conception, but the soul energy is still absolutely one with the universe. We might say that it has not yet become individualized. The soul energy begins to bond with the energy field of the pregnant woman, while the fertilized egg begins its journey. The soul energy is not yet ready to fully bond with the fertilized egg; the process of fully bonding with the fetus begins approximately two months into the pregnancy and may take anywhere between two and three months to complete.

During this process, the universal consciousness that is one with the soul energy begins to create ripples within itself to create the sense of individuality, to make it possible for the soul energy to bond with the physical body of the fetus. This is a very difficult process, and any pregnant woman who plans to abort should do their best to abort the pregnancy before the start of this process (which starts from seven to eight weeks after conception). The bond between the pregnant woman's energy field and the soul energy of the fetus strengthens as more time passes. The connection between these two energies is like no other in humans and throughout the animal kingdom. The bond between these two energies is as close as you can get to absolute unity. For that reason, many mothers throughout the animal kingdom would fight to the death to save the lives of their newborn.

The soul of the newborn child will feel a tremendous loss once you separate it from the biological mother. It does not matter how loving the adoptive mother is, she will not be able to replace the energy of the biological mother in the short time after birth. For that reason, many adopted children will grow up with the feeling of abandonment, no matter how loving the adoptive family may be. Imagine that you spent every second with someone for nine months, so close that you heard their heartbeats. Your energies are so intertwined that you cannot tell where you begin and end. In essence you are both one, and suddenly you come to this world and get separated from them. It would feel like half of you has been separated from the other half. This is similar to what a baby will feel once he or she is born into this world and then adopted. That is why it is so important for babies not to get separated from the mother after birth for any length of time.

I would personally prefer to be aborted and come back to a better situation, than come to life and get separated from the energy that I have bonded with for nine months. There are also no guarantees as to how well a child is treated after the process of adoption. I am neither for nor against adoption, or abortion. I am simply explaining the cause and effect regarding each decision. Ultimately the burden of the decision is on the pregnant woman. Remember that nothing dies in this world, the energy simply moves from one experience to the other. Life always balances itself, so don't take everything so seriously. If you are a woman who has come to such a decision, do not worry about making the right decision. Life is with you; the right decision is what you feel in your heart, you are God's consciousness.

Choice 3: Birth

This option is one that requires a major commitment and so it should not be taken lightly. You are signing up to be role models for many years to come when you choose to become parents. So you might ask yourself, are you prepared to give the child the care that he or she needs to become a healthy adult? Are you willing to sacrifice, and to put the needs of the child before yours? Are you emotionally healthy, so that you can bring an emotionally healthy child into adulthood?

How to raise children properly

I'm going to break down the growth of the child from birth to adulthood, and discuss the most important issues regarding that particular era.

It is well known in the scientific community that a child's brain develops very fast in the first five years of life, and particularly in the first three years. Every time the child has new experiences, new neural connections are made in the child's brain. This will affect the way the child learns, feels, thinks, and behaves for many years. Tremendous effort will be required to change thought patterns and behaviors after these neural connections are made. In fact, meditation is the only way you can sever these neural connections and make new ones.

Once a thought has entered your mind to behave a certain way, if you intend to stop that thought pattern and behavior by focus, it weakens the neural connection that supports that particular thought pattern and behavior.

In order to sever the connection completely and change the way we behave, we will have to try to stop that thought pattern and behavior over and over again until we become successful. This is why using mantras is an effective way to counteract a particular thought pattern and behavior.

The best way to prevent bad behavior is to make sure the right connections are made in the first five years of the child's life. The child's caregiver and environment play the biggest role during that time. Babies require a tremendous amount of love and affection in the first five years. Constant physical touch and soothing sounds stimulate brain growth, which improves emotional health.

The importance of mothers

The mother's presence is required during the first five years, and particularly the first three years of its life. I have already talked about how the baby's soul energy bonds with the mother's energy field. Any separation after birth will have a significant negative effect in the baby's emotional health. He or she will surely have a feeling of abandonment if separated from the mother for an extended period of time. That is why I asked, are you prepared to give the child the care that he or she needs to become a healthy adult? Are you willing to sacrifice, and put the needs of the child before yours? Because if you're planning to have a child, and put them in daycare, you are abandoning your child.

I know that what I'm saying may not be popular with many people who choose to put their children in daycare, but that does not change the facts. Children left in daycare at an early age will suffer both mentally and spiritually, so do your best to avoid this. This effect gets worse the younger the child, so if you are a mother who works outside of the house, try to delay going back to work as long as possible by timing your pregnancy. Leaving your child with a grandmother or a loving relative is better than leaving your child with a nanny. In addition, leaving your child with a new mother who has a child of her own and is looking to make some extra money would be better than leaving your child with a nanny. Leaving your child with a nanny is a lot better than taking your child to commercial daycares; commercial daycares are the absolute worst-case scenario.

I knew someone very close to me who owned a daycare. She was a very nice spiritual woman who did her best to take care of the children left in her daycare. However, she simply did not have the time to attend to every child's needs because to make a daycare profitable, the ratio between children and caregivers has to be very high. Different states or provinces have different standards, but on average the ratio for commercial daycares is one caregiver for every four infants or one caregiver for every eight children. You need to ask yourself, would one caregiver be able to give the same amount of care and attention to four infants or eight children that a mother could give to her child or children? Logically the answer is no; the amount of care, attention, and love that could be given by a caregiver in commercial daycares could not even come close to what a mother could give to her child or children. That is simply a fact, without even considering the loss and damage caused by the child's separation from the mother's energy field.

The next important phase after infancy begins when the child begins to talk and comprehend vocabulary. Newborn babies can only communicate through an emotional outburst. They cry and show an emotional reaction when they are in pain or hungry, or when they are uncomfortable because their diaper needs to be changed. They get frustrated and show anger when they want something and cannot communicate that with you. It is extremely important to change this behavior once they develop the capability to communicate with you. This is extremely difficult, but extremely important. The ramifications of not changing this behavior will follow the child for the rest of their life. Parents make life difficult for themselves if this issue is not dealt with as soon as possible.

Remember that when children are born, a repetition of certain behaviors will strengthen the neural connection supporting those behaviors. So the longer the behavior continues, the harder it will become to sever those connections. It is possible to sever the connection and change the behavior no matter how late in life, but it will be significantly harder. In fact, the spiritual journey is about severing the neural connections that support certain behaviors and conditioning, and replacing them with new neural connections that support love, unity, and respect.

To wean off children from showing anger and other emotional reactions when they are not pleased with a situation, the parents need to be disciplined in how they react to a child who is having an emotional reaction. Once children have developed the ability to communicate and comprehend, let them know that you will not engage with them until they are no longer showing anger and an emotional reaction. Remain calm and be disciplined while the event is happening. Children can read facial expressions and body language when you are communicating with them. You need to be both patient and consistent to change the behavior, so let's look at an example that we have all experienced.

We have all seen situations where a child wants something in a shopping center, and the mother or the father says no, and the child begins to cry. The parents can react in many different ways. They may ignore the child, or threaten the child with a punishment if he or she does not quieten down, or take more drastic measures to quieten the child because they feel embarrassed by the noise the child is making. Engaging the child in order to quieten him or her down is the worst thing that you can do, because you are telling the child that you will respond to an emotional reaction. Whether it is positive or negative, you are responding to that behavior, so the neural connection that supports that behavior strengthens because of your reaction to that behavior. Ignoring the child altogether would not be the worst thing that you could do, but telling the child that you will be willing to discuss the matter with them if they stop crying is the right course of action. This may or may not stop the crying, but if you stay disciplined and repeat it over and over again, eventually the child will decide to try discussing the matter. If that happens, you do not need to cave in immediately, but you should support the change in behavior with positive reinforcement, such as promising them something they enjoy at a later time. It is important not to promise them something they enjoy while they are showing an emotional reaction. Positive reinforcement should only come after the crying has stopped. This will encourage children to communicate instead of having an emotional reaction. Understand that change is difficult for children, as well as for adults. Just think how difficult it is for you to change something in yourself, so take your time and be patient. Your consistency will determine whether you are successful or not, whether you are trying to change the behavior of a child, teenager, an adult, or yourself. The basic principles are the same in all situations: you will never be able to change any one, or anything, if you are arguing and fighting with them. That would only strengthen the neural patterns supporting their behaviors.

How to discipline older children

Dealing with older children and teenagers is slightly more complex, but the principles remain the same. You must first calmly and clearly discuss your expectations and boundaries with your older children or teenagers. Then you need to let them know exactly what the consequences will be if your expectations are not met, or what will happen if they cross the boundary lines. Make your consequences severe enough to put some fear in them. A healthy fear of parents is absolutely necessary, but also put in place a reward system in terms of which they will be rewarded if your expectations are met and no lines are crossed. Choose the consequences of their bad behavior wisely. For example, taking away video games, TV privileges, or a cell phone for a period of time will not be useful, because they know that they will only have to wait a certain time to get them back. A better consequence for bad behavior would be to take away every privilege without giving them any specific time when they will get them back. If the time comes where you are implementing this type of discipline, wait until they're not at home and then remove everything from their room, and store them completely out of reach. Only leave them the bare minimum of what they absolutely need for daily life. The shock factor has to be at its maximum. You would only need to do this once if you do it right. The most important part when they get home is for you to remain completely calm and emotionless no matter how they react. Calmly explain to them why their belongings are gone, and let them know what they need to do to earn them back, one item at a time. Do not give everything back to them all at once after a certain period of time. Allow them to earn everything back one item at a time. I know that this works, because I was a recipient of it once, and that was enough for me to make a significant change about how I behaved at home.

My mother had given me and Telly specific instructions about coming home from school. I was to go straight home from school, while behaving properly on the bus with my friends. One day my mother wore a disguise and followed me from school to home. First of all, I was horsing around with my friends on the bus. Then we all went to the shopping center nearby, and then I played a couple of quick games of soccer down the street from our home, before I finally went home. My mother's disguise was so good that I did not realize that she was near me the entire time. She came home while I was playing soccer just a few blocks from our home.

Once I came home, she called me to the kitchen, and asked me how my day had been and why I was late. I told her a tale of a sequence of events that had never happened. After I finished, she calmly told me that she had followed me from school, and then she went through every rule that I had broken that day. She then told me that I was grounded, and restricted to my room for a full month. My father's corporal punishment was nothing compared to the psychological warfare that my mother presented with this punishment. I was completely caught out and had nothing to say, so I went to my room. Once I got to my room, I realized that she had completely removed everything from my room, other than my schoolbooks and some clothing. She had removed all the electronics, the fictional books that I liked reading, my ping pong racket and ball —

basically, everything that I could possibly use to entertain myself. I was not allowed to come out of my room except to go to the bathroom, and to take showers. I felt as if I was going mad after only a week; but no amount of apologizing was sufficient to end this punishment. Even though it was difficult for my mother to see me suffer, she did not give in, and stuck to the time period for the punishment. After the end of my punishment, I was allowed to come out of my room, but I did not get any of my belonging back for a long period of time. She told me that I could earn them back only with good behavior, and by being honest with her.

This was a critical junction in our relationship. The experience of being grounded for a full month without anything to entertain myself was so severe that I knew I would never want to experience it again. I realized that she could follow me in disguise at any time, so I knew that I had to change how I behaved. After that event, I learned to communicate and compromise with her, and I always kept my end of the bargain. As I said, if you do this right, you will only have to do this once. Remember that it is extremely important for you to hold your children accountable for their bad behavior, no matter how difficult it is for you to see them suffer. They have to know that you will not give in after you have given them a punishment.

Never have an emotional outburst when you are disciplining a child or a teenager. All they will learn is the wrong way to react when they are not satisfied with a situation, and they will continue with the same behavior once they become adults. This is not just about teaching them how they need to behave at home, it is also about teaching them how to behave when they're not pleased with a situation, and you need to be the perfect role model.

It is very important that you behave the same way with your significant other in front of the children. Fights among parents are extremely damaging to the child's behavior. How can you ask your children to control themselves when you cannot control yourselves as adults? This is why it is so important for couples to meditate and deal with their anger before they start having children. They will watch your every move, copying how you behave with them and with each other. This is what I meant when I said you are signing up to be role models when you have children.

One of the most important responsibilities of any parents is to give their children the necessary knowledge and tools to live independently from their parents when they become adults. This will include cleaning and eating healthily.

Many mothers take care of every aspect of their teenagers' lives, which includes cleaning, cooking, and doing laundry. They think they are being loving by doing everything for their children, but that is not love, that is bad parenting. You need to transfer the responsibility of taking care of themselves as early as possible. First make them responsible to clean up after themselves at a very young age, and then give them cleaning responsibilities around the house. This will teach them to clean their living space when they are older and move out. I remember that when I was young, my mother cooked, but my sisters and I were responsible for putting the dishes away and cleaning the house completely. I am very happy that she made us responsible for cleaning, because as adults all of our living spaces have always been clean. She also showed us the importance of eating healthily and demonstrated by teaching us how to prepare simple meals. These were not complicated dishes, but whether you are a man or a woman you need to know how to make basic meals.

Diet and healthy living for your children

I am very passionate about diet and healthy living. Obesity is rampant in Western societies because of the availability of junk food, and fast food restaurants selling food with little or no nutritional value. Obese parents have children who also become obese. It is very important for any couple to address their personal and emotional problems before they have children. God has given you free will to live your life as you please, and take any path that you like, but when you sign up to have children the burden is higher, because you are taking responsibility to influence the path of another soul. This responsibility is sacred, and should not be taken lightly. Fix what is broken in you, before you take responsibility for another soul, because the karma and the cycle will repeat itself in your next life, until you break the cycle.

Let me give you an example: a person who is born into an obese family and is not taught how to eat healthily becomes obese. There will be two possibilities for this situation. One possibility is that he or she will continue with unhealthy eating and have children who follow in his or her footsteps because they don't know any better. In that case he or she will reincarnate into an obese family again in their next life, and the cycle will repeat itself. The second possibility is that the person will finally decide to change their bad eating habits, learn to live a healthy life, transfer that knowledge to their children, and break the cycle once and for all. Once you learn your lesson and stop the cycle it will not repeat itself, so why not do it in this life? Do not buy junk food. Reduce the temptation for everyone by not having any unhealthy products at home to begin with. Never introduce your children to fast food. If you already have, cut it out altogether. Once they get the taste of greasy and sugary foods, they will not have a taste for healthy food. That should be obvious to everyone. You would not allow your children to get addicted to drugs, so why would you allow them to get addicted to greasy and sugary foods? They are one and the same; addiction is addiction, no matter how you look at it. Life does not differentiate between the types of negative effects that you are having on your children. In your next life you will receive back the effort that you put into this life with your children, that is guaranteed, that is karma. Break the cycle, change your behavior; it is never too late to change.

You need to make sure that your children are living a balanced life. A common problem with older children and teenagers is they spend too much time on social media and video games. Most parents have no ability to control or monitor any of their children's activities because they give into requests from their children and buy them smart phones, which give them access to the Internet 24/7. If you're worried about their whereabouts, buy them regular phones, or restrict their data so they cannot connect to the Internet anytime they want. Monitor their homework and Internet activities by placing their desk with computer in a common area in your apartment or house. You can buy them noise-canceling headphones if they complain about noise while they're doing their homework. Make an effort to monitor their activities; it will pay off in the long run by ensuring they do not go astray, because it would require much more effort on your part to bring them back in line once they have gone astray.

You also have to make sure that they are involved in some type of physical activity in order to open up their chakras and draw in universal energy. Team sports that require focus are a natural form of meditation, so playing those types of sports will help them with focus, as well as opening up their chakras for a free flow of energy. It is up to you to help them manage their time, and ensure they live a balanced life. It is more likely for a teenager to live a balanced life as an adult, if he or she lives a balanced life at their parents' home. When your child is 13, talk to him or her about the importance of focus, and explain to them how it would benefit them in their school, and playing sports. I explained in an earlier chapter how focus and meditation can help children, teenagers, and adults in their daily life, so teach them how to meditate. This has nothing to do with spirituality – better focus can help everyone to perform any type of task.

Using drug tests on your children

Teenagers using alcohol and drugs are a problem for many parents around the world. The problem is that many parents talk to their offspring about alcohol and drugs, but they do not monitor them regularly to see if they are using or not. I suggest that you talk to your children about alcohol and drugs before they become teenagers, but at the end of your conversation let them know that you will randomly perform drug tests. Have a drug test kit ready and give them their first drug test. Drug tests are very inexpensive; there are many companies that do drug tests for a very reasonable price. For example, one company charges less than ten dollars for their most comprehensive urine test, which you can perform at home, like a pregnancy test. They charge less than a hundred dollars for their hair test, which is more accurate and shows you which of the most common drugs have been used in the preceding 90 days.

People who do the wrong things only do it because they think they can get away with it. Take that away from your teenagers. Let them know before they have any chance of trying drugs that there is zero chance of them getting away with it, by giving them random drug tests. If you wait until you catch them in the act it will be too late. They will already be addicted to drugs and you will have to spend thousands of dollars on getting them sober, as well as deal with the consequences of their actions which may include: poor performance at school, getting into trouble with law, and spending time with a bad crowd. The best scenario is to make sure they will never touch drugs to begin with, and the chances of them ever doing so will be significantly reduced if they know there is no way they can get away with it. Talk to them about losing all their privileges until they are 18 years old if they test positive for drugs.

We also have the means to significantly reduce crimes in Western societies by having a mandatory DNA test for everyone in our country. Politicians have not moved in that direction, citing privacy issues. We need to understand that as societies, if we are serious about eliminating and reducing crime, it is absolutely necessary to have such a database. People who do not commit crime have nothing to worry about. People who do not agree with this proposal may not necessarily be criminals, but they're not one hundred percent sure of themselves. Criminals would hate such a database because it would reduce the chances of them getting away with crimes significantly. Honest and law abiding people should put pressure on politicians to make this happen for the safety of the entire population. Imagine the effects that such a database would have on crime rates like murder and rapes. Why wait for someone to commit a serious crime, before we get their DNA? Is our privacy more important than the lives of the human beings who would be saved by the existence of such a database?

Some parents face very tough challenges growing up, and go through tremendous difficulties to make a life for themselves. Once they have children of their own, they do their best to make sure that their children don't experience the same types of difficulties growing up, and that is a huge mistake. The reason those parents became successful was due to the struggles that they experienced growing up, which resulted in their personal growth and success. Not allowing their children to struggle and face tough challenges will result in inadequacy once they become adults. Growth comes from struggle. We evolve when we face challenges and overcome difficulties. If you're interested in your children's success and well-being, you have to prepare them for the challenges that they will face when they become adults. The only way that you can prepare them for what Life throws at them is to put in place a sequence of events where they struggle to overcome challenges. Do not shield them from pain and suffering, because once they are adults they will have to fend for themselves. If you have not prepared them, they will get overwhelmed and crumble under pressure.

Don't shield your children from negative experiences

Parents who don't prepare their children for adulthood properly tend to rescue their children, whether they're teenagers or adults. Nothing will ever change unless you take the training wheels off and let them fall down. It is okay to feel pain, and it is okay to fail. Tremendous growth comes from failing. Pain and suffering only make you tougher and stronger. You would do a great disservice to your children if you shield them from negative experiences.

I personally made that mistake with Naz. I began to work when I was 19 years old and moved out of my parents' home when I was 20. I worked more than 80 hours a week to pay for my own expenses and help my family. I worked in many low paying jobs such as 7/11 stores, gas stations, and cleaning companies before I worked in our family business. I always held two jobs to make enough to live on my own, and even worked throughout the years that I went to school to study electrical engineering. Those experiences made me grow and evolve as a human being.

But when I started to make good money working in the family business and nightclubs, I made sure that Naz, who was 14 years younger than me, never faced any difficulties growing up. I bought her the best shoes, computer, rollerblades, and so on. My father paid for her first car, and I gave her fifty dollars a week just for spending money throughout her time in high school, on top of what she got from our father. She had everything that she needed, but she struggled as an adult to survive on her own. She was not ready to face the difficulties and challenges that Life threw at her, so we rushed to rescue her over and over again. The more we helped her the more she relied on our help, until Life connected and instructed me to pull away and allow her to struggle on her own without my help.

This was very difficult for me to do because I love her and couldn't watch her suffer. But as soon as I pulled away and told her that she was on her own, she started to pull herself together, and survive on her own even though she was facing very difficult challenges in her life, including significant physical injuries due to a car accident. She is still struggling, but I am no longer worried about her because I know that she's capable of pulling through. I know that many parents are facing similar situations and the only way to help their children is by pulling away and allowing them to struggle on their own without any help.

God has given every soul free will to decide what they want to experience in their life. Some parents try to dictate their children's every move as a teenager and as adults. Many of them attempt to live vicariously through their children, and that is not fair. We all get a chance to live our life the way we want to; parents should give their children the knowledge and guidance to navigate the twists and turns of life, but they cannot go with them on that journey. Every soul has to take this journey on their own and make their own decisions and their own mistakes. Mistakes and struggles go hand in hand, and are necessary for growth. Many times I tried to prevent Naz from making mistakes, and failed every single time, as if Life was telling me to leave her alone. Allow your children to choose their path whether you agree with them or not. If they make a mistake, it is okay, they will learn from it.

I will tell you that the biggest lesson that Life taught me when my third eye opened was to discipline myself and not to help anyone unless I was specifically asked to. Do the same for your children. Give them tools and guidance to navigate through life, and help them to find what it is that they are passionate about. I promise you if they find it, they will become successful. Sometimes it takes time for someone to develop and find what they are passionate about, so be patient. I'm not telling you to baby them and keep them at home when they're adults, but if they're not ready to go to college and university when they finish high school, give them time to figure it out.

It is up to you whether you want them to move out on their own or continue to live at home, but make sure that they go to work and are responsible for their own living expenses. Make sure that they contribute at home both physically and financially. I personally think that it would be more helpful for them to live on their own separately from the parents, because they will get a better idea as to what it takes to live on their own, and it would instill in them a sense of urgency to figure out what they want to do with their life.

Love, sex, and relationships

One of the most profound human experiences is an intimate relationship with another human being. This is a very complex encounter that has significant effects on our physical and spiritual body. Most people have a complete lack of understanding of what takes place when these meetings occur, which results in confusion, hurt, and pain. We tend to make mistakes that affect our lives significantly for long periods of time because we don't understand how intimate relationships affect our physical body, as well as our spiritual energy. Love and sex are so intertwined that sometimes it is difficult to know what the other person is truly feeling when sexual intimacy happens. I have heard people say that they love, but really their action suggests that they have no understanding of what love really means. So let me define the true meaning of love.

What is love?

Love is absolute unity, love is what binds us together, the "I" has completely disappeared and ego has been dropped. Love is without judgment, expectation, or condition. Love is absolute acceptance, there is no conflict and there is no struggle, the energy field has become one at every level.

By definition, God, love, absolute unity, and absolute acceptance are synonymous. This is the definition of love at the highest level. It should be the goal of every relationship to experience love at its deepest level. Unfortunately, a very small percentage of people experience true love in their lifetime, either as couples or as friends. We are multi-dimensional beings. In previous chapters I described the seven chakras and the seven layers of our energy field. The problem with experiencing love is that our energies bond with each other at different levels of the body at different times when we become intimate with another consciousness, whether in a friendship or a sexual relationship. Experiencing love at the level of physical body, lower layers, and higher layers are very different from each other. At the same time there are significant differences between how sex and love affect men and women, both at the physical and spiritual level. So I want to go through the effect of sex and exchange of energy between the two consciousness at every level of our energy field. I want to focus on couples and sexual relationships in this section, and how we can elevate relationships to the point of experiencing true love at every level of the spiritual energy field.

Sex is the expression of love at the physical level, but there are two possibilities with any sexual encounter: the physical body, and energy exchange at every level of the spiritual energy field.

Let us look at our physical and spiritual connections at every level and see how we can elevate our connections from the lowest, which is physical, to the highest, which is enlightenment.

The physical body

In any sexual encounter the physical body begins to produce and release many chemicals that affect our brain and physical body on many levels. These chemicals and their effects are included in the following list.

- **Endorphins** make you happy, and naturally relieve pain, lower stress levels, and boost confidence.
- **Dopamine** is a neurotransmitter that affects the brain's reward and pleasure centers. An increased level of dopamine is also associated with craving and dependency, which can result in dependency between the participants.
- **Norepinephrine** is similar to adrenaline, which increases the heart rate and produces excitement. Norepinephrine in combination with dopamine produces elation, intense energy, sleeplessness, craving, and focused attention.
- **Testosterone** increases sexual desire in both men and women, but men produce more testosterone than women, so for men this desire is more pronounced. For that reason, sex is extremely important for men and they feel loved when they have sex. Women on the other hand need to bond at a higher spiritual body

to feel loved. This is a significant difference between how men and women view sex. I will discuss this further shortly.

- **Oxytocin** is a hormone that also acts like a neurotransmitter. Oxytocin is the physical representation of love. Oxytocin is called the love hormone or the cuddling hormone because it causes you to feel a connection and bond with your lover. It is a natural tranquilizer that lowers blood pressure; it also lowers our defenses and makes us trust people. Women produce more of this hormone than men, and for that reason they feel more bonded after a sexual encounter than men do. Sex is more meaningful for women than for men at an emotional level, which is another significant difference between men and women.

Release of all these chemicals in any sexual encounter can cause a feeling of love between couples who have been together for a significant time, or two people who have just met. So it is important to be aware of the natural effect of these chemicals and how they can affect the way you feel about your partner. It is very important not to allow the effects of these chemicals to cloud your judgment when you meet someone new and start a sexual relationship, because these chemicals can mimic a feeling of love with new couples who do not have an emotional connection.

Sexual experience is the only human experience besides enlightenment where the energy fields between two consciousness completely mesh into each other. Energy cords form and connect the chakras of different bodies to each other, and a tremendous amount of energy is exchanged through these connections between the two individuals. These energy cords begin to form at the early stages of the relationship and strengthen as more time passes. The strength and speed at which these cords form can increase with more sexual encounters. The energy is exchanged at every level of the spiritual energy field, but during the sexual encounter itself, the energy exchange is much more intense at the first and fourth layer of the spiritual energy field relating to the etheric and astral body respectively. The chakras for the first and fourth body go into overdrive during the sexual act. The etheric body is the first layer of the spiritual energy field that is in direct contact with the physical body. A considerable amount of energy is exchanged through direct transfer from the male to the female at this level.

The sexual energy of men and women

Positive energy is male energy (yang), and negative energy is female energy (yin). **The polarity of the energy at the etheric level for men is positive (male energy),** while **the polarity of the energy for women at this level is negative (female energy)**. On the other hand, the **polarity of energy at the astral level, which is the fourth body for women, is positive (male energy), while the polarity of energy for men at this level is negative (female energy)**.

To summarize, men have positive energy in their genitalia and negative energy in their chest, which is why men's nipples are not very sensitive. For women the opposite is the case, they have negative energy in their genitalia and have positive energy in their breast. For that reason, their breasts are very sensitive and men need to caress them in order to arouse women. Positive energy is male energy (yang), and negative energy is female energy (yin).

		Women Energy polarity	**Men** Energy polarity
Cosmic body	seventh layer	neutral	neutral
Celestial body	sixth layer	neutral	neutral
Spiritual body	fifth layer	neutral	neutral
Astral body	fourth layer	positive	negative
Mental body	third layer	negative	positive
Emotional body	second layer	positive	negative
Etheric body	first layer	negative	positive

Women need to warm up with positive energy before they're ready to engage with their negative energy. As the sexual act progresses, energy continues to build up in their respective areas. This buildup continues as long as the male can hold his orgasm. When a man orgasms he releases the built-up positive energy in his etheric body directly into the woman's etheric body. Sex is not just a physical act; there is a significant spiritual component in this process. Women also release positive energy that has been built up in their astral body through their breasts into the man's fourth body, but the amount of energy that is released is significantly lower than what they would receive in the sexual act. However, the amount of positive energy released through their breasts changes depending on how they feel about their partner. They open up the fourth chakra more and release more positive energy if they are in love with their partner. The most amount of energy is exchanged when chakras lineup across from each other. For that reason, the missionary position is the most popular position.

Women will feel more sexual when the connection with their partner strengthens at the astral level, which is the reason why women prefer to have sex when they feel loved. This is the complete opposite of what men feel. Men feel loved when they have sex, which is the connection at the etheric level. This has to do with the opposite polarity of energies in different layers of the spiritual energy field for men and woman.

Positive energy, which is the male energy, is much more intense than negative energy, which is the female energy. The difference in intensity in each layer of the spiritual energy field is the reason why men and woman experience the same events in life differently from each other and sometimes have difficulty seeing their partner's point of view.

Overall in this energy exchange women are the winners, as their energy field gets stronger with the sexual act, while men feel weaker after sex. If you ask any man, he will tell you that he feels drained after he has had an orgasm and cannot immediately have sex again. Men need time to rebuild positive energy through their root chakra before they can have sex again.

I now want to clarify why men like to roll over and separate from women for a short time after orgasm. Before the orgasm the man has positive energy and the woman has negative energy at the etheric level, so opposite polarities attract each other. However once a man has had an orgasm, he has unloaded all his positive energy at the etheric level and becomes neutral, while the woman is still negatively charged at that level. There is no longer any attraction for the man to remain attached until he has rebuilt positive energy through his root chakra. On many occasions before my celibacy, my girlfriends got upset with me when I wanted to roll over and separate from them for a short time after orgasm. I could never explain why I needed to do that, so I feel it is necessary to explain why this separation is required for a short period. It gives the man a chance to rebuild his positive energy.

This energy exchange has significant repercussions for both sexes. The first and the most important is that this energy transfer literally transfers part of your consciousness to the other party. Your consciousness makes up your personality, experiences, and characteristics. In this energy exchange you give them a piece of you and get back a piece of them. So if you look at couples who have been together for long periods of time, you will see that they will start to pick up some of the characteristics of each other. In fact, this is how Life balances people who do not meditate and take charge of their own personal development. This energy exchange happens at every layer of the spiritual energy field and affects the strength and weaknesses of both partners. This is why opposites attract. We tend to choose friends who have similar attributes to ourselves, but we choose sexual partners to address the weakness that we see in ourselves. So when you consider dating someone it is very important to ask yourself, would I like to see their characteristics in myself? Because whether you like it or not, this energy exchange will happen, so be more selective of whom you choose to be in a relationship with.

A man whose energy field is made up of 60% male and 40% female energy within the first four layers of spiritual energy would look for a woman whose energy field is made up of close to 40% female and 60% male. During the exchange of energy through portals that connect the chakras together, each layer energy level is affected, and as more time passes, the energy difference between each layer gets closer and closer to each other. This is a very effective way of balancing out each other, but it also has a negative side effect. The negative side effect is that when couples initially meet because of polarity differences, they're very attracted to each other and have sex frequently. As more time passes and more energy is exchanged between the two, the polarity difference between them diminishes and they have more of themselves in the other person. This results in less attraction towards each other and more attraction and desire to be with someone else. This is a problem for every couple that has been together for an extended period of time, but there are remedies to counteract this problem that I will go through.

The importance of complete faithfulness

Sexual energy is universal energy. We are this energy, and through our chakras we continuously draw energy from the universe and exchange energy through our energy field with each other and experience ourselves through it. We experience the universe and each other through our senses, but ninety percent of our energy is directed through our eyes. A blind person does the same thing with their other senses.

You have to understand that when you look at something, a piece of your energy goes out to that object and does not come back. If you desire it, a substantial energy is dedicated to that desire. In fact, that is how we manifest. The problems with couples who have been together for a long time begin when the polarity of their energies gets closer to each other, so they start to look at other people, or pornographic videos, or fantasize about being with someone else. Men are very visual and love to look at sexy women or pornography when their partners are not around. Both men and women fantasize about being with someone other than their partners. The problem with fantasizing is that even if you don't act on any of your fantasies you have dedicated a significant amount of your sexual energy to that fantasy, which is not coming back. This sexual energy could have been dedicated to your partner. Lack of sexual energy between the partners will result in less intimacy, and ultimately the breakup of their relationship. The same applies when you look at pornographic images or sexy people. A piece of your sexual energy goes out and doesn't come back. When a man is constantly looking at women who are in close proximity to him all day long, what is he going to have left when he gets home to his partner? Not much.

The other effect of looking and fantasizing is that when you look at something other than what you have, a desire will rise in you to have it. Once this desire has risen, you will not be content and happy with what you already have. This has nothing to do with how attractive your partner is. You could be going out with the most beautiful woman or handsome man, but as long as you look at other people you will never be happy with what you have at home. This is the nature of any human being. This is apparent in couples in Hollywood. You may look at a beautiful actress or a handsome actor and say, "If I was with them I would never cheat on them!" But we continuously hear that couples break up in Hollywood because they're constantly in touch with other actors and actresses in movies, and other men or women who throw themselves at them. So if they're not disciplined and allow themselves to desire people other than their partners, it will result in infidelity and unhappiness.

An abstinence experiment for married couples

I'm challenging every couple to do an experiment for six weeks. Close your eyes and your thoughts to all other stimulants and desires. For example, do not masturbate, or look at any pornography or attractive people. Do not fantasize about anyone other than your partner. If you're watching a movie and there is a sexual scene, just close your eyes for a few seconds until it is over. Something amazing happens when you do this: your chakras continue to build up sexual energy inside of you without any outlets. One day you will come home and just rip off your partner's clothes and ravish them like you have never done before. This works better if both partners participate, but even if only one of the parties implements this technique, the other will feel the difference and notice the change. This is the only way you can remain happy in a long-term relationship or marriage. The couples who remain happy with each other over the years dedicate themselves to each other. Remember that **the moment you desire something other than what you have, you will no longer be content with what you have.** This is true about sexual partners or any physical object; a desiring mind is a sick mind that is never happy and content. You're going to have to choose which is more important to you, a quick fix and short-term gratification while being miserable at home, or a happy partner and long-term happiness.

I understand that what I'm asking you to do is unorthodox, and may seem difficult to do (especially for men), but I want you to keep an open mind and just try it for six weeks. You don't have much to lose other than six weeks of your time. But if I am right and this technique works it can save your relationship or your marriage and make you happy. I promise you that you will be happier in the long run.

Once I was talking to a friend who was complaining about the lack of intimacy in his relationship, and telling me that his partner was not taking care of herself the way that he would have liked. So I used myself as an example and told him:

"I have been celibate and sexual energy has been building inside of me for a long time. I do not look at women and fantasize about them because there is no point, but let's hypothetically say that I break my celibacy. Do you think I would care if the woman who I have sex with were very attractive? Or has make-up on? There is so much sexual energy inside of me that having an outlet to get it out will be the most important part."

This will also be true if you close your eyes and thoughts to outside stimulants completely for a period of time, and direct all your energies towards your partners. Suddenly your partners are going to look much more attractive than ever before, and you won't care so much about every little annoyance or problem.

One other point that I would like to make is that there is no problem with anyone who is single who likes to watch pornographic videos, masturbate, or look at and fantasize about being with attractive people. This will not have a negative impact as long as it is done in moderation, but these activities will be detrimental to any long-term relationship or marriage.

Using tantric sex to maintain intimacy in a relationship

There is a second solution for lack of intimacy between couples that have been together for a long time. The polarity of energy between couples who have been together for a long time reduces with time. To counteract this effect, you can extend the period when you are building energy during the sexual act. Tantric sex in the east was created on this premise. In tantric sex, reaching orgasm is delayed for as long as possible. The goal is to build sexual energy and delay orgasm for as long as possible. Tantric sex is sex combined with meditation. Increased levels of dopamine during the sexual act naturally increases your focus. Choose positions in which you can be comfortable for a long time, slow down the rate of thrusting; remember that speed is the enemy, so take your time. Once the man is close to reaching orgasm he should stop, but not pull out. Both partners should remain playful through touch and feel. Enjoy the sensation of touching each other, but keep your minds silent and do not talk to each other. The man should only start thrusting again if he feels he is losing his erection, then continue until he is close to orgasm and stop again.

Repeat this process for as long as you can. Eventually both partners will have built so much energy that their orgasms will be much more intense. Just like everything else, using this technique is going to be challenging at first, but your orgasms will become much more intense and enjoyable. You will develop the ability to last longer and longer as you practice this technique. The goal is not to have a sexual encounter in that fashion every time, but you need to add other dimensions into your sex life in long-term relationships to prevent sexual boredom. Having quick or rough sex can become one-dimensional within a short period of time in a relationship, and orgasms achieved will not be as intense as tantric sex. You can look up positions that are more suited for tantric sex online and experiment to see which ones you like the best. Men need to control the pace in order to delay orgasm, but women also have a good sense of when a man is ready to finish, and they can stop or slow the pace down. This technique works much better if both parties participate.

This will have a secondary effect that will be beneficial for men. The pelvic floor muscle at the bottom of the base of the penis restrains the release of semen. This muscle has both a physical and spiritual dimension to it, because it physically holds back the semen and the spiritual energy, and releases them at the same time. There are other body parts that have both a physical and spiritual dimension to them, such as your eyes. Using this technique will strengthen this muscle and allow men to stay erect longer when having sex. It is like when you work out in the gym and strengthen your biceps by putting pressure on them when doing bicep curls. When you force a muscle to work longer, it will get stronger over time. You need to be patient; it takes time to build strength, but it will be rewarding in the end. Having sex in this way helps men who suffer from premature ejaculation.

You can also strengthen this muscle without having sex by doing Kegel exercises. It is easy to find this muscle. Next time you go to the bathroom to urinate, try to stop the flow. The muscle that you use to achieve that action is the pelvic floor muscle. Once you find which muscle it is, you can repeat the action without actually urinating. Slightly tighten the muscle and your rectum at the same time and release. Do ten to twenty repetitions, four times a day. Strengthening the pelvic floor muscle will help men to delay orgasm, stay erect longer, have a stronger erection, and have more intense orgasms, as well as helping with a healthier prostate.

And when men are able to maintain an erection longer, they are more able to bring women to climax.

Men who are single can use the same technique by masturbating while watching a pornographic video. Continue masturbating until you feel you're close to having an orgasm, and then stop. Continue watching the pornographic video, and as soon as you feel that your penis is going soft, start again and stop just before orgasm. Continue this process as long as you can, using lubrication to mimic the inside of a vagina. You will have much more intense orgasms and strengthen the pelvic floor muscle at the same time. If you are a father who is reading this book and have a teenage son, please teach them this method of masturbation, because while you are helping them to be better lovers in the future, at the same time **this exercise strengthens their root chakra and that is significant**. This is why I have spent so much time talking about this, because the root chakra is the single chakra at the bottom of your energy field. Strengthening this chakra has a significant effect on your overall energy field. Your teenage sons will masturbate whether you teach them or not, so they might as well learn how to do it properly, which benefits them both spiritually and sexually.

One of the most common techniques that men use to delay orgasm is by thinking about something that has nothing to do with sex to take their minds off reaching orgasm. This technique does delay orgasm for a short period of time, but once you start thinking about something else the root chakra becomes less active and the solar plexus chakra, which is the chakra for the third layer, becomes hyperactive in order to create the thought. This will cause your consciousness to become focused on the third layer and in doing so, takes away focus from the first layer. This will take away from what your partner will be feeling from you and reduce the pleasure that is felt by them. The better way to delay orgasm is by strengthening the pelvic floor muscle.

Women can use the same technique when masturbating, or do Kegel exercises to strengthen their pelvic floor muscle, which results in stronger root chakra. Find the right muscle by trying to stop the flow of urination while relieving yourself. Once you have found the right muscle, contract it for five seconds and release it for five seconds. Repeat this sequence for ten to twenty repetitions, three to four times a day.

Strengthening your root chakra strengthens your energy field, and gives you better connections to your physical body and the physical world around you.

Love in the emotional (second) body

Sex is the expression of love at the physical and etheric body, but we do not truly feel loved until we connect with our partners through the second layer of the spiritual energy field. The second layer is the emotional body, and we connect through its center, the sacrum chakra. Polarity of energy in this body flips for both men and women compared to the etheric body. The polarity of energy in the emotional body is negative for men, and positive for women. For that reason, women are more emotional than men in this state of consciousness.

In this body we experience opposite emotions like happiness and sadness, fear and fearlessness, love and hate. I call the love in this layer the **dirty love,** because this love automatically comes with hate. You cannot possibly love anyone in this body without hate showing its ugly head at some point. You can look at any couple that has been together a while and see them behave very lovingly towards each other for a period of time, but suddenly without any notice or any good reason, they will start to fight. This cannot be helped, because when you experience love in this layer, every moment that you are loving, at the same time your anger is building momentum to swing the other way. The pendulum will always swing the other way, it is guaranteed.

Anger is the medium that we use to go from love to hate. For that reason, in order to experience love beyond this body, we need to break this bridge and transcend beyond the duality that exists within this layer. Most human beings have never developed the ability to experience love beyond this layer, because they have never dealt with the anger that has been building inside of them ever since childhood. You need to meditate and relieve yourself of the anger within you, and transcend beyond the second body. Love is who you are, and once you have destroyed the bridge between love and hate, hate will simply disappear. Love is absolute unity and acceptance. Hate is absolute separation. The spiritual path is to travel from separation to absolute unity. You can achieve this in your lifetime if you choose to do so, and experience true love.

We cannot experience love in the mental body, which is the third layer of the spiritual energy field, with its center chakra the solar plexus. The polarity of the energy in this body flips again compared to the previous layer, which is the emotional body. The polarity of energy in the mental body is positive for men, and negative for women. For that reason, men in general are more logical than women. The mental body deals with the mental aspects of our existence and sense of logic. The issue is that love is beyond logic, love is beyond reason. You cannot use tools to fix and understand something that is beyond its capability. For example, I want to help you understand how your computer works, but I give you a book about learning how to read English. You cannot possibly use that book to learn about how your computer works. The same is true about using reason and logic to comprehend love, love is beyond both.

I have loved four women in my lifetime. I never said, "I love you" unless it really meant something to me. I only said it if I was willing to put my life on the line for them. I remember that one of my girlfriends (Melanie) used to ask me, "Why do you love me?"

And for the life of me, I could never tell her why. I would think about it, but I could not come up with a logical answer, and she used to think that there was something wrong with that. But there's nothing wrong with not having an answer to that question. In fact, if you ask someone why they love you, and they are able to tell you why, they do not truly love you, they just think that they do. I want to be clear about something here. Many people are in bad or even abusive relationships, and they use love as an excuse to stay in a bad environment, and they say I'm staying in this relationship because I love my partner. That is not what I'm talking about here. I'm talking about when you are in a caring and loving relationship, and there is true love, which includes mutual respect and admiration between the two parties.

Believing in God is the same thing. There's no logical reason why anyone should believe in a God or a higher power. There is no scientific proof of such an existence, but love and faith are both entities beyond reason and logic. I'm asking you to use the techniques given to you in this book, so that you can increase your vibration and elevate your consciousness to experience love and God. But I am appealing to your sense of logic by giving you all the reasons why you should. It is a paradox that cannot be explained by logic, which is why it requires faith.

After all that, I'm going to tell you something very interesting about the third body. Unless couples connect to each other at the mental body, they will not be able to experience true love in the fourth body, which is the astral body. The astral body is the highest spiritual body that has a physical dimension to it. Experiencing love at the astral body is the highest love that can be experienced between two physical consciousness. But in order to get to this level, you need to connect to each other at the level of the mental body. This is because the mental body and the mental aspects of our consciousness can help us travel from experiencing love at the emotional body to experiencing love at the astral body. You need to develop the ability to communicate with your partner without anger in order to elevate your love that exists in the emotional body to the love that exists in the astral body, which is the true love, a love without hate.

It's like this: if you want to learn how your computer works, you cannot use a book about learning English. But you need to learn to read English, so you can comprehend the manual that comes with your computer.

Most people get stuck with love at the emotional body because they cannot connect with each other at the mental level. Eventually anger takes over, which results in the breakup of the relationship or marriage. When I practiced energy healing I talked to many couples that complained about an inability to communicate with each other properly. The problem is not communicating what they are trying to say to each other, the problem is connecting and comprehending what the other is saying. This problem comes about because when couples are communicating, anger can quickly enter into the equation and move them down to the emotional body.

To be clear: **you can only experience yourself in one of the seven layers of the spiritual energy field within a three-dimensional space at any one time**. So you are constantly moving from one of the layers of the spiritual energy field to the next, depending on your state of consciousness, thoughts, and feelings. When you try to communicate with your partner or anyone else, you move to the third layer and try to connect with them at the mental body, which deals with thoughts, reason, and logic. During this connection, if anger comes into the equation at any time, you immediately move down to the emotional body. Once you have moved onto the emotional body, your reason and logic goes out the window, and there is no chance of reaching a solution. There is no way to have any kind of reasonable conversation with anyone who is in the emotional body. This is why no one can possibly win an argument, or have any type of productive conversation with anyone, while they're angry. To achieve that goal, you need to remain in the mental body so you can use the mental aspects of your consciousness and connect with each other at the third layer. How can we keep our anger in check and remain in the mental body during our communications?

There are two things that can be done to achieve that goal. One will help you in the long run, and one will help you in the short term. The long-term solution is to meditate and get all the anger that has been built up inside of you since childhood out of the second body, so that there is no anger left. This is what we talked about earlier: transforming the anger energy and transcending beyond the second body.

The short-term solution to this problem is to communicate meditatively, in order to make sure anger does not come out during conversations. A significant number of couples spend thousands of dollars on counseling, because they need a referee when they talk to each other. In essence the presence of the counselor in the room assures that they do not get to the point of yelling at each other. This will not be necessary if you take steps to keep anger out of your conversations.

I will tell you how to communicate with each other meditatively, after we have discussed experiencing love at the higher layers of the spiritual energy fields, as well as looking at the dynamics of choosing a partner and the dating process. We also need to look at the actions that cause negative reactions in our relationships, which result in breakups.

True love in the astral (fourth) body

True love can only be experienced when we connect with each other at the astral body, which is the fourth layer of the spiritual energy field, with its energy center the heart chakra. The polarity of energy in this body flips once more compared to the previous layer, which is the mental body. The polarity of energy in the astral body is negative for men and positive for women. For that reason, women in general are more nurturing and loving than men in this state of consciousness. Let us look at what true love would look like for people who are able to connect with each other at the astral level.

Love is unity, love is what binds and connect us together. The "I" has disappeared and the two consciousness have completely surrendered to each other. Love is without judgment, expectation, or condition. **Love is acceptance, there is no conflict and there is no struggle**. The spiritual bodies of two consciousness have strong connections through the first four layers of the spiritual energy field. This love is not just a desire for companionship and does not come out of need. When you love at this level you are ready to give without expecting anything in return. This is a state of consciousness of **being in love.** The other has become the center of gravity in the relationship. You each live for the other, and when both parties are in love with each other something magical happens. There is a melting into each other that results in complete unity between the two. Energy current is freely exchanged at the first four layers of the spiritual energy field; the sexual encounter becomes making love. This is the highest type of unity that can be experienced between two consciousness that occupy physical bodies. Take note that I have removed the word **absolute** from the definition of true love at this state of consciousness, because no two people or couples can ever reach a state of perfection while they're in the physical body and experiencing love in the first four layers.

The transformation of love in the fifth layer

Love is transformed in the fifth layer. The fifth layer is the spiritual body, with its energy center the throat chakra. **The polarity of energy in the upper three layers of the spiritual energy field is neutral.** For that reason, the upper three layers are beyond the duality that exists in the physical world. Once you have reached love in the astral body, which is free from hate, add meditation to it. Then it would be transformed into compassion. Compassion is the highest form of love. You need to have compassion to see beyond people's conditioning, faults, and shortcomings. This is absolutely necessary to transcend beyond the fifth and the sixth layers, which are the spiritual and celestial bodies, respectively. God is absolute unity, absolute acceptance. There can be no judgment whatsoever. This is the definition of love at the cosmic level. To reach God and experience absolute unity, you need to become one with all of its parts, you need to become one with the best and the worse.

I understand that it is difficult to imagine becoming one with a child molester or a murderer, but that's what would be required to experience enlightenment. This does not mean that you need to condone anyone's bad behavior, but you need to develop the ability to see other people's conditioning. You need to have compassion to go beyond good and bad. Remember that there is only one of us, and if you meditate enough, Life will allow you to experience that unity. That is what I experienced in December of 2005. That is enlightenment. No one else but you exists, every living being on this planet, the universe, and beyond is you in some form. You need to understand that, and not only should you be devoid of any negative feelings, but you should have compassion for others in their struggle to find their way home.

Here is an example. Imagine that a woman who is a heroin addict and lives on the street gets pregnant and gives birth to a boy. This boy is born with heroin in his blood, already addicted to one of the deadliest drugs. He's born with mental illness and chemical imbalances in his brain. He is born with low genetic IQ and has no chance of a real education. He has to steal to survive, living on the streets. This is an extreme example, but there are millions of people on this planet who grow up in such situations. You judge them based on your life, IQ, genetics, and experiences that you have had, not based on their life, IQ, genetics and experiences that they have had. All this becomes clear to you if you meditate enough and reach the point of compassion.

Now that we understand the true meaning of love and compassion, we can look at how we choose partners, and what we need to do in order to experience love and unity with them at the highest levels. I have talked about how our past conditioning can affect our reactions and daily decisions. Now, let's look at how our past conditioning can affect our choices in partners and in relationships. Our experiences in childhood play a big role in how we react to our environment when we are adults. That includes whom we choose as friends and lovers. We have discussed how neurons in our brain form to support behaviors that we experience growing up, especially in the early stages of life. As adults we tend to create situations that are familiar to us, by perpetuating some of the deficiencies that existed within our families growing up. Of course in all families there are both good and bad behaviors. The key to having successful relationships is to continue with the good behaviors, and work to resolve the issues and deficiencies that exist within each one of us **before we attempt to seek love**. Otherwise your relationship is doomed to be unsuccessful, or fail altogether. There is a chance that you may make it, but it will be with deficiencies and devoid of true love. You may never realize its true potential.

There are two options to resolve past conditioning from our childhood. One is to seek therapy for many years, and the other is to meditate and resolve all the issues internally. Tremendous growth comes from meditating; it is the only way to permanently break apart the neurons in our brain that support undesirable behavior. Once you have removed all the negative energy from the emotional body through meditation, you will be devoid of any deficiencies within yourself, so you will not be looking for someone to fill the hole that existed in you before the start of the process.

Here is an example. The parents of a six-year-old girl separate and get a divorce. The mother gets full custody and the father is not much involved with their daughter. The father eventually gets married to another woman and has more children with the new wife. The little girl grows up with major deficiencies in her life; no matter how hard the mother works to fill the hole that exists in her heart. There are many possibilities as to how her deficiencies could manifest themselves, but when she becomes an adult, one thing is guaranteed. She will be afraid that the man of her choice will leave her at some point in the relationship. Now there are two possibilities. She might find a man who is similar to her father in order to recreate the familiar scenario that she experienced in childhood. Or she will find a good man who is committed to her, but because of her insecurities, every time there is a disagreement, she is going to question his commitment and assume that he's going to leave. Our mind is extremely powerful, and our imagination plays a big role in creating our reality. If she imagines that he's going to leave, he will leave, no matter how committed he was at the beginning. We have all had deficiencies in our lives that can result in insecurities. It is important to meditate and come to peace with the deficiencies that we experienced growing up. I know that I probably sound like a broken record repeating the same thing over and over again, but I feel that I need to demonstrate how meditation affects every single aspect of your friendships, relationships, and life.

How meditation affects every aspect of our lives

The effect of meditation in this scenario goes beyond coming to peace with deficiencies. We not only need to be at peace with our deficiencies growing up, but we need to be at peace with our own mind. We have all heard that you need to love yourself, before you can love someone else, but what does that mean? Does that mean that you need to go and stand in front of a mirror every day and tell yourself, "I love you"? Absolutely not! Loving yourself means being at peace within your own mind. You don't need to be occupied at every moment, because you're not overwhelmed with your thoughts when you are by yourself. You can be alone and be comfortable without anyone else. You don't need someone else to complete you; you are complete all by yourself.

When you're afraid of being alone, you are likely to cling to somebody or some relationship. That is loneliness. There's a big difference between being alone and loneliness. Being alone and comfortable in your own skin has a quality that cannot be measured by anything. Meditation is about happiness in your own aloneness. You close your eyes and stop occupying yourself with outside stimulants. You dive into the darkness of your mind and find peace with the past. Once you find peace within yourself, you find the eternal light that shines beyond the darkness of your soul; then you are whole. In loneliness, you are missing something. You go into a relationship because you need something. You depend on the other person to fill a hole that exists within you, and that dependency on the other causes you to lose your freedom. Love can only happen when you are free, and you are free when you are whole all by yourself. It is never too late to begin your inner journey and find the peace that already exists within you; all you have to do is to dive in and find a pearl that is hidden underneath the sand.

The next step is choosing a partner who is right for you. This is the most important step in the dating process.

People always present the best of themselves at the beginning of an encounter, so you need to be indirect to find out who they really are. When you meet someone, ask them about the dynamics of their family in childhood; you will be able to find a lot of useful information. See how they interact with their friends and family. Also examine their daily life, and how they operate on a day-to-day basis. For example, are they in close contact with their parents? If a man has a close relationship with his mother or sister, he will be in touch with his feminine side, which results in better understanding of women. By the same token, if a woman has a close relationship with her father or brother, she will be in touch with her masculine side, which results in better understanding of men. A person is more likely to be affectionate, if they are affectionate with their mother. Are they living close to their family? Because if someone has moved 2,000 miles away from their family, it is likely that family is not the most important thing in their lives. Do they need to be occupied all the time? If so, this is a sign of neediness. Are they open with you about their friendships, or are they trying to keep you away from their friends and family?

The most important thing to look for is to see if they are living a balanced life. Of course the personality of people is dependent on many things, and too complex to analyze by asking some questions or looking at their behavior for a short time. In general, there are more problems with people who are egotistical, because it will always be about them. Love and ego are the complete opposite of each other, so you need to put them in situations to see how much they are willing to bend for you at the beginning of the relationship. If they're not willing to do it then, there is no chance of them doing it in the future. Love is about giving, so test and see how much they are willing to give.

I personally believe that the reason so many relationships and marriages break apart is due to looking at things the wrong way. When two people meet, they begin to size each other up. Almost everyone looks at the attributes of the other person, but the success of any relationship does not depend on anyone's attributes. It has everything to do with what their negatives are, and whether you can live with those negatives. Love is unity, and will not be possible without acceptance. So when you meet someone, look to see what their negatives are, and whether you can live with their negatives without trying to change them. Because if you can completely accept them just the way they are, then it will be possible to experience true love. On the other hand, you will never be able to experience true love if you cannot fully accept someone's negatives, no matter how positive their other attributes are.

I want to be clear about something. There is no judgment of anyone for setting high standards as to their requirements for whom they want to date. In Western societies, we are free to choose our partners. You can decide what is acceptable and what is not acceptable for you, so take your time and find out the other party's attributes and negatives. Once you have that information you can make an informed decision as to whether what they offer is good enough for you. The waiting period for deciding whether to marry needs to be at least two years, because people tend to hide their negatives for as long as possible, but almost no one can hide their negatives for more than two years. It is your fault if you don't see their negatives within two years, because you have chosen to close your eyes to the red flags and odd behaviors that you have seen along the way.

Once you have accepted your partner's positive attributes and negatives, you cannot bully them into doing what you want them to do. You cannot force them into submission if you do not like certain behaviors. You have the choice to leave them and find someone else, but you cannot ask anyone to change into what you want. **Love is unity, and unity is not possible without acceptance.** Once you have chosen to stay with someone after seeing all their negatives, you have no right to complain when you see those behaviors – but there is a paradox here. Once both parties have agreed to accept each other's negatives, they need to make every effort to at least maintain themselves at the level at which they have accepted each other. No one should tolerate a partner who does not take care of themselves or give one hundred percent of themselves to the relationship. It is not acceptable for people to let themselves go and make no effort to remain attractive, and say that if you love me, you accept me no matter what.

Experiencing enlightenment is no different than experiencing love with someone else. The seeker does everything he or she can to align themselves with All That Exists. Life only accepts seekers who are willing to give one hundred percent of themselves in this relationship. Love is unconditional, but that does not mean that you can do whatever you want and receive the same amount of love and affection. Do you think

I would have received the same amount of love and affection from Life, had I chosen to remain with the organized crime family? Absolutely not. I would be in jail by now. I would have been forgiven and eventually reached the light, but not until the end of time. I would have reached the light at the end of the line, after everyone else. Life also has very high expectations when it comes to making an effort in this journey. On many occasions where I have felt tired and not kept up with my disciplines, Life has connected to me and reminded me that unity will not be possible if I do not remain vigilant with my disciplines and make a full effort every step of the way. I have also been required to fully take care of my body and maintain physical health and balance in this journey.

The reason I am making this comparison is to tell you that if you want to experience true love at the astral level with someone else, the same requirements have to be met. You will have to take care of yourself and be healthy, so love can grow inside of you. Only then will you have something to give. You need to become whole, so that your love is not coming from a place of need. You need to make every effort to make the other happy. Love can only happen when you give, just for the sake of giving.

Many relationships go down the drain because the moment people feel secure in their relationships, they stop making an effort. Love is about making an effort to experience unity, so you must do everything you can to align yourself with the other. This should not stop once your relationship has progressed to the point where the other has fallen in love with you. The institution of marriage has become the biggest love killer, because many people get comfortable and stop making efforts in their relationship once they get married. Instead of making more effort for each other, they make less effort and allow their ego to take over. It goes from being about the other to being about themselves. They let themselves go and gain weight. The pressure of raising children sometimes result in less healthy diets. All of this results in many people getting stuck with love at the emotional level. This love has a negative side effect; it comes with hate.

Experiencing true love at the astral level is very difficult because it requires a lot of effort, both individually and as a unit. Both parties have to constantly work on themselves to grow together spiritually, and they also need to maintain their physical health. Remember that reaching love at the astral level is a spiritual connection and it requires the health of your body, mind, and soul, which is your spiritual energy. Physical health and spiritual energy directly affect each other, so it's not just about looking good. Both parties have to raise their spiritual energy to the astral level in order to connect with each other at that level.

Looking for love in all the wrong places

People sometimes look for love in the wrong places. You cannot go out with fixer-uppers and think that you are going to save them. You cannot marry them and have children, and then when things don't work out complain and act like a victim. If you chose a fixer-upper, it is not their fault. You need to take responsibility for closing your eyes and choosing someone with major deficiencies. It is up to you to work on yourself to accept their faults and shortcomings, not to put pressure on them to change. End your relationship as soon as possible if you do not have children and there are significant problems in the relationship. But if you have children, work on yourself to accept your partner's deficiencies for the sake of your children, because they will suffer the consequences of your separation from each other. Unless there is physical abuse, or drug and alcohol abuse, try to stay with your partner until your children grow up and become adults. Then do what you want with the rest of your life.

The chances of you breaking up the family and finding an emotionally healthy partner are very slim, because there must be a reason why you chose someone with major deficiencies to have a child with in the first place. You need to meditate and go on a mission of self-discovery and find those reasons before you even consider breaking up the family and looking for someone new.

Your children will not benefit from a broken home or seeing their parents date new people. Remember the karma that will follow you into your next life. Your children suffering will become your suffering in your next life. But if you persevere and take responsibility for your mistake, and accept your partner's shortcomings, tremendous growth will come from your acceptance. I want to emphasize again that you should feel free to leave if you have no children. But when you take responsibility for another soul the burden on you is much higher.

Children who live with a single parent do better when their parent does not openly date other people in front of them. There is a tremendous amount of emotional distress for children who have to share their single parent with someone else and possibly with other children. It is hard enough to see your parents separate from each other. Your children should not suffer because you have chosen the wrong partner and cannot keep it together. I understand that people cannot become celibate after a breakup or a divorce, but at least you can keep your dating away from your children until they reach adulthood. According to studies, 67% of second marriages and 73% of third marriages end in divorce. Children do not need additional commotion in their life after the first divorce. Disagreements on how children should be raised and disciplined are the most common problem in second and third marriages. If you are divorced, you're better off just dating and keeping your love life separate from your children. Do not drag your children on an emotional roller coaster as you date one person after another.

I had a close friend who got divorced. At the time, she had a vibrant and happy teenaged daughter. After two years, my friend began to date another man who had two daughters of his own. They decided to move in together. The teenaged daughter suffered a great deal as a result. The new man would try to discipline and correct her behaviors. Within a short time, my friend's daughter became depressed and her grades suffered in school. She just wanted her mother to herself. She had already suffered from her parent's separation, and did not need this disruption in her life. These type of relationships are often bad for the children, so just be aware that what goes around will come around in your next life.

There is a paradox here; there are divorced parents who take the time to resolve their past issues through therapy or meditation and self-reflection. These type of parents allow themselves to grow and learn from their mistakes after their divorce. If you do this inner work, there's a possibility that you could choose an emotionally healthy partner who will support you and your children. The difference between the two is doing the inner work. It is obvious that if you do the inner work and become emotionally healthy, then it is possible for you to choose a partner who is also emotionally healthy. In that case it could in fact benefit the child to have an emotionally healthy stepparent.

In short, if you are a divorced parent and you still want a family, do not date for a long period of time and do the inner work by meditating or seeing a therapist and become emotionally healthy. Then you can start dating, but keep it away from your children. Take your time to see if your partner is also emotionally healthy. After a two-year period, when you are confident that you have a solid relationship and an adequate understanding that they are not to interfere with how your child is disciplined and raised, then introduce them to your children. A stepparent should never discipline their partner's children. Do not rush this process. Emotional connections between you and your partner, and your child and your partner, take time to develop, so be patient, or you may end up divorced again.

The dynamics of dating

I want to look at the complicated dynamics of dating and see how some actions or inactions break up relationships. Let us look at the honeymoon period. I have always heard that the honeymoon period is not realistic, and that people show their true self after the honeymoon period. Initially when we meet someone, we dress up and make ourselves look attractive. If they ask us to go somewhere that we don't like, we go for their enjoyment. If they ask us to do something for them, we do it without giving argument. We show the best of ourselves, we give because we want to. There is unity, so we feel love, but the moment we start to feel secure, our ego begins to show its ugly head. In the honeymoon period everything is about them, but the moment your ego comes into the picture, it is no longer about them, it is about you. The moment "I" or "me" enters into the equation love disappears.

However, it does not need to be this way. You just have to control your ego and realize that love is much more enjoyable than hate. You need to work on yourself to keep your ego in check, and it is easier than you'd think. Any negative feeling that you have comes from separation from the other, and love is unity. So avoid any action that brings up any type of negative feeling. That is how you keep track of your ego. Avoid taking any action or having any conversation that causes negative feelings. You can choose to accept what is, or leave and find someone else. **The process of dating is for you to determine if you are a good match for each**

other, that is all. You should not use this process to try to mold someone else into what you want them to be. There should be no hard feelings along the way. Either you can live with their negatives or not. It's not that complicated. It only gets complicated when you try to compromise. Love cannot be reached with compromise, because compromise and acceptance are the exact opposites of each other. You may be able to form a partnership with compromise, but you will not have a true loving relationship. Love is without condition and compromise. You have to understand that this is not about who is right or wrong. Even if you are right and a deficiency exists with your partner, you cannot ask them to change for you. You have to accept them as is with all their deficiencies, or leave the relationship and find someone else, because love will not be possible with compromise. Compromise always results in resentments, and you cannot be in love with someone and resent them at the same time.

I was once engaged to a beautiful woman who was a high school teacher. She was very soft and calm. Her personality complemented mine, because I was naturally aggressive. She came from a very good and loving family. When I was a child, my mother was physically very affectionate towards us. She always bombarded us with lots of hugs and kisses, so naturally both of my sisters and I were very affectionate towards each other. Naz is 14 years younger than me. I often babysat her. She walked for the first time when Telly and I were playing with her. My father was a great provider but absent for emotional support, so I filled that role for Naz. Always talking to her, guiding her every step of the way. I would give her hugs, hold her tight for a long time, and give her big kisses on the cheek on a regular basis.

At the time of my engagement to the schoolteacher, Naz was 14 years old. My fiancé had grown up in the family where her father was very loving, but not affectionate towards her. So my physical affection towards Naz was very unusual for her, and it made her uncomfortable. She discussed her feelings with me, and insisted that I tone it down. I became very upset. I wanted to marry this woman, but I decided that I could not do what she wanted of me, and decided to end the relationship. My mother really loved the schoolteacher and told me that if I was serious about getting married, I needed to compromise. I thought about it, and chose to take her advice. We continued with our relationship for two years after that event, but my relationship with Naz suffered because of this compromise. She felt the change in my interactions with her. One day when I went for a visit to my mother's apartment, I gave Naz a hug and she burst out crying. I asked her why she was crying. She said, "You never hold me tight, squeeze me, or give me big kisses like the way you used to."

Naz had suffered for two years. I was so afraid of repercussions from my fiancé that I had completely changed the way I interacted with Naz. This hurt me a great deal, and I ended my relationship with my fiancé within a month. I should have never compromised in that situation. She did not truly love me; her love came with a condition. Compromising on who you are will make you miserable, it will end in resentment and it does not work. You can compromise about which movies to watch, or where to go for dinner, but you should never compromise on your values, and who you are as a person.

The moral of this story is that what is normal in one family may not be normal in another. Right and wrong are very subjective, depending on the dynamics of family situations. I want to give another example. Some parents are dishonest, and lie in front of their children on a regular basis, so the children learn that is acceptable to be dishonest. These children may grow up and continue to be dishonest adults. If you date such a person and discover their dishonesty, you cannot ask them to change. Dishonesty is a bad behavior, but we do not have the right to force our morality onto someone else. You have a choice to leave, or stay and accept them as they are. You can choose what you want for your life. You can choose to stay or leave, you can choose to direct your life in any way that you see fit, but you cannot choose a change for someone else. That is the spiritual path, you do not have to condone any behavior or participate, but you cannot judge or change someone else.

Transcending beyond the positive and the negative

You may well ask, "What about ISIS? And people who commit horrible crimes in our societies? How do we accept their behaviors?"

An enlightened person has transcended beyond the positive and the negative. He or she knows that the criminal is really just himself or herself in another body. He or she knows that there is only one of us. He or she would see their conditioning and see their shortcomings, and not judge. Life is everyone's teacher, and has a plan for each one of us to reach the light. It is not up to any one of us to change someone else, but we have the right to defend ourselves and to stop such people from committing crimes and hurting others. But we need to do this with compassion, because they are us in another form. I understand that this is difficult to accept. But if you meditate enough, you will get there and understand that they are you in another body.

Finding what negatives you can and cannot live with is the most important aspect of dating. I personally believe that no one should consider getting married until their late twenties, because your own personality changes considerably from eighteen to the late twenties. Combining that with the changes of the other person during that time, if you get married in your early twenties you could both be different people in eight or ten years. We should use that time to date many people, and determine what negatives we can accept, and what negatives are unacceptable. You cannot possibly know what you can accept if you have not experienced it. People have different negatives, so if you only date one person for a long period of time in your twenties, you would only experience certain type of negatives. I'm not suggesting that you should have sex with multiple people. I am only suggesting that you should try to gain experience by dating as many people as possible, so you can make an informed decision when you have matured and are ready to be in a committed relationship. The experience of dating many people will make you better at recognizing good and bad characteristics. You also get better at seeing signs of what you like and don't like.

Life always gives you a helping hand in the dating process. I want you to go back and think about the people that you have gone out with for any significant amount of time, but had serious problems in the relationship. Think deeply about the beginning of the relationship. I promise you that an event happened when Life showed you a red flag, where you saw an odd behavior, or something that did not make sense, which you ignored. Life always gives us a glimpse of what it is to come, and then it is up to us to connect and listen to our own gut instincts. Remember that there is a part of you that is one with them. So ultimately you know the truth, just trust yourself and don't waste your time when you have a bad feeling about someone.

Deciding to have sex should be an informed decision

However, the dating process is very complex because people present the best of themselves in the beginning. You need to figure out the other party's negatives and positives as quickly as possible, and decide if they are a good match for you. You need to make this assessment as soon as possible because energy cords begin to form between the two parties and strengthen over time. This bond strengthens with sexual interactions, as well as with spending time with each other. It is better if you do not have sex until you have made an informed decision on whether they're a good match for you. Sexual intimacy can create a false bond and affect your judgment. We can usually leave someone within the first month of dating without much effect on our energy field, but breaking these cords will hurt more as more time passes. The other effect of delaying the sexual encounter for at least a month is that it will give you a chance to connect with them at the emotional level, which is the second layer of the spiritual energy field. The emotional body will give you a better glimpse of who the other party is at the emotional level. You can also see if they are only interested in having sex, or having an emotional and bonded relationship.

Both Christianity and Islam have portrayed sex as sinful for those who are not married. But there is definitely a double standard when it comes to men and women who want to have sex without an emotional connection. Women are looked down upon for having a sexual relationship, without wanting to be in an emotional or a committed relationship.

This really disrupts the unconscious, and how men and women develop their relationships, and I will tell you why. Many of us have been told that it is wrong to have sex before you get married, so subconsciously many people feel bad when they have sex outside of an emotionally committed relationship. This mindset results in many bad long-term relationships that have no chance of success because many people, particularly women, date someone who does not meet their standards, but convince themselves that he or she is good enough, so that they can continue having sex without feeling guilty. In doing so, they try to mold the other into what they're looking for, which results in a poor outcome and a bad relationship. There's nothing wrong with just having sexual intimacy without an emotional connection, if you're not yet ready for a committed emotional relationship, as long as you are open and honest about it. It is better to be honest with yourself and the other party about what your intentions are, and how you feel about them, without feeling guilt. In previous times, people got married very young. But today, people get married at an older age, which is better, because we are wiser and able to make better decisions with more experience. It is not reasonable to expect people not to have sex until they're married or ready for an emotional and committed relationship. People would be more honest about their intentions if there was not such a stigma attached to wanting sex without an emotional connection. Different people are ready at different times for an emotional and committed relationship. There should be no judgment about when that happens.

Let me be clear. I am not suggesting that people should be promiscuous. This is not about being right or wrong, for every action there will be a reaction. You deny yourself growth and access to the deeper meaning of love if you have sex with many people without an emotional connection. However, it is better to have sex without an emotional connection with multiple people, than to find someone who is not a good match for you and try to turn them into what you want, or lie and convince yourself that they are the right one for you. Be honest with yourself. If the other person is not a good match for you, but you still want to be sexually active, do not feel guilty. Go into it with awareness, and then you will see the emptiness of sex without an emotional connection. Tremendous growth can come from that.

This is not about right or wrong, this is about you deciding what you want to experience in your life. Are you going to remain alone and work on yourself until the right person comes long? Or you are going to have sex without an emotional connection with multiple partners? Or are you going to find someone who is not a good match for you, and try to turn them into what you like? The choice is yours, but the last choice will be detrimental to your growth.

Complications in relationships between men and women

Now let's look at other aspects of relationships and why so many of them don't last. One of the most common issues between couples who have been together for a while is constant bickering over the most mundane things. I want to first look at different characteristics of both the male and female energy. Remember that we are made of both those energies, but women are female-energy dominant, while men are male-energy dominant. Depending on the situation, we can identify with our male energy or our female energy.

Male energy is the positive energy and is associated with these characteristics: intense, expressive, doer, aggressive, analytical, logical, organized, hard, controlling, left brain, protector, confident, decisive, direct, performance, simple, serious.

Female energy is the negative energy and is associated with these characteristics: calm, reserved, observer, submissive, intuitive, creative, structured, soft, seductive, right brain, nurturer, friendly, responsive, indirect, vitality, complex, playful.

Our energy field is made of both male and female energy, so we all have all these characteristics within us. Men have male-dominant energy, and women have female-dominant energy. Both men and women have strengths in some areas and weaknesses in other areas, depending on the percentage of male and female energy and how it is distributed in the first four layers of their spiritual energy field, plus the strength of neutral energy in the upper three layers. It is very important that we become aware of our strengths and weaknesses in order to achieve our goal. This becomes very apparent in relationships. I believe that many women in our societies have completely lost touch with what their strengths are when dealing with men. Men are also guilty of the same thing, but to a lesser degree, because female personality is more complex and naturally in control of the path the relationship takes. Men on the other hand naturally have a simpler personality. Unfortunately, women are identifying more with their male energy than female energy. This has caused turmoil in many relationships all over the world.

Women tend to complain or argue with their men when things don't go their way. This causes disruption in many relationships and marriages on a regular basis, straining the relationships. Men are male-energy dominant and naturally aggressive, they are born to fight. When woman argue or fight with their men, they're also identifying with their male energy, but they have less of it. They can never win the fight. A man will never back down in a fighting situation, so the fight continues until they are both exhausted and stop. In any situation where there are disagreements between the couple, this approach is futile. There is a better way for women to approach man when they want something from them. Let me give you an example.

Men have male-dominant energy. Aggression is one of the characteristics of male energy, so men are like a fighting bull. You will not be able to get a fighting bull to do what you want by grabbing his horn and wrestling him down. The fighting bull is born to fight, so waving a red garment in front of him only brings out his natural aggression and is an invitation to a fight, which cancels out any chance of a happy ending. On the other hand, women can easily neutralize men's aggression with affection. Women can simply walk up to the fighting bull, rub his head and whisper into his ear to lie down, and most likely the fighting bull will obey the command. Male and female energy complete each other, one needs the other to be at ease. The male energy needs the female energy's affection to neutralize his aggressive tendencies. This is a need, it must happen. Without it he will feel incomplete; male energy is starving for affection. If a woman is aggressive towards a man, this will only add to his unrest.

The female energy's characteristics are seductive, affectionate, and friendly. Women are female-energy dominant, and they need to use their strength when dealing with men. I once observed my mother trying to get my father to do a chore. He was having a lazy day and did not want to do it. My mother continued to force the issue by nagging him, so I quietly told her, "Why don't you walk up to him, run your hand through his hair a couple of times, give him a kiss on the cheek, and then ask him to do it?"

"I don't want to do that, because that is manipulating. I am asking him nicely, so he should simply do it," my mother replied.

I would like to tell all the woman in the world that if you ask a man if he would rather be nagged, or manipulated with affection, most of them will choose manipulated with affection. There's nothing wrong with women controlling the situation by using seduction and affection. In fact, that is exactly what's needed when they are dealing with male energy in a romantic relationship. There is a time and place for women to identify with their male energy and demonstrate confidence and independence outside of their romantic relationship. Women simply need to understand the dynamics between the male and female energy and balance the use of their female and male energy. The approach of seduction and affection will work with the majority of men. If you have a man who does not respond to seduction and affection, you need to dump him as soon as possible. A man who does not respond to that type of treatment is a bad man. I want to emphasize that simply asking nicely is not sufficient. Affection plays a big role in neutralizing the natural aggressive tendencies in the male energy.

Most men in our societies also suffer from an imbalance between identifying with their male and female energy. Many men feel it is wrong to identify with their feminine side, because they see it as a sign of weakness. This has caused problems not only in many relationships, but even between countries. Female energy is a powerful force, which brings balance to the natural order of things. I promise that if more men would identify more with their female energy, our planet would not be in the grim situation that it is in today. Female energy is what binds us together. It brings calm and vitality to the energy field of our planet. I'm asking all men and woman around the world to use this powerful force which is within them in their daily life, and solve issues both personal and outside of their home. Men feel that their strengths come from their male energy, but female energy is strong as well.

Let me give you an example. Before I became the head of security for a nightclub, my predecessor was a strong man who ruled with an iron fist. He was respected and his orders were followed, but he was not loved. I used a different approach once I took over the position. I was working with 17 alpha males who were full of testosterone. I was also strong like my predecessor, with a strong presence of male energy, but I gave them love and affection instead of ruling with an iron fist. My affection was very subtle, such as embracing them with a close hug, or simply placing my hand on their shoulder for a moment. I developed a close bond with all the members in the unit. The difference was that I was loved as well as respected. The men were willing to go above and beyond to do their job, and protect me and each other if it was needed, because of that love.

Both men and women need to balance the use of their male energy with their female energy to get the best results in any given situation. Men should not be afraid to talk about their feelings in their romantic relationships and also outside of that environment. We need to change the way we look at men who show emotion and talk about their feelings in our societies, so they will feel more comfortable with identifying with their female energy. Balance between the use of male and female energy is key to a successful relationship between a man and a woman. I suggest that everyone carefully read the characteristics of both male and female energy, and see where it would be more suitable to identify with each one. Remember that you are made up of both male and female energy, and not using both of their characteristics to your advantage in different circumstances is denying yourself the use of powerful forces that exist within you.

The need for intimacy in relationships

One of the other issues that couples in long-term relationships face is the fading of intimacy. Intimacy is extremely important in any relationship, whether romantic or platonic. Consciousness is one, meaning we are all one entity and are connected to each other. Vibration in any part of consciousness is felt throughout the universe and beyond, but at close range, tremendous amounts of energy are exchanged between two energy fields. The closer you are to each other, the more energy is exchanged. For that reason, long-distance relationships have a very low chance of surviving. The bond and closeness that we feel towards each other strengthens with intimacy and fades with distance. Intimacy between couples in romantic relationships is one of the most important aspects of the relationship. I'm not simply talking about sex. I'm talking about the closeness and bond that is felt between the couple. This bond strengthens with the smallest touch, because more energy is transferred when we touch each other with the palm of our hands and fingers. We also exchange tremendous amounts of energy when our chakras line up close to each other. For that reason, the missionary position is the most common sexual position used by everyone throughout the world.

People in our societies are extremely busy. Lack of balance in people's lives has made people become tired and exhausted. Sexual intimacy requires a lot of energy and effort, so when people are tired that is the first thing they cut out of their lives. Men and women who work come home tired out. Those who are married with children have to do more work when they are home with their children. Gradually they become so overwhelmed by their activities that intimacy becomes an afterthought. Before they realize what's happening, the bond between them weakens and they grow apart from each other. It is extremely important to become aware of this fact. I want to emphasize again that I'm not just talking about having sex; I'm talking about simple touches and a show of affection towards each other on a regular basis. I'm talking about conversing with each other, complementing each other, and caring about each other, so that the bond between the couple remains strong, even through the most difficult times. It's not realistic to be intimate sexually every day, but it is important that couples remain sexually active, no matter what's happening in their lives. Sexual intimacy creates the strongest bond between any couple. The problem with not having sexual intimacy regularly is that once you stop having sex, it becomes more and more difficult to have it, especially when you're physically tired. It's like an engine that has not worked for a long time does not start with ease. The more active you are sexually; the more sex drive you will have.

I recommend that every couple dedicates a short time every day to be physically intimate with each other. I am only talking about simply touching each other. Maybe just a quick shoulder massage, or rubbing each other's hands. Perhaps snuggling with each other or simply kissing each other for twenty seconds. These small connections every day maintain the couple's bond with each other, even if they don't have sex. Sometimes these small connections get the engines running, so they naturally turn into having sex, which is wonderful. If you want to have sex with your partner and your partner does not seem to be in the mood for it, don't ask them about having sex. Simply start with small touches to get their engine running. Once that happens they may be good to go. Getting into the mood is the tough part, and talking about it does not get you in the mood. However, kissing, rubbing, and touching each other causes your body to release the hormones that get you in the mood for having sex.

The difference between physical intimacy and verbal communication

I want to differentiate between physical intimacy and verbal communication. I've seen many couples simply tell each other, "I love you" on a regular basis without having much feeling behind it. They seem to think uttering the words, "I love you" many times a day counts as intimacy. Nothing can replace physical touch between two people, not even saying the words "I love you." However, if you hold your partner in your arms and look into their eyes, and then say, "I love you," then you have put feeling behind what you're saying. When you transfer energy while you are holding them, this "I love you" is meaningful and effective, while just saying the words is not as effective.

Don't fall into a habit of saying things without putting feelings behind it, because not only will it not be effective, but it can actually put some distance between a couple. People know the difference between a verbal communication that has feeling behind it and one that is just said out of habit. Speed is the enemy; take your time when you are conveying emotions to your partners. I'm not talking about minutes; I am only talking about seconds. Instead of just uttering the words "I love you" quickly and going, walk up to your partner, hold them in your arms, look into their eyes, and then say, "I love you," and then walk away. It only takes ten extra seconds to do it the right way, but there is a world of difference between what it is felt by your partner.

The most important thing in the dating process is to learn from your mistakes and from your experiences. It is useful to think about your past relationships and try to see patterns that continue to happen over long periods of time. One of these patterns is that Life always gives you an exact replica of your last relationship, to see if you have learned your lesson. The pattern will not stop until you demonstrate that you have learned from your mistake and will not repeat it again. For example, let's say you dated someone who was not being truthful with you early on in the relationship. But even though you saw some odd behaviors, you ignored your instincts and continued dating them. Eventually things got really bad and you broke up with them. You are guaranteed to meet someone who is very similar to the partner in your last relationship, and the same pattern will repeat itself. It's up to you to demonstrate that you're not going to ignore the odd behaviors, and end the relationship right away.

Recognize the patterns in your relationships

I would like you to take the time to contemplate past events in your life, including your relationships, and connect the dots. The best way to learn is to see these patterns in your life, because it will help you to recognize the next ones when they happen. One of the biggest mistakes that new couples make in our societies today is moving in with each other early on in the relationship. I have talked about how love cannot happen when it originates from a place of need or convenience. I understand that at times, moving in with each other can be cheaper, and more convenient, but it has a devastating effect on the course of your relationship. Many people who move in together stay in bad relationships because it is too difficult to separate from each other. Breakups are extremely difficult at the best of times. Tearing apart energy cords that bind you together is extremely hurtful. When you add moving out on top of the emotional distress that is caused by the breakup, the mountain might look too hard to climb, so you may stay in a bad relationship a lot longer than you should. Moving and breaking up are both hard things to do, so you should avoid doing them together. The difficulty of doing these tasks together can cloud your judgment. The other factor is that you don't really get to know someone in the first two years of the relationship. You do not want to tie yourself down when you barely know someone. This move is a lot more detrimental if there are minor children involved.

Not all relationships are meant to last forever

You also have to keep in mind that you are not meant to stay with everyone whom you date for the rest of your life. Life sometimes brings someone into your life for a specific reason, at a point in time. He or she may have strengths in their energy field that could address a weakness in yours, or vice versa. Meeting them could also benefit you or them in another fashion. Sometimes dating someone causes you to learn something about yourself, or simply to learn a lesson. Sometimes dating someone makes you realize what it is that you don't want. In doing so, you also realize what is it that you're looking for. There is a theme to all this, you just have to look at it with awareness and then you see it. You never meet someone by accident; Life brings people together for a purpose. What I recommend is to look at the patterns in your life and take the cue from what's happening in your life. These events in your life are trying to tell you something. For example, if you have been with someone for a significant time and suddenly a sequence of events happens where you question your relationship, or you see odd behaviors, or you see some characteristics that do not line up with your values, Life is trying to tell you that it is time to separate. You may have received what you were supposed to out of that relationship, and it may be the right time to separate. This is why I say that couples should not move in together too quickly, because we're not aware of how long we are supposed to date someone. You have to allow Life to help you on this journey, and once you openly accept Life's help in this matter, and accept the signs that come to you, everything will go a lot smoother.

I want to give you an example that happened to me. After the events of December of 2005, Life asked me to become celibate. At the time, I was going out with a beautiful woman (Melanie) whom I loved. She had told me that I was the only man she had ever fallen in love with. Separating from her was very difficult, as we had been going out for two years. Once Life asked me to become celibate, I stopped touching, and having sex with her, but we still spent time together. This was very difficult for both of us. She used to sleep in my bed and asked me, "Can you please just give me your hand because it gives me comfort?"

Deep inside I knew that I needed to separate from her completely, but I could not get myself to do it, so Life started to help this process. I noticed that without any logical reason, she would get extremely angry and fight with me. After her anger would subside, she would tell me, "I don't know why I acted that way, I am sorry."

But the same thing would happen the very next day, and the next day after that. We had issues before, but nothing like that.

Sometimes we know that we need to separate from someone, but it's too painful to break those energy cords. So Life puts in a sequence of events that cause you to fight with each other, in order to build enough courage and resentment at the same time, so you can go ahead and break apart. I would like you to always remember that **you are the life that I am talking about.** Remember when I gave you the example of the teacher, and the student who is learning how to drive. You are both the teacher and the student, but when the teacher wants something to happen, it will happen. If Life decides that a couple needs to separate from each other, a sequence of events happens, such as that they keep fighting with each other, until they break it off. It is better to take your cue as soon as possible, so as to shorten the amount of suffering before you break it off.

Moving in with each other is a wise thing to do only if you have been together for at least two years and you have got engaged and are planning to get married. It is not a bad idea to live together for a six months period before you get married. Living with someone under the same roof day and night is different than dating someone. So it may not be a bad idea to get a feel of what it is like to live with them before you make a lifetime commitment. Also, I highly recommend that everyone do premarital counseling before they get married. It is important to know all the negatives of your partner before you get married. You may not know all their negatives even though you may have dated or even lived with someone for a long time. Marriage brings about new issues, such as children and other family members. A professional premarital counselor can bring up issues that you may not have thought about or experienced in your current relationship. An experienced counselor has seen it all, and can guide you in the right direction.

You should also look at marriage like a contract. When two people are doing something together, it is better to have a good understanding of how things should be. It is difficult to come to understandings and make them up as you go, once you have got married. Your expectations of how things should be could be very different from your partner's, and these are the sorts of things that will be discussed in premarital counseling. It may cost you some money, but it is a very good investment to make. It will save you from a lot of grief in the future. That is why people sign contracts in the business world, because they provide a guideline of how both parties should proceed in the future. Marriage, in some ways, has a lot of similarities to the business world. It is always better to have a clear understanding of how to proceed in different situations, before they happen.

The division of labor in modern Western families

In Western societies, the dynamics of marriages have considerably changed in the past fifty years. More families have both partners working outside the home. Previously, one person worked outside the home, and the other worked at home, keeping house and taking care of the children. The division of labor was clear, but in a partnership where both partners work outside the home to earn income for the family, the division of labor has shifted. Traditionally, men worked outside the home to earn income to support their families, while women stayed home to take care of the children and the household. In families where both parents work outside the home, the labor has not been fairly divided. Many women who work outside the home to earn income are still responsible for the majority of the household work, including taking care of the children. This results in the woman in those families overworking.

The division of labor has to shift. Men in those families need to take a bigger role in taking care of household chores and children. Women are the pillars of the family structure, and a woman who is exhausted will not be able to maintain balance in her life. Then, the entire family will suffer from this imbalance. A woman who is exhausted cannot be a good lover, may not be able to provide healthy nutrition for the entire family, and so on. It is very important that the woman in the family is healthy, because she is the driving force of the family.

Overspending and poor budgeting are two other issues that put a lot of unnecessary stress on many families. It is much better to live a simple, happy life, than a stressful life with a better car and house. These are very simple issues that have very big consequences for the entire family. Many parents get so obsessed with having the best material possessions that they forget what is most important: the relationships between the parents and the children in the household. Life is about evolution, and spiritual connections. Our family life is where we make our deepest connections and closest bonds with our partners and children. So don't lose sight of what really matters in your life.

Remember that love and unity are natural states of consciousness. When you are in a serious relationship or marriage, use that opportunity to experience unity and love. Your goal should be to experience the highest form of love. If you remain focused on that goal, everything else will work itself out. All the negatives will become small irritants and slowly disappear. Individuality is not real; you have never been separated from each other and All That Exists.

How couples can discuss serious matters meditatively

Now that we have looked at different aspects of relationships and marriages, it is time to see how couples can discuss serious matters in their relationship meditatively. Before I move into that discussion, I would like to mention one big difference between men and women. Earlier, I mentioned the different characteristics of male and the female energy. Male energy is simple and direct, while female energy is complex and indirect. Men and women have all the four characteristics mentioned above, but because men are male-energy dominant, they have simpler personalities and are more direct than women who have complex personalities and are indirect. This causes a lot of problems in many relationships. I advise women to pay good attention to this: you need to be clear and direct when you want something from your man. It is very important for you to specify clearly what it is that you're expecting and are looking for. Men are not very good at reading signs and indicators.

To be precise you need to be clear and direct, so let me give you an example. Let us say one day you had a really bad day, and you're looking for emotional support. You see your partner and tell him the story. Once the story ends, you need to clearly communicate with your partner as to what you want him to do. For example, say: "I want you to come and hold me," or "I want you to rub my shoulders to take the edge off," or "I need you to take me out to get my mind off what happened today."

Do not expect your man to read your mind, and react the way you think he should. Men are generally not very good at that. This goes for every situation that you could think of. You need to be very specific about what you want to happen. Male energy wants to serve and protect. Once men receive the information as to what is required of them, they immediately go into the serve and protect mode, which shifts into doing. Male energy is the doer; female energy is intuitive and creative. Men are weak in that department; they're not good at reading and knowing how they can create the environment that you're looking for. But if you give them the specifics of what you're looking for, they will be very good at doing and bringing your creation into reality. In some rare situations the roles could be reversed, if there is a woman with strong male energy presence and a man with a strong female energy presence. The members of the LGBT community are no different. One of the couple has a stronger male energy presence, and the other has a stronger female energy presence.

Before I discuss the technique for having discussions meditatively, let's look at a typical argument between couples. There are three possibilities with couples. First are the couples that have recently met, and do not have a long history of arguments between them. Second are the couples that have spent a significant amount of time together, and there are some resentments and anger due to past events. Third are the couples that have spent a significant amount of time together, but there is a lot of pain and anger based on past events like infidelity. To have discussions meditatively in the second and the third scenarios is going to be more difficult, but not impossible to accomplish.

First, let's look at a typical argument between a couple. There is an issue that needs to be discussed, but long before the discussion takes place, each party goes over what they want to say to each other. They go over past events and how they relate to the current situation. They begin to interact with their thoughts. Pain and anger they have felt from past events mingle with their thoughts about the current situation. By the time the couple are together, they have already thought about exactly what they want to tell each other. The conversation begins, and is usually about blaming the other party. Once one of the party starts talking, the other does not listen to what their partner is saying; instead, they are thinking about how they're going to respond. They may be looking at each other, but no one is really listening and comprehending what's being said. Each one is focused on making their own point. To do so, they start to talk faster in an attempt to dominate the conversation. But once you start to talk faster, you begin to breathe faster, and your heart rate beats faster to support the lungs. This is the perfect condition for anger to come out. Remember that the energy of anger requires a fast heartbeat with rapid breathing. Our intellect and logic requires our consciousness to be focused on the mental body, which is the third layer. The moment anger comes out, our consciousness gets focused on the emotional body, which is the second layer. So the moment anger comes out, there is absolutely no chance of reaching a resolution. Couples who have been together for a long time know exactly what they need to say to get a rise out of their partner. They begin to bring up events from the past that were hurtful. All the resentment and anger from the entire relationship surfaces. The discussion turns into a big fight, and eventually they are both exhausted and separate from each other.

All arguments and disagreements between couples that have been together for a long time have some of the elements that I have mentioned above. The problem with all those discussions is that anger enters into the equation at some point, and once both parties have focused their consciousness in the emotional body, the mental body, which controls the mental aspects and logic, goes into hibernation. This removes any chance of a productive conversation. The goal of communicating meditatively is to put in place a structure where both parties can control their emotions while communicating with each other, so they can use their mental body to reach a logical solution. This is easier if both parties agree to this form of communication, but it is still possible to communicate meditatively if only one party of the couple participates.

The long-term solution to communicating meditatively is to meditate individually and let go of your anger and past pain and suffering. But in the short term you need to keep past events out of your current discussion, and only focus on the resolution. I understand that in some cases this may be very difficult to do. For example: if one of the party has been involved in an affair, how could you keep away the anger that is felt by the other party? After any major event such as this, a period of cool-down is absolutely necessary. Couples should only attempt to have discussions if sufficient time has passed and the anger has subsided. Once you reach a conclusion in your mind that you would like to work things out, that is the time to have discussions. There is no point in having any discussions if your anger is still on the surface. This technique only works if you're at the point where you are ready to reach a resolution, whatever that might be. Ultimately the long-term solution is to meditate and release all the anger within you, but in the short term, you will have to let go of all your anger, pain, and suffering for the duration of the conversation with your partner.

The first step for the participants is to focus on the resolution: what they want to achieve with the discussion. Each party may come up with their own resolution, but it needs to be identified in clear terms. The enemy in every discussion is the speed with which couples communicate their point of view to each other. Remember that anger does not become activated if couples talk to each other at a slow pace, and breathe slowly as they talk. A discussion should not be a one-hundred-meter dash; it should be a marathon in which both parties take their time to communicate their point of view.

The goal of every conversation should be understanding the other person's point of view. You may or may not agree with that point of view, but it is very important to understand that once a point of view has been communicated to you, you should repeat back to your partner your understanding of what was just communicated to you. This procedure guarantees that you are listening to what's being said, rather than thinking about your response. Ask your partner if they are willing to do the same. Do not allow the conversation to pick up pace. Limit your conversation to the current events; there's no point in rehashing old wounds, because they will bring with them the anger and pain that was felt at that time. Love is acceptance; think about how you can understand and accept their point of view, or at least parts of it. A compromise could be reached if you can accept parts of each other's point of view.

At any time, if you feel anger surfacing, take a deep breath for two seconds, then hold it for two seconds, and then breathe out for two secondsRepeat this process until you feel calm again. Do not allow yourself to get frustrated. Remember that frustration also requires a fast heartbeat and rapid breathing. This entire process is about keeping down your heart rate and breathing. Don't rush to reach a conclusion. As long as you breathe slowly you remain in the mental body. Make sure that you sit across from each other in close approximation. If you are on good terms, hold hands while talking to each other. Allow the energy cord between the two mental bodies to strengthen during your conversation. A resolution reached with this method will strengthen the bond between the two of you. This is the only way you can reach love at the astral level. This cannot happen in a single event, but repeated conversations meditatively allow you to grow and evolve together. Regular meditation allows you to release the energies relating to past events that have caused pain and suffering in your life. Tremendous growth and transformation can come from the combination of these exercises.

Meditation techniques and the art of meditation

All that we have talked about brings us to this important point, which is how to meditate and become the master of your mind. The ability to silence your mind is the most important thing in your spiritual journey. I'm not saying that understanding intellectually how everything works is not important, but even more important is knowing how to silence your mind and raise your vibration. Because if you actively meditate and raise your vibration, you will experience and understand intellectually everything that I've talked about so far. The transformation and change comes from raising your vibration. In my experience, many people love to learn and understand the spiritual path, but when it comes to the actual work of transformation through meditation, they lack effort and conviction. This is not entirely their fault, because many people do not understand how to climb this mountain. At first glance meditation seems like a very easy thing to do. You sit down and close your eyes, and by all accounts you should feel silence and tranquility, but the exact opposite happens when people begin to meditate for the first time. I remember many years ago before the events of December of 2005, I was speaking to a friend about meditation, and I thought that I was going to start meditating. I went to a park, sat near a tree and closed my eyes. It felt good for about five seconds, but then suddenly my thoughts consumed me up more than ever. It was so overwhelming that I stopped after only a few minutes. I was not prepared, and did not know how to deal with the onslaught of thoughts. This is a typical experience for someone who tries to meditate for the very first time.

After that fateful day in December of 2005, I tried to meditate again, but this time, things were different. I could clearly hear thoughts coming from my higher self, guiding me on how to meditate. I was learning meditation from Life through direct contact, so I began to use several techniques to improve my focus. After about three years, when the period of separation ended, I began to research meditation. Only then did I realize that all the techniques that I had been using all along were actual meditation techniques taught by different masters for thousands of years.

There are more than a hundred different types of techniques used for meditation throughout human history, but I feel that knowing that many techniques for an average person could become confusing. So I wanted to take you step by step through the exact sequence of techniques that Life taught me. I knew nothing about meditation and started from zero, so my goal is to transfer this knowledge to you exactly as it was conveyed to me. Meditation techniques seem very simple, but they are extremely complex as to how they affect your energy field. This journey begins with simple closed-eye meditation, progressing to open-eye meditation, and ending with third eye meditation while performing any type of activity. My goal is to get you to a point where you can focus and meditate doing anything, so you no longer have to dedicate a specific time to meditation. Once you reach to that level, any type of activity could become meditative. I have researched different techniques that are used by many people. I don't want to put down what is being taught by others, but what I am teaching here has come directly from Life itself. It is wise to at least give this a try and then decide what works best for you. What I ask of you is to completely read the entire section several times to clearly comprehend the material before you attempt meditating. More experienced meditators can read the material and decide which category suits them better: closed-eye meditation, open-eye meditation, or a more advanced third eye meditation while doing any type of activity. There is a specific closed-eye meditation that I'm going to teach you specifically for raising your vibration. No matter how advanced you think you are, if you have not tried this specific breathing technique, please make sure that you use it for at least six months.

I'm going to break down this part into three sections: Meditation postures; meditation techniques; and the art of meditation.

Meditation postures

There are various postures for meditation to choose from, depending on your preference. The most important thing to consider when choosing a meditation posture is to be absolutely comfortable. But do not lie down on a bed because once your breathing has slowed down, you will likely fall asleep. The level of comfort in meditation is extremely important because the muscles that support you to sit in any position burn calories. Your heart and your lungs have to work a little bit harder to supply nutrients and oxygen to those muscles if you're not comfortable in that position. The more comfortable you are in any sitting position, the less calories you will burn. In turn, your heartbeat and breathing process slows down. The goal of meditation is to help you silence your body and mind in order to raise your vibration, while opening up your chakras to exchange energy more freely with the universe.

You have to make sure that your spinal cord is straight and as close as possible to 90° with respect to the ground. I am going to discuss four common meditation postures that are used around the world, and tell you the benefits and disadvantages of each one.

Sukhasana

Sukhasana means easy pose, and is used in Buddhism, Hinduism, and yoga. In this position both knees are bent and the legs cross at the shins, just above the ankles. Position each foot so that it is under the opposite thigh. Open your chest by expanding your chest outwards while resting the back of your palms on your lap. You can bring your thumb and any of your other fingers together. There are two variations of this pose, as seen in the diagrams.

Padma Sana

Padma Sana means sitting in the Lotus position, which has two variations. Ardha Padma Sana is half Lotus. In this position, cross your legs at the shins just above the ankles, but position one foot on the inner edge of the opposite thigh with the sole pointing upward, and rest the other foot under the opposite thigh. Open your chest by expanding your chest outwards while resting the back of your palms on

The first variation of meditation posture Sukhasana (easy pose)

The second variation of meditation posture Sukhasana (easy pose)

Meditation posture Ardha Padma Sana (half lotus)

your lap. You can bring your thumb and any of your other fingers together as seen in the photo above.

Padma Sana is full Lotus. In this position the legs are crossed at the shins just above the ankles, but this time both feet are placed on the inner edge of the opposite thigh with both soles pointing upward. Open your chest by expanding your chest outwards while resting the back of your palms on your lap. You can bring your thumb, and any of your other fingers together.

Virasana

Vira means brave or strong in Sanskrit. In this position you sit on your shins, while keeping your thighs together. The outside of your hips rests on the heels of each foot. You can either rest the palms of your hand on your thighs or you can bring your hands together, with the backside of the left hand resting inside of the palm of the right hand. Make sure you open your chest by expanding your chest outwards in all these positions, because it will help to keep your back straight. You

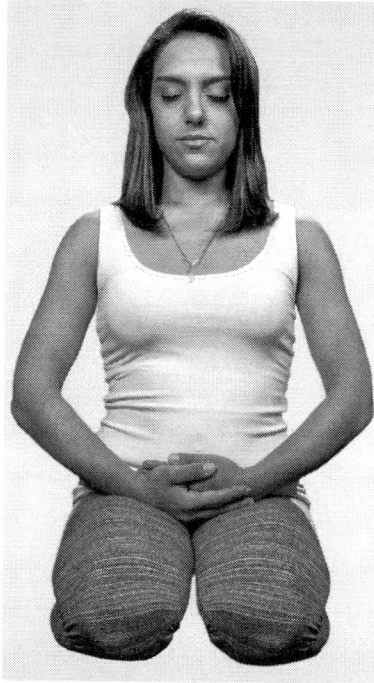

Meditation pose Virasana (brave pose)

can also use a cushion under you to make sitting in these positions more comfortable.

These variations complete the meditation postures that can be used while sitting on the ground. Next, let's look at the benefits and disadvantages of each one.

Benefits and disadvantages of meditation postures

There are three main disadvantages with these meditation postures. Many people always focus on the main seven chakras, but there is a chakra on the bottom of the feet that is just as important as the other seven. This chakra connects you to Mother Earth. Connection of this point to the ground stabilizes your energy field and strengthens the energy currents that travel through the body. Unfortunately, none of these sitting-on-the-ground meditation postures connect the bottom of your feet to the earth, making these meditation postures less desirable. Even though these postures have been very popular in Buddhism, Hinduism, and yoga, there is a meditation posture that addresses this particular issue, which I will discuss shortly.

The knees are bent excessively in all of the above meditation postures, restricting the flow of blood, as well as energy through our legs. People with even minor injuries to their knees or lower back will have a difficult time sitting in these positions for extended periods of time. Lotus postures are even more difficult for people who are not very flexible.

Sukhasana and Padma Sana are better than Virasana because crossing your legs causes your root chakra to open to its maximum capacity, strengthening your energy field. Opening your chest and straightening your back will cause your front and back chakras to open up more, resulting in an increase of energy flow and strengthening your energy field.

Meditation postures sitting on a chair

S it on a chair that has a 90° angle, and is completely flat on the back. Any amount of curve on the supporting side of the chair will cause your back to curve, which is not desirable. If you cannot find a chair that is flat with a 90° angle, move slightly forward, push your chest out by expanding your chest outwards and sit as straight as possible (see the photo opposite). Open your legs as far apart from each other as possible by pushing your toes outwards. Lay the palm of your left hand on your

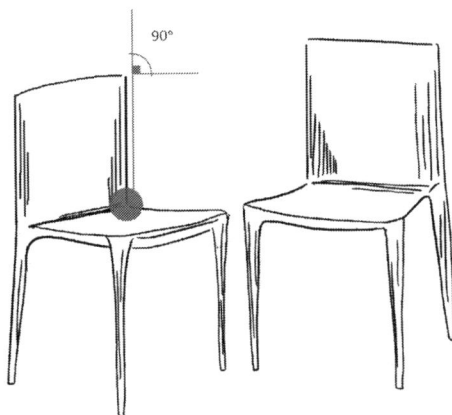

An example of a preferred type of chair for the sitting-on-a-chair meditation posture

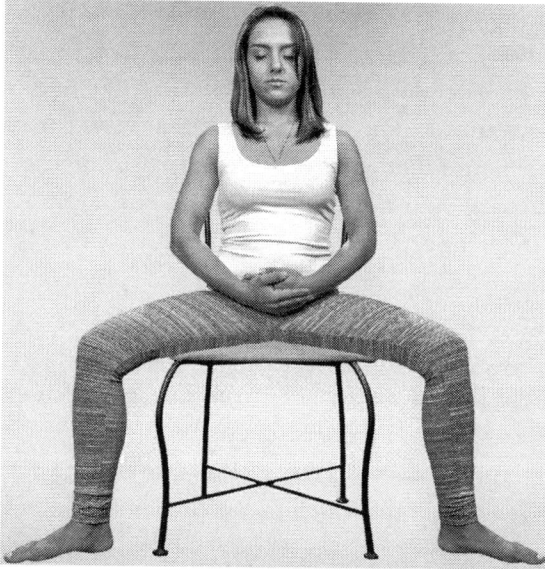

Front view of the sitting-on-a-chair meditation posture

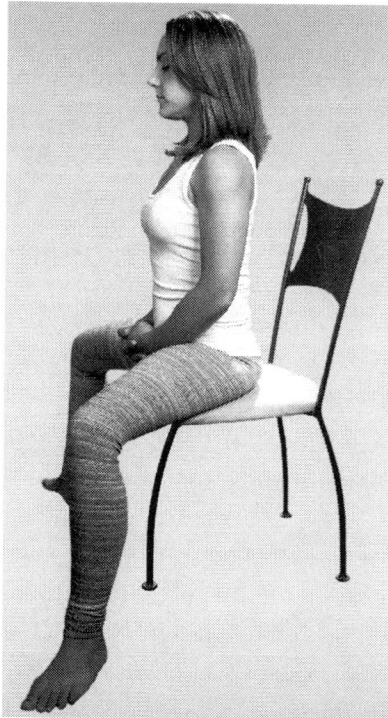

Side view of the sitting-on-a-chair meditation posture, using
a chair whose back is not set at a 90 degrees angle

belly, and then place the palm of your right hand on the top of the back of your left hand.

Sitting on a chair with a 90° angle and flat back is by far the best and the most advanced meditation posture, because the best meditation posture is the posture that allows you to sit with the minimum amount of work required by your muscles to support sitting up straight. Resting your back on the supportive structure of a chair with a 90° angle allows the back muscles to work less, in turn using less calories and oxygen. This results in a slower heartbeat and less frequent breathing. The 90° angle of the chair assures that you will keep your back straight throughout the meditation. Make sure that you open your chest to promote opening up the front chakras. Opening the legs as far apart as possible with your toes outward allows your root chakra to open up to its maximum capacity, with the bottom of your feet fully touching the ground. This fully connects the foot chakra and promotes better energy flow throughout the system. The knees are only bent at approximately 90°, rather than completely bending to zero degrees as happens in the sitting-down-on-the-ground postures.

There are also chakras located on the palms of our hands as well as the tips of our finger. Instead of pulling energy into our energy field, these chakras push energy out of our energy field. In this meditation posture, placing the palm of the left hand on the belly and resting the palm of the right hand on top of the back of the left hand causes the energy that is flowing out of the palms of your hands to go back to your core instead of leaving the body. Under normal circumstances, the energy that flows through the palm of your hands exits the body, but pushing this energy back to your core allows you to build energy in your energy field at a faster rate.

A tremendous amount of energy is drawn in during meditation. It is best to try to retain as much of it as possible, and placing the palm of your hands on your belly ensures that most of the energy stays within your energy field.

I completely understand that many experienced meditators would not want to change their meditation posture, but spirituality is about evolving. Even though it might be slightly uncomfortable to try a new posture, I assure you that you will get used to it, and it will benefit you more in the long run to sit and meditate on a chair that has a flat back set at a 90° angle.

Meditation techniques

Meditation techniques are tools that allow you to focus on something other than your thoughts. Remember that the consciousness that is occupied by your senses is who you know yourself to be. This consciousness, which is the small part of you, also identifies with thoughts in your mind. The same consciousness uses imagination to create its reality. The reality is that the thoughts in your mind are not really yours. I will explain this phenomenon shortly in the next section about the art of meditation. The goal of every meditation technique is to give you tools to focus on something other than your thoughts. There are more than a hundred different meditation techniques that have been used around the world throughout human history. All of these techniques either focus on the five human senses, which are seeing, hearing, feeling, tasting, and smelling; or they focus on the power of imagination. You can pick any of these aspects, and create a unique type of meditation.

Let me explain this more fully. You normally experience your reality through your five senses, while thoughts circulate in your head. You are processing all of the information coming to your senses, at the same time as thinking and identifying with the thoughts in your head. Your consciousness is divided between all your senses and the thoughts in your head. All of the meditation techniques force you to focus on one or more of your senses, instead of thinking and identifying with your thoughts. Meditation techniques are meant to be temporary tools to help you silence your mind. Once you improve your focus, you will have to drop that technique in order to move on to the next level. There is only one technique that you could retain and continue to use until the point of enlightenment that is achieved through surrender. That technique is to focus on the third eye, which I will explain shortly.

I am not going to go through all of the meditation techniques because many of them are not suited for an average meditator. Instead, I am going to focus on meditation techniques that Life directly taught me when I began meditating after the events of December 2005. I'm going to take you through the same sequence of meditations that Life took me through. The popular belief is that you need to focus on a single technique during meditation, but that is not true. Life taught me to mix and create hybrids of different techniques in order to silence my mind more effectively. In time, as I got better, I began to drop the techniques one at a time.

I started with the easier closed-eye meditation, and then moved on to the more difficult sitting open-eye meditation, followed by meditating while doing various activities and focusing on the third eye. The goal is to get you to a point where you can focus and silence your mind while doing any type of activity.

This is very important: the progression of going from closed-eye meditation to sitting open-eye meditation to meditating while doing various activities and focusing on the third eye has to happen. Every time you want to go from one stage to the next, it is going to be initially frustrating and uncomfortable, because it is slightly more difficult. Once you have become good at silencing your mind in the lower stage, you have to transition to the next stage which is a more complex and difficult meditation. This is what evolution is all about. Your spiritual development depends on you being brave enough to take the next step and continuously improve your focus. I will give you some guidelines as to when would be a good time to take the next step, but do not forget that your higher self will guide you through this process. The answers are always within you.

I believe it is best to learn each technique by itself, and then learn how to mix them up and create hybrids. Each technique has its own unique effect on your energy field, so it is important to understand how each technique is affecting you. The other factor is that we are all different from each other, and some techniques are better suited for you than others. The only way to find out is to try different ones and find which one you like better. This is no different than trying different types of food. I might like one type of food and you may like another. This is why I chose to mix different techniques together, so you can decide for yourself what works better for you.

There are also universal techniques that everyone should include in their meditation, because of the special effect of that particular technique, such as raising the frequency of your vibration. Before we go through the individual techniques one by one, I want to talk about one important thing that can make a big difference in our lives, and that is using mantras.

USING MANTRAS TO
FOCUS YOUR CONSCIOUSNESS

Using mantras can be an effective way to focus our consciousness on a specific issue. Mantras can be used to stop or redirect a thought, overcome a fear, or change a specific behavior or reaction. I was able to overcome many of my fears, and change many of my reactions and behaviors by using mantras. I also used mantras to calm myself down when I felt overwhelmed. Repeating any sentence or a word over and over again can change the way you feel or behave in any circumstance. For example, when you are worried or overwhelmed in a situation, if you continuously throughout the day repeat "**I am okay,**" or "**Everything is okay,**" you will eventually feel okay. You can effectively tackle any fear or change any behavior by using mantras over and over again over a period of time. Your perseverance will determine the rate of your success, but if you stick with it I promise you with one hundred percent certainty that you can change any aspect of yourself no matter what it is. I want to give you some pointers about choosing mantras for your specific issues.

Make your mantras a positive sentence that empowers you in any situation, rather than focusing on the issue itself. For example, if you're worried about not having money, do not focus on saying I'm going to be okay for money, rather say: "**I'm strong and can overcome any obstacle.**"

Always have a written copy of your mantras somewhere visible, and take two minutes every morning to read them repeatedly and remind yourself to use them throughout the day. Repeat the same process before you go to sleep.

Only focus on three or maximum four separate issues at any one time to work on, and once you have overcome a fear or changed a specific behavior, move onto the next challenge you want to tackle.

Be vigilant about using the specific mantra that you have set for yourself every time a thought regarding that specific issues enters your mind. Your perseverance will determine your success. These are some of my favorite mantras that I used throughout the years.

I'm strong and can overcome any obstacles.
(Used when I was going through severe financial difficulty or when I was stressed.)

Calm and collected I am moving forward.
(Used when I felt agitated or intense.)

Everything is happening exactly as it should.
(Used when I was worried about the outcome of a situation.)

At ease, my brother.
(Used when I was upset with someone or felt overwhelmed or stressed.)

There is no conflict, there is no struggle.
(Used when I was upset with someone.)

Make your own mantras and see what works for you the best. As you meditate more and improve your focus, your mantras become much more powerful and effective.

Buddha's breathing technique

There are many variations of this technique. In this technique the meditator becomes aware of their breathing. This technique focuses on feeling the sensations in various stages of the breathing process. You are not normally aware of the sensations that occur during the breathing process. You do not attempt to control how fast or how slow you are breathing. You are not aware how deep or how shallow your breathing is, because you are always occupied by your thoughts. The goal of this meditation is to become aware of every moment during the entire process from the beginning to the end. This is one of the most important universal techniques that everyone should try, because learning to become aware of your breathing will raise your awareness, increase the frequency of your vibration, and help you to control your emotions. This technique will particularly help you in the moments where you feel anger coming out, because if you develop the ability to focus on your breathing and slow it down, you will be able to control your anger and frustration. The tips of our noses are very sensitive, when you breathe, you can feel the sensation of air touching the walls of insight of your nose. In this meditation, focus to constantly feel that sensation. This sensation is very mild, but definitely noticeable; remain aware of this sensation throughout your breathing.

Once you have read the entire section on meditation, including "The art of meditation," sit in your preferred meditation posture, and begin by taking a deep breath in. Stretch out this breath as long as possible. Focus on feeling the air touching the tip of your nose. Do not rush through it. Once you have inhaled as much air as possible, hold your breath for two seconds, and then breathe out with the same speed as you took your breath in. Do not rush through breathing out. The two seconds is only an approximation of the length of time, so you should not be counting the numbers one and two in your head. Also, the length of time that you can breathe in and out will depend on your lung capacity. As you improve and expand your lung capacity, try to stretch out the length of each in and out breath.

Be aware of the same thing during breathing out, feel the sensation of air touching the walls of the tip of your nose, as it exits your body. This is a universal technique that everyone should do, to not only to help you control your anger but to raise the frequency of your vibration. You normally take very shallow breaths with great frequency. The frequency of your vibration is directly affected by your heart rate, and breathing more frequently results in lower vibration of your energy. Therefore, the frequency of your vibration is always in a state of flux, depending on your heart rate and breathing.

Our brain burns more calories than all the other organs. Our hearts have to work harder and beat faster to supply oxygen and nutrients to our brain when we think. The more you develop the ability to silence your mind, the less oxygen and nutrients will be required by your brain, resulting in a slower heart rate, and a decrease in the frequency of your breathing. In turn, this results in the increase of frequency of your vibration in your spiritual energy field.

Remember that your energy field is made up of seven layers in three-dimensional space, and the consciousness within each body vibrates at its own frequency. The frequency of each layer increases as you go up the ladder towards the crown chakra. So once you silence your mind, the frequency of your vibration increases during the time of meditation. The deeper your silence, the higher the frequency will be at that time. This means that the chakra relating to that frequency at that time becomes hyperactive and draws in much more energy into your body with the higher frequency. This increases the density of energy with higher vibration in your energy field. The higher frequency energy that is drawn through that chakra travels down your spinal cord, filling up the lower layers with energy that has higher vibration, transforming them in the process. This is the spiritual process that allows you to evolve yourself at a much faster rate. The more you meditate, the deeper your silence will be and in turn, the faster you will increase the vibration of your energy.

For this reason, it is not important how much you believe in the material that I have talked about so far. What is important is that you meditate and increase the frequency of your vibration, because once that happens, transformation happens and you experience for yourself everything that I have talked about so far. You can reach enlightenment with this technique, if you become completely aware of every moment, without the presence of any thoughts whatsoever. But your awareness and silence has to be effortless for enlightenment to happen.

The other factor in meditation is the muscles around your chest and back that help you to expand your lungs during the breathing process. Since you have been taking shallow breaths most of your life, those muscles may be weak (unless you're an athlete who is involved in frequent cardiovascular exercise). Taking deep breaths in this breathing technique will help you to develop those muscles and in time, as you practice this meditation more, you will develop the ability to take even deeper breaths and silence your mind more, resulting in the increase of the frequency of your vibration. If you have never meditated, in the beginning you will realize that one moment you are aware of the sensation of air touching the tip of your nose, and the next moment you are thinking about something.

Do not get discouraged, this is normal. You're going to go in and out of awareness. Simply, once you catch yourself thinking about something, go back on becoming aware of the sensation of air touching the tip of your nose.

Meditation is like everything else in our lives. In the beginning of starting anything, you're not going to be good at it, but with constant work and dedication **you will get better**, that is guaranteed.

The second breathing technique, "holding on to breath"

The previous breathing technique focused on being aware of every moment by feeling the sensation of air touching the tip of your nose, while increasing the frequency of your vibration was secondary to being aware. This technique mainly focuses on the frequency of your vibration, while being aware is secondary. I mix this particular technique with other meditation techniques in order to create hybrids. I will discuss these hybrid techniques shortly. This technique may not be suited for people with mid back or shoulder injuries. You should stop if you feel an increase in pain at any time while you are meditating. Consult your physician if you have any concerns about the effect of this particular technique.

Sit in your preferred meditation posture. Begin by taking the biggest breath possible, make it as long as you can. Feel the air filling up your lungs, feel your chest and stomach expand as they are filled with air. Once you have inhaled as much air as possible, hold your breath for as long as possible.

One thing you need to understand is that the process of thinking relies on the movement of consciousness inside your energy field. The movement of consciousness in your energy field is dependent on breathing. Once you hold onto your breath, the process of thinking slows down considerably and you will have an easier time controlling your thoughts.

The second thing that happens is that holding your breath for as long as possible causes oxygen deprivation in your blood system. Your brain senses this deprivation and sends a signal to the muscles in your chest and back to expand even more, so you can draw more oxygen in. This effect results in an increase in your lung capacity over time. You have not used anywhere near your maximum lung capacity in your entire life, even if you're an athlete. This technique forces you to push the boundaries of your lung capacity.

The question is, when is a good time to breathe out, and take another breath in? The moment you feel your stomach deflating, breathe out all the way, and then take another big breath in. I do not want you to feel like you are suffocating, and I do not want you to experience any physical discomfort during this meditation. Once you start, after a few minutes you will know the right timing for you. Do not forget that during the time of breathing out, focus on your belly and chest pushing the air out. Become aware and feel your chest, and stomach expanding, and retracting while you breathe in and out.

The longer you can hold on to your breath, the higher the frequency of your vibration will be at that time. You will require less oxygen and nutrients for your brain as you silence your mind more, resulting in you holding your breath longer and longer.

The throat chakra is the center of the spiritual body with a frequency of 384 Hz. Remember that spiritual energy with this frequency has a neutral polarity. You need neutral energy in order to transform the lower bodies with positive and negative energies. So if you can push yourself and reach that frequency, the energy drawn by this chakra will help you go beyond positive and negative in the lower bodies. This technique is specifically designed for raising the frequency of your vibration.

Listening techniques

This technique focuses on the sense of hearing. Next to the sense of seeing, hearing is the second most dominant sense. For this reason, listening techniques are commonly used as a device to silence the mind.

Listening techniques are especially good if you are just starting to meditate, but in time you will have to drop this technique and move on to more difficult techniques in order to enhance your focus. There are two different variations of listening techniques: guided meditation and listening to the sound.

Guided meditation listening technique

Guided meditation is a type of meditation in which you listen to someone talk. The topic can be anything. The speaker tries to focus your attention on what he or she is saying. This talk is usually combined with some type of sound or music. There are thousands of scripts available online for this type of meditation. The topics of these scripts could be good for sleep, anxiety, deep relaxation, healing, positive energy, and so on.

I personally do not think that guided meditation is truly a meditation. Don't get me wrong, guided meditation can improve your focus, but meditation is about silencing your mind, so as long as there are words spoken, silence cannot be reached. Guided meditation is direct thinking and direct thinking is a step before meditation. This type of meditation could be more suited for elderly people who have never meditated before. I hope that you are brave enough to try one of my hybrid combination meditation techniques that I will discuss shortly. There's not much to guided meditation. Simply sit in your preferred meditation posture and focus yourself on listening what is being said.

Listen to the sound, and let it touch your soul

The effect of different sounds on our consciousness is undeniable. Listening to different types of music is part of the daily life of almost every human being around the world. Like consciousness, different sounds have different frequencies, so depending on how we feel, we choose to listen to different types of music. The sounds that we listen to definitely affect the frequency of our vibration, so choosing the right sound for this meditation technique is extremely important. Many people choose music that is very relaxing, but music that helps you relax does not help you to become alert. Awareness cannot increase without becoming alert, so music that helps you relax is not a good choice for this particular situation. You should also not choose music that has any type of vocals in it.

Crystal bowls

My personal recommendation is to choose the sound of crystal bowls. Crystal bowls are instruments that make sound waves at a specific frequency. Crystal bowls are made with specific frequencies to match the frequency of the seven chakras in our spiritual energy field. You can go online and choose from any of the seven frequencies that relate to each of the layers in our spiritual energy field. Remember that the energy in the first four layers have positive and negative polarity depending on if you are a male or female, so it would be better to choose a crystal bowl that corresponds with the fifth or the seventh body. The energies within these bodies have neutral polarity, so they are better for transforming the lower layers. You can use the crystal bowl that corresponds to the sixth layer if your third eye is open, or you are specifically trying to open your third eye. The live sound effects of crystal bowls are undeniable. For some reason the sound effect of crystal bowls that are downloaded from the Internet is much lower than when you listen to it live. I highly recommend that you try to find a location where you could meditate to the sound of crystal bowl live.

For meditation at home, sit in your preferred meditation posture and listen attentively to the sound of crystal bowls downloaded from the Internet. Remember that your center is listening to the sound, so follow the sound from your ears to your center, which is located at your bellybutton. Follow the sound until you have reached your center; once you are there, you will find your true self and experience enlightenment.

You can reach enlightenment through this technique, but your silence has to be absolute and effortless before that happens.

Looking techniques

There are different variations of looking techniques, but all open-eyes meditations are by far the most difficult type of meditation because of the movement of our eyes when they are open. Eyes function like the cursor of a computer. We move our eyes in different directions in order to activate the right or left hemisphere of our brain. The left hemisphere allows us to activate the consciousness that has to do with our past experiences. The left hemisphere also deals with functions such as analytic thoughts, logic, reasoning, mathematics, and science. The right hemisphere is used in creativity, imagination, intuition, and insight, as well as art and music. We are literally divided, with male energy controlling the left side and female energy controlling the right side. Our eyes are constantly moving to the left and the right depending on what we're doing or thinking about at the time. God is unity, and you can never become enlightened as long as you are divided, so the focus of all looking techniques is to focus your eyes and not allow them to move at any given time. If you do not allow your eyes to divide you, you will become one with All That Exists.

Your eyes want to constantly move. You are not normally in control of their movements and will have difficulty focusing your eyes on a specific point for an extended period of time. Pay attention next time you are driving or sitting in a vehicle that is moving. Your eyes constantly fixate on one thing for a moment, and then quickly fixate on something else the next moment. One moment you are looking at the car in front of you, the next moment you are looking at a sign or an advertisement on the street. Your eyes cannot help themselves, they are constantly moving from one point to another, and in doing so they randomly activate different thoughts in your head. One moment you are thinking about one thing, the next moment you are thinking about something else altogether. There are two ways to focus your eyes, and that brings us to two variations of open-eyes meditation.

Look at everything at once, and see that you are everywhere

God is everywhere. This technique focuses on looking at everything at once, without allowing your eyes to focus on a specific object or a point. Sit in your preferred meditation posture in a room, outside in a garden, or somewhere suited for meditation. Peripheral vision for a person with healthy eyesight is about 180° for both eyes from side to side. Try to look at everything together within your peripheral vision from side to side. Do not allow your eyes to fixate on any one thing within that range. This is an extremely difficult thing to do for a long period of time. You can try to do this anywhere where you are sitting for any length of time. You have to be aware that the muscles that control your eyes are not used to doing this for an extended period of time, so start with just minutes at a time and add to it as you become more comfortable. You cannot move your eyes to the left or to the right if you are looking at everything at the same time.

Once you stop the movement of your eyes, it becomes easier to silence your mind because the thinking process requires your eyes to move. You can still activate the left and the right hemispheres without moving your eyes, but it is more difficult to do. You still are going to struggle with your eyes looking at everything at once in one moment and then fixating on something the next moment. Simply go back to looking at everything once you catch yourself fixating on an object. You can reach enlightenment using this technique and see that you are everywhere, if you can completely silence your mind without any tension felt by the muscles that control your eyes.

Fix your eyes on a single point, and allow consciousness to lift off your body into the corners of the universe

This open-eye meditation is more practical and easier to do for extended periods of time. Life taught me a hybrid meditation technique that included this technique in combination with a breathing technique that I will be discussing shortly. We looked at everything at once in order to prevent the eyes from moving in the previous meditation technique. However, in this technique, we fix our eyes on a single point in order to prevent the eyes from moving. The best way to practice this meditation is by taking a flat-headed tack and coloring the head with a black marker pen. Then take a blank sheet of 8½ by 11 paper and find its center by connecting the opposite corners using a long ruler and a pencil. Once you have found its center, remove the lines with an eraser. Preferably find a wall that faces east, and place the 8 ½ by 11 sheet of paper on the wall. Push the colored tack into the center of the blank paper that you place on the wall. The white sheet of paper in contrast with the black colored tack makes the point pop. Use tape to attach the four corners of the blank sheet of paper to the wall. Sit in your preferred meditation posture approximately six feet away from the wall. Focus both your eyes on the tack, without allowing them to move. Your eyes cannot divide you if they are both fixated on a single point.

The same thing happens with this technique. Without the movement of your eyes the thinking process slows down considerably. Become one with the tack, and focus all your consciousness on that point. When we look at something a piece of us moves to that object. Once your focus becomes absolute, your consciousness moves out of your body and into the single point. In doing so your entire consciousness lifts off your body, and travels to the corners of the universe.

Open-eye meditations are the last step before you move on to meditating while you're performing any kind of activity. This technique prepares you for the next step because you learn how to stop your thoughts with your eyes open. You should not attempt these techniques until you have got good at silencing your mind with your eyes closed. The open-eye meditations are the next step after closed-eye meditations. Once you can comfortably stop thoughts with your eyes closed, you are ready to move on to open-eye meditation. Take your time transitioning between the two, by switching between the two for a while. Transitioning from closed-eye meditation to open-eye meditation is always difficult, because it feels like you're going backwards, but it's a necessary step in your spiritual development.

There is a very important hidden aspect in both of these techniques. Both of these looking techniques help to activate and open your third eye. Both looking at all objects at the same time and fixating on a single point naturally focus your consciousness on the third eye. You may not even be aware of this, but it happens naturally. So it is in the best interest of your spiritual development to get to these meditations as quickly as possible. You have to understand that even if your third eye does not open in this lifetime, the focused consciousness will have a lasting effect on your energy field into your next life. Your meditation efforts will never be wasted.

Third eye meditation

Focus your consciousness on the third eye and let the light touch your soul. In the previous meditation technique, we learned to focus our consciousness on a single point outside of our body. This meditation technique uses the same principle, but instead of focusing your consciousness on a single point outside of the body, we focus our consciousness on a single point located right in the center of our forehead.

Once you can focus all your consciousness on any single point regardless of its location and can absolutely silence your mind without any effort, you can become enlightened. This point can be located outside of the body, or anywhere inside the body. Once you are absolutely focused on a single point, you are no longer divided and a consciousness that is not divided becomes one with the whole.

There are two reasons why we focus on the third eye. The first reason is that the point located on the third eye craves attention. In almost all activities that require a great amount of focus, you naturally focus on the third eye without even realizing it. Focusing on the third eye naturally balances your energy field and strengthens the connection to your higher self. Once you're focused on the third eye you get addicted to being there. You will not be able to control it; it draws you in so that it is easier to focus on the third eye than to focus on your big toe.

The second reason is that the third eye is the sixth chakra, which opens the door to the spiritual realm of consciousness. This realm of consciousness contains energy, insight, and all the knowledge that exists within the collective consciousness. **You are connecting to All That Exists.** Once I tell people that my third eye is open, I'm always asked if I have any special powers, so I want to clearly explain how this connection works.

I have already talked about the three possibilities with regards to opening the third eye. The first possibility is activating the third eye by focusing on a single point, or on the location of the third eye itself. The second possibility is the ability to see with the third eye, just the way you see with your normal eyes. The third possibility is the ability to open the sixth chakra and draw energy directly from the spiritual realm of consciousness. This energy is a powerful neutral energy that is beyond positive and negative. This energy travels down the spinal cord and replaces the energy within the lower five layers of the spiritual energy field, transforming you in the process.

Now let me explain how that affects our reality. Our universe is God's playground, and just as you can program a 3D printer, Life can program whatever it wants to experience, and it will come to fruition. Every one of us has access to this playground. We are God's consciousness, and we create our reality by vibrating what we want to experience. When you focus on anything the universe latches on to your thoughts, and initiates a sequence of events to make that thought into reality. But the strength of your connection with the universe depends on the frequency of your vibration.

Let me give you an example. We connect and perform tasks on the Internet at different speeds. Some of us have weaker connections, so it takes a lot longer to perform certain tasks, but some of us have high-speed connections, so we can connect and perform the same tasks at a much faster rate. The third eye connection in some ways is similar to having an uninterrupted and strong connection to the Internet. The difference is that Life makes available to you all the information that exists within the entire system at exactly the right time with the right sequence.

Let me expand on this example a bit further. You have access to the Internet so you have access to the knowledge within the consciousness that exists within our planet, but all the knowledge is in bits and pieces scattered all over the net. The available information is not organized or cohesive for the seeker. The connection through the third eye connects the seeker to the collective universal consciousness, but the seeker receives the exact information that it needs at the exact right time and sequence. This connection goes beyond the exchange of information. The energy that passes through the third eye into the seeker transforms the seeker from within, preparing him or her to experience absolute unity with Life itself.

The other effect of this connection is that **the seeker "witnesses" the movement and the future of the human evolution.** The main reason for writing this book is for Life to communicate with our generation about the platform that human evolution is moving towards for centuries to come. The key word in the highlighted sentence is "witness," which is why there is so much emphasis on silencing your mind. The seeker is **prohibited** from projecting themselves to try to make changes to the system without the approval of Life itself. This is why I practice **surrender**. I stop all thoughts and desires that rise within me twenty-four hours a day, seven days a week. I am not a supernatural being with special powers. In fact, the "I" in me does not really exist anymore. I am focused on receiving information from Life, and aligning myself with that information at all times. Everything that I have told you so far has come from Life itself.

My recommendation to anyone who wants to open their third eye is to align themselves with the information in this book. In doing so, if you commit and effectively silence your mind, Life will open your third eye and vibrate through you just the way it has vibrated through me.

Once your third eye opens, your life will never be the same. Just remember that your intentions must be genuine; after all, you and Life are one.

The third eye is located right in the center of the forehead, but it is very difficult to focus on that point right away without any practice. The muscles that support your eyeballs are not used to pushing your eyes up towards the center of your forehead. If you try to do that for a long period of time without practice, you may get a severe headache.

The best way to prepare is by sitting in your preferred meditation posture, facing towards the east in order to align yourself with the energy of the sun. Then at first, close your eyes and focus both of your eyes on a single point right in between your two eyebrows. Meditate on that point for ten-minute intervals. Slowly relax your eyes and move the focus of your attention from between your eyebrows towards the center of your forehead. I have described earlier how you might be able to locate your third eye in front of a mirror. There may or may not be a physical representation on your skin. Sometimes the opening is just below the surface of the skin. I can visibly see mine, which has grown in size slightly since the beginning of my journey. It would be good if you could see yours as well. It is a very small knob right in the center of your forehead. There may be hundreds of similar looking knobs on your forehead, but there should be one exactly in the center. The meditation is simple: once you develop the ability to focus on that point, remain focused there with great intent. The thinking process slows down as your focus improves. Once you have gotten good at focusing on the third eye with your eyes closed, you can try to focus your attention on the third eye with your eyes open. This is the only type of meditation that you can do while performing any type of activity. It actually improves your performance, because it greatly enhances your insight, intuition, and accuracy. This is the ultimate meditation, which you should strive to perfect.

Pretend to be dead so you can free yourself from your fears

This meditation uses the power of imagination as the device to enhance your focus, in order to help you silence your mind. There is a secondary effect with this meditation, and that is helping you get over the fear of death. I have already talked about death on several occasions, so I will not discuss it in great detail again. But in short, we never die, we are eternal, so there is no reason to fear death. Unfortunately, in our societies, families do not talk to their children about death, and all children see is crying and sadness when someone dies. This creates a deep fear in our consciousness when we become adults. I remember when growing up, my mother was so afraid of losing one of us in an accident that we were not allowed to talk about death in our household. The fear of death grew in me even more after my grandfather died when I was eight years old. I remember thinking that I am still young and have many years left, so I don't have to worry about it now. I don't think that I ever pictured myself dying. This is how the fear of death goes deep into our consciousness, and grows as we get older. Many people involve themselves in death-defying stunts or have dangerous occupations, but that does not mean that they're not afraid of dying.

Whether they are atheist or spiritual, parents need to talk about death with their children. You do not need to talk about an afterlife if you are an atheist and don't believe in God, but you do need to explain death as a process of life in some fashion. The unknown part of death will only increase the fear in children.

Death needs to be celebrated, and being afraid of it is foolish. Imagine that you are an Olympian and have won a gold medal in a sporting event. You have worked all your life to get to that moment, but when you are on the podium to receive your gold medal, you become fearful of it. This is directly analogous to the way we regard death. All the challenges and difficulties that we have faced in our lifetimes lead us to the moment of death. That is when we are rewarded for all the pain and suffering that we have endured.

This meditation will help you to get over your fear of death by imagining that you are dead, and making peace with that thought. Imagination can be a powerful tool in meditation. We often underestimate the power of our thoughts and imagination. Imagination is a state of mind. Feeling good and fearful cannot occupy the same space at the same time, so if you can feel good while you imagine yourself dead, then the fear will slowly dissipate. This will not happen quickly, so be patient. You might be worried that you may manifest your death if you imagine yourself dying. I can assure you that every birth and every death is perfect. This means that there are no accidental births or deaths. There is no way for you to manifest your death; your time of death was predetermined before you were born. This question only rises in you because you are uncomfortable about imagining that you are dead. Please push past this discomfort; it will dissipate as you progress in this meditation.

This is one of the few meditations that can be performed lying down on the ground. Please understand that your imagination is as good as your conviction regarding this matter, so you are going to have to want this. You can play around with this meditation to get your preferred posture. First, lie down on your bed or on the ground in a very comfortable position. Imagine in your mind how you would like to die. This is important, because you are convincing yourself of this death. You have to pretend that it has happened. If you are afraid of dying, start by pretending that you have died from natural causes and are lying down on a hospital bed. Visualize yourself on that bed and imagine any supporting facts that go with your scenario.

The only thing to watch for is that you are witnessing this imagination in your mind as if the person that is lying on the bed is actually someone else. Remind yourself that you are dead, if any thought enters your mind. Focus yourself on the events in your scenarios. To help convince yourself of this imagined scenario, do not move around. If there are any thoughts in your mind, remind yourself that you are dead. How could there be any thoughts? The better you convince yourself of this scenario, the more successful you will be in enhancing your focus and eliminating your fear of death.

You can imagine different scenarios in which you have died. For example, dying in a car accident, or if you're brave enough, a homicide. Play around with it. I want you to get the feeling that death is not a big deal. The more you become peaceful with your imagined deaths, the less you will be afraid of dying. It is better to attempt this meditation when you are in a good mood. It is not necessary to do this meditation lying down if you can ignore the fact that you are sitting in a meditation posture. This will depend on how imaginative you are as a person. Naturally, some people are more imaginative than others.

I want to mention one last thing. Some people might be afraid of dying from a particular illness due to some past events, so they may be uncomfortable imagining themselves dying. For example, a woman whose mother has died from breast cancer may be afraid of dying from breast cancer herself. The fear has sunk deep into her unconscious. The more she avoids thinking and talking about this fear, the deeper she suppresses the fear. A fear that has been suppressed is much more dangerous than a fear that is on the surface, because you can release a fear that is on the surface, but you cannot deal with and release a fear that has been suppressed. It is in everyone's best interest to bring their fears to the surface and make peace with them, because if you do not Life will have no choice but to make that fear into reality, so you can overcome it. This can become a vicious cycle that can transcend beyond a single life. So for the woman in our example, it would be better to bring that fear up to the surface and make peace with it, rather than suppress the fear.

There is an extremely important factor with this meditation: do not visualize coming to the moment of death. Always imagine from the moment of death and after. This is because you can interact with the thought if you're thinking about coming to the moment of death, but after the moment of death you are dead, so you cannot interact with the thought. In our example, the said woman could imagine that she has already died from breast cancer, and is lying down on a bed in the hospital. She needs to make peace with that visualization. She can continue to visualize seeing her children grow and watching over them, but not interacting with them, just being a witnessing consciousness. Make your visualization a positive one, so imagine seeing them in happy moments. But always be a witness in your imaginations, do not imagine that you are interacting with them. Just remember that you are dead, so how could there be any thoughts or conversations? Witness these events as if you are watching a movie. This is a powerful meditation if done correctly.

Make sure that your focus is strong so you do not fall asleep. Fight sleepiness if you feel tired.

Hybrid meditations

Now that we have discussed the important individual meditation techniques, it is time for me to teach you the combinations that Life taught me from the beginning stages to the point of meditating with focusing on the third eye while performing any type of activity.

First hybrid meditation

The first hybrid is a combination of Buddha's breathing technique plus listening to the sound of crystal bowls corresponding to the frequency of the throat chakra. This hybrid is straightforward. Sit in your preferred meditation posture and begin by taking a deep breath in. Stretch out this breath as long as possible. Focus on the tip of your nose as air touches the inner walls of the tip of your nose. Once your lungs are full of air, hold your breath for approximately two seconds without counting the numbers, then breathe out, but take your time and do not rush through it. Maintain focus on the sensation of air touching the inner walls of the tip of your nose as it exits the body. Focus on the sound as it touches your eardrums. Follow the sound to your core located at your bellybutton. Repeat this sequence over and over again. You have so many things to focus on that you will have a difficult time thinking about anything. I will discuss with you in the next section, "The art of meditation," what to do with the thoughts that sneak in. I will also talk about the duration of meditation.

Second hybrid meditation

The second hybrid meditation is the combination of open-eye meditation (looking at a single point on the wall) plus holding your breath. Sit in your preferred meditation posture, place a blank sheet of paper on the wall with a black-colored tack in the center of it, as we discussed previously. Focus both of your eyes on the point, without allowing your eyes to move. Take breaths that are as deep as possible. Feel your chest expanding as your lungs fill with air. Once your lungs are full of air, hold your breath as long as possible. Once you feel your stomach is deflating, breathe out, but make it as long as possible, and feel your chest retracting. Once you have completely breathed out, repeat the same sequence over and over again.

I became so good at this technique that I can hold my breath for about forty-five seconds before I need to take another breath. On one occasion Life pushed me to reach about fifty seconds, and at that point my consciousness lifted off my body, and I experienced nirvana and absolute silence without any effort. It is important to understand that you need to be able to silence your mind with focus while you are holding your breath for around fifty seconds, before your consciousness lifts off your body. Holding your breath by itself will not do the trick. Silencing your mind with ease is a necessary part of this sequence.

Third hybrid meditation

The third hybrid is a combination of holding your breath plus focusing on the third eye. Sit in your preferred meditation posture. Take a breath that is as deep as possible. Feel your chest expanding as your lungs fill with air. Once your lungs are full of air, hold your breath as long as possible. Once you feel your stomach is deflating, breathe out, but make it as long as possible, and feel your chest retracting. Once you have completely breathed out, repeat the same sequence over and over again.

To make the transition from the last combination to this one, you can add to this variation by listening to the sound of a crystal bowl. But the goal is to drop the techniques one by one as you get better. Do not add the technique of listening to the sound of a crystal bowl if you are okay with just holding your breath and focusing on the third eye together.

These hybrid techniques are just recommendations. You can make your own hybrid combinations by combining two or even three of the individual meditation techniques together. But as you get better, you will have to drop the techniques one by one until you are only using the open eyes third eye meditation while performing any types of activity. That should be the progression of anyone's meditation journey.

Meditating while moving around and performing various activities

These combinations together gradually prepare the meditator for the next step, which is meditating while moving around and performing various activities. Each one of these techniques has a specific effect on your energy field. Feel free to move between the techniques and see what works best for you. Both open-eye meditation and the third eye meditation are advanced techniques that you should strive towards. You need to go from these combinations to meditating with a single technique of third eye meditation or open-eye meditations. Once you can silence your mind while using only one of the two techniques mentioned above, you are ready to move on to focusing on the third eye while performing any type of activity. Once you are at that point, you no longer need to sit down to meditate. Your life is meditation, focusing becomes second nature. Whatever you are doing can be turned into meditation just by focusing all your consciousness on that activity. Be total and present for the duration of that activity. Do not multitask. If you are driving focus on the third eye and everything that is happening around you. If you're riding a bicycle or a stationary bike, focus on the movement of your legs going up and down. If you're cooking or using any tools, focus and be present. If you are running, focus on the tips of your toe as they touch the ground. Whatever activity you're doing, engulf yourself in it in such a way that there is no place for thoughts to remain. Dedicate all of your consciousness totally to that activity. Focusing on the third eye brings balance into whatever it is that you're doing. It is the only technique that can be used in any type of activity. You only have to get used to focusing on that point with your eyes open.

I'm not going to sugarcoat it, these transitions are going to be difficult, but if you stick with it, I promise you that it will change your life. You will go beyond experiencing the positive and the negatives in your life. It will only be a matter of time before you become the master of your mind. You will no longer be a slave to your mind; instead, your mind becomes the servant, and you the master. A master is in complete control of his or her emotions and reactions. A master of the mind moves calmly and collectedly, without any fear or anger. You were meant to experience life in this way, and such a life is within your grasp. All you have to do is reach and grab it by performing these meditation techniques.

This world is real

There is an issue that I would like to address. Many spiritual leaders have called this world an illusion or Maya, and given a wrong idea to people about this world. This world is real; there is no illusion about the existence of this world. The illusion that exists is created by your projections because you are living in a dream world. Listening to music while working, driving, working out, and many other types of activities is popular among people around the world. The problem is that you are not really listening to the songs attentively; you are using those moments to project and imagine different things in your mind. This world is not an illusion; you are creating an illusion in your mind. Whether you're listening to music or not, you're always dreaming and imagining different scenarios in your head. Music only creates a better environment for your illusions. You are not real when you are dreaming and imagining. You have created a world in your mind that does not exist.

It's important to understand that reality cannot compete with your illusions, so when you have to deal with reality you suffer. You have to stop these illusions and live in the real world. The only way that can happen is for you to be present in everything you are doing. There is nothing wrong with listening to music, as long as you remain in the present moment, but unfortunately most people have a habit of imagining and dreaming as soon as they listen to their favorite tunes. You may have to reduce the amount of time that you listen to music, until you have improved your focus and can remain present while listening to music.

The art of meditation

In this segment I'm going to talk about different aspects of performing meditation techniques, as well as give you an understanding of how to deal with the thoughts that intrude during meditation.

Duration of meditation techniques

Often when people start to meditate, they expect to become silent and relaxed right away, but the exact opposite will happen. You're always occupied with something throughout the day, so the activities that you're involved with occupy your mind to a certain extent. You may have about fifteen to twenty thoughts circulating in your head waiting for a chance to get in. As you are doing your daily activities, these thoughts constantly go in and out. The reason watching TV is so popular is that when you watch an interesting program, you are so focused on it that your consciousness does not allow any other thoughts to come in. Basically, all you are doing is taking a break from the thoughts that are circulating in your mind. Once you close your eyes to meditate for the first time, there is nothing occupying your mind, so all the thoughts can easily get in without much resistance. This is why starting to meditate is a daunting task. The new meditator feels overwhelmed, and stops the meditation.

I have heard many people say "I don't like meditation because of ..." This usually indicates that a meditator has tried to meditate and has got overwhelmed, so he or she is looking for an excuse not to have the same experience again. Starting to meditate is similar to starting to work out. You cannot go from not doing any exercising, to a vigorous workout. Your body will get very sore, so you will not want to do it again. Performing meditation techniques for the first time is the same. You should not go from zero to twenty-five minutes overnight. Choose your preferred meditation posture and meditation technique. Set your alarm clock for five minutes, so you don't have to open your eyes to see how much time has gone by. Five minutes is such a short time that no matter how difficult meditation might be for you the first time, you can suffer through it. It will go by fairly quickly; in this way you will not feel overwhelmed and stop meditating all together.

Add one minute to your meditation every other day, so go from five minutes to six, from six to seven, from seven to eight, and so on, until you reach at least twenty-five minutes per day. The gradual addition of time also allows the muscles in your eyes and chest build strength gradually. The reason reaching twenty-five minutes per day is important, is that our thoughts are layered, similar to an onion. I have talked about thought patterns earlier in the book. You have daily activity thoughts, interactive thoughts, random thoughts, creative thoughts, daydreaming thoughts, and thoughts that come from your center. The focus of meditation techniques is to stop the daily activity thoughts, interactive thoughts, random thoughts, and daydreaming thoughts. Similar to peeling an onion one layer at a time, you have to peel away these thoughts one layer at a time. Buried beyond these layers are your anger and fears, so in order to reach that deep, you need to discard the top layers. The longer you meditate the deeper you can go. Once you are meditating regularly, you will have less layers to go through the next time you meditate, and you can discard the layers faster and with better focus. Twenty-five minutes is the minimum amount of time required daily for you to make some headway getting through these thick layers of thoughts. An hour at a time is ideal to get through to the deepest and darkest part of your consciousness. As you meditate more and more, you will go back in time to anger and fears from your childhood. Suddenly a thought will pop into your head during the meditation, making you wonder, where did that come from? When that happens, you know that you are making progress. I want to emphasize again: be very gradual with increasing the time of meditation in one sitting because if it becomes too much, subconsciously you will create situations that make it difficult for you to meditate.

One other thing to consider is that you don't always need to meditate in perfect conditions. Throughout the day, you can meditate anytime, anywhere, even if it's just for five minutes. You could be riding the bus, or you could have got to work five minutes early, or you could be at home and your children are taking a nap. It does not matter if there is a lot of noise around you, or if you are standing instead of sitting. Close your eyes and focus on your breathing or on the third eye, for any amount of time. The important thing is to improve your focus every time you have the opportunity. I used to meditate in loud environments, where it would be difficult to focus. Meditating in more challenging environments can help you get better at focusing when conditions are more ideal. So meditate any chance that you get throughout the day, regardless of time and place.

Your attitude towards meditation

Unlike physical workouts where you see changes to your physical body quite quickly, meditation has a very subtle and gradual effect on your energy field. So it is more difficult for an individual to motivate themselves to meditate on a daily basis. Meditation is the most important thing that you can do in your life. You should never forget that the main reason you have been put on this planet is to evolve and raise the frequency of your vibration. Energy continues to grow and rise within your energy field, and with some effort you begin to transform. This transformation takes time, so you need to be vigilant along the way. Your attitude towards this effort could affect how much you improve and progress along the way. Meditation must not be a chore in your life; remember that. When you're not happy being somewhere, your mind is going to try to go somewhere else. The whole point of meditation is to remain in the present moment, so if you regard it as a chore, that will hinder your effort to become silent. Your attitude towards this effort can make or break you. Just like working out, meditation is a difficult task, especially after a busy day at the school, at work, or at home taking care of children. No one really wants to do it, especially when they feel tired, but you need to push past the tiredness and persevere. Go into it with a positive attitude, knowing that you are doing something very important in your life, and remind yourself of that regularly. Every day, once you sit in your preferred meditation posture, just before you start your meditation, imagine in your mind that during the time of meditation energy is flowing and building inside of you. Having a positive mindset about meditation can take you a long way on your journey.

The effect of two opposite energies on meditation

The popular belief is that you need to be relaxed while performing meditation. This is only half of the equation, because if you are too relaxed you will get sleepy, and will not be able to focus on stopping the thoughts in your mind. You also need to bring intensity to every moment remaining being calm, but how much intensity and calmness do you need to have the perfect balance?

Nirvana or absolute silence can only happen in the state of perfection where the two opposite energies within your energy field are activated at exactly the right amount to balance each other. Let me give you an example to make this clear. A woman who is made up of 60% female energy and 40% male energy needs to activate the male energy more to offset the imbalance that exists within the two opposite energies. The right balance for every individual is going to be different, because the percentage of male/female energy is different for every person. The way we activate the male and the female energy in our energy field is by identifying with their characteristics. Male energy is intense, while female energy is calm. The balance between these two characteristics affects your focus at all times, particularly under pressure. Let us look at some examples of pressure moments that could be affected by these two characteristics.

Has it ever happened that you have studied really hard for an exam and felt that you knew the material really well, but suddenly at the time of the exam, you found that you couldn't remember the material that you had studied? Or you have prepared for a presentation, but suddenly at the time of the presentation you felt nervous and gave a poor presentation? Or have you experienced feeling nervous during a job interview, and not giving good answers to the questions? Have you seen a professional basketball player miss an easy free throw at the end of a tied game? Or a professional golfer missing a two-foot putt that could seal the championship? Or any professional athlete choking under pressure? All these events happen because of an inability to activate the right energy combination at that particular moment. Intensity is a male characteristic, while calmness is a female characteristic. Maximum focus is available to you when you have the right amounts of intensity and calmness to balance your male/female energy. This balance is different for every individual, since we all have different energy combinations. So when you are facing a moment of pressure that requires a great deal of focus, you will have to bring the right amount of intensity and calmness to that moment. The woman mentioned above who is made up of 60% female energy and 40% male energy, needs to bring about 60% intensity with 40% calmness to have the maximum amount of focus. She is in a state of perfection when she has balanced her energy field with the right amount of intensity and calmness.

This is easier said than done because many things affect our intensity and calmness at any one time. For example, you might have some anxieties about an interview you are going to, which can affect your calmness. You might feel tired, so you may lack intensity at that moment. A professional athlete could go into a situation with too much intensity and end up tensing up, or go into it too relaxed because he or she thinks that the task will be easy. Both situations can result in a lower amount of focus, which can result in missed opportunities. This phenomenon has effected every one of us at some point in our lifetimes in some way. Like everything else, meditation requires focus, so in order to reach pure silence, you need to bring the right amount of intensity and calmness to every moment.

How to achieve a balance of intensity and calmness

The question now is how do we achieve this state of perfection in which we have optimal focus and balance? For the purpose of our conversation, I may use "**at ease**" instead of "**calmness**" because they are synonymous. I have found that it is easier to start with bringing **intensity** to every moment, and then adding being **at ease** to balance it out. Once you get the right balance between the two, you naturally activate the right amount of energy every time you need to focus on something.

Start your meditation by bringing intensity to every moment for five minutes; silence your mind as if your life depends on stopping your thoughts, and then quietly in your mind tell yourself to be "**at ease,**" as if your higher self is telling you that. I found that it is more effective if I say it as if my higher self is telling me to be at ease. This worked best for me, but you may say whatever you want to put yourself at ease, while maintaining your intensity. You could also come up with your own solution to finding the right balance between intensity and calmness. These meditation practices will help you when you are faced with pressured situations or situations where you are worried about something or have anxieties. Once you find the right combination in your mind, anytime you are worried about something or have any type of anxieties or anger, just tell yourself: **"At ease my brother,"** or **"At ease, my sister,"** as if Life is telling you to be calm. Your mind can quickly activate the right amount of male and female energy to balance you in that moment. The more you practice, the easier it will become for you to achieve that state of consciousness when you need to. The state of consciousness in which you activate the right amount of the male and the female energies within your energy field to offset the imbalance that exists within you is **the state of serenity**. Do not forget that you need to have the exact amount of intensity and calmness in every moment to reach that state of consciousness.

There is a simple exercise that you can do to speed up the time required to find the perfect balance. Purchase five ping pong balls and a small garbage basket. Place the basket far enough from you so it would be challenging to throw the ball into the garbage basket, but not too far that it would be too difficult to get any balls in. Practice for a minute to get used to the range. When you are ready, play a game with yourself in which you win if you successfully throw three balls into the basket, and you lose if less than three go into the basket. Imagine that your life depends on you winning the game, or make it interesting by rewarding yourself with something if you win, and punishing yourself with something if you lose. This will bring intensity to the moment of you throwing the ball, but before you throw the ball, take a deep breath in and exhale all the way out, and then throw the ball. This sequence is similar to when a pitcher of a professional baseball team throws a pitch. This is also a form of meditation, because you need to silence your mind and activate the exact amount of opposite energies to maximize your focus. You can increase the distance to make it more challenging once it becomes too easy for you. Practice this exercise every day, until you can naturally focus yourself without much effort.

Once you have learned to focus yourself, apply this technique to everything that you do. When you are performing your meditation or any type of activity, prevent your mind from wandering by bringing intensity to every moment, while being at ease at the same time. This is an important aspect in meditation that is often overlooked.

What to do with the thoughts that sneak in

We do two things with thoughts that enter our mind. We either identify with the thoughts, or we interact with them. The goal of meditation is to create a separation between you and the thoughts that enter into your mind, or the way you react to certain thoughts. The reality is that the thoughts in your mind are not yours. In fact, there is no entity within you that is called "mind." All thoughts come from a universal field. Your consciousness is vibrating at a specific frequency and receives the thoughts dedicated to your consciousness, similar to a radio tuning into a specific frequency. Once you receive a thought that has been dedicated to your consciousness, you identify with it or you take an action to support that thought; only then does it become yours. We also have memories of thoughts or past experiences that are randomly activated by another thought or a stimulus, such as seeing something familiar. The same thing happens once you identify with that thought or interact with it. You strengthen the memory by giving energy to it.

During the time of meditation, we actively focus on the meditation techniques so we can stop identifying with and interacting with our thoughts. To understand this process better, let us look at identifying with thoughts, supporting our thoughts with some action, and interacting with our thoughts.

How to stop identifying with your thoughts while meditating

Identifying with our thoughts is based on past experiences and conditioning. When something happens, based on your past experiences, you identify with a thought that relates to that experience. For example, you see a man throw a piece of garbage out of a moving car. Based on your past experience and upbringing you either condemn this action with a thought, or you think that it's okay. Either way, you are identifying with one of the two scenarios. The goal of meditation is to go beyond identifying with any type of thoughts. In this way, you can go beyond positive and negative, and beyond judging in general. You need to stop identifying with all thoughts, regardless of being right or wrong.

Once you stop identifying with all thoughts, you become a witnessing consciousness. God's consciousness is a witnessing consciousness. All That Exists is not judging you for your actions, and in order to align yourself with it, you have to become a witnessing consciousness. This does not mean that there will be no consequences for the actions of the man who threw the piece of garbage out of the moving car. Karma is a separate system that is in place to automatically balance the cause and effect. Every action will have a consequence, regardless of your thoughts or feelings about that action.

So when a thought enters your mind during the time of meditation, do not identify with it; do not say this is good or bad. Do not give any energy to it, just look at it as if it's somebody else's thought. Imagine you see a cloud moving in the sky. Look at your thoughts the same way: just watch them come in and then leave without paying any attention to them. Earlier in the book, I talked about an exercise in which you would not speak unless you were spoken to for periods of time. This exercise is great for creating separation between you and your thoughts. When you are practicing this exercise, thoughts enter your mind but you do not say anything, so you keep watching thoughts entering your mind and then leaving without you uttering any words. Normally you tell people around you whatever you are thinking about. Once you practice this exercise, thoughts enter your mind but you stay silent, and so the separation between you and your thoughts strengthens as time passes. I highly recommend everyone to try this exercise, **"do not speak, unless you are spoken to"** for periods of time on a weekly basis. It is a great way to control whether or not you identify with a thought that enters your mind.

How to control your reactions to events while meditating

The second technique that you can use to create separation between you and your thoughts is by controlling your reactions to events that are happening around you. For example, while you are driving a car, another vehicle cuts you off. There are different possibilities as to how you could react to this action. You could condemn this action in your mind, by flipping your middle finger, giving the other driver a dirty look, sounding your horn loudly and swearing at them, or simply shaking your head. In all of these scenarios, you have identified with a particular thought or reaction. Identifying with a thought or a reaction is one and the same. The best thing you can do is show no reactions at all and move on as if nothing happened. Controlling your reactions in different scenarios allows you to have more control over how you react to certain thoughts when they enter your mind. The purpose of all these exercises is to give you control over your thoughts, your reactions, and emotions. Once you get to the point where you can exert control, then you can spontaneously react to every situation as you wish in the present moment consciously, not out of habit and past conditioning.

I know what I'm saying is extremely difficult to do, but you need to work on yourself and get yourself to the point where you are in complete control of your thoughts, your reactions, and emotions. During the time of meditation do not react to any thoughts that enter your mind. As I said before, just watch them pass by as if they were someone else's thoughts.

How to stop interacting with your thoughts while meditating

Interacting with your thoughts occurs when a thought enters your mind and you start projecting into the thought by giving energy to it. This thought could be positive, negative, or part of your imagination. We often interact with our thoughts as if they are live events. In our mind we have conversations with people or imagine scenarios in which we are doing things with them. This interaction gets more intense when we have had disagreements with others. We may find ourselves obsessively thinking that we should have done this or should have said that. Daydreaming is another way of interacting with our thoughts.

The focus of meditation is to stop all interactions with our thoughts by focusing on performing the meditation techniques. If you find yourself interacting with your thoughts during the time of meditation, just remind yourself that "**I am just watching,**" just as you would watch a cloud passing over the sky. Or imagine that your thoughts are a television program and you are simply watching. You do not interact with a television program when you're watching TV, so reminding yourself that "I am just watching" creates a separation between you and whatever is in your mind. Imagination is a great tool if used properly during the time of meditation.

It will take time to separate yourself from your thoughts. Do not expect to see results immediately after saying, "I am just watching" a couple of times. Focus on the technique of the meditation, and then when thoughts sneak in, do not identify with them; instead, watch them as if they are not your thoughts. Remind yourself that you are just watching and witnessing, then focus on the meditation technique again. This is the battle that you have to fight every moment during the time of meditation. One moment you are focused on the meditation technique, the next moment you will catch yourself identifying or interacting with a thought. You will go back and forth with this, but as you meditate more and more, you will get better at stopping these thoughts and maintaining your focus on the meditation technique. Some days it will be easy to stop the thoughts and some days it will be more difficult, but if you keep fighting and persevere, I promise you that you will win in the end.

The witnessing consciousness is already within you. Your higher self is watching you without any judgment, it sees what you see, hears what you hear. The silence that you seek is already there; all you have to do is stop the excess noise that has been created by your mind.

Negative experiences are a necessary part of life

Now what should you do when you are thinking about someone who has hurt you, or you remember an experience that was painful for you? These types of thoughts and experiences contain negative energy that needs to be released, and when they come up during the time of meditation, it is a perfect time to release them because deep breathing and a lower heartbeat opens your aura. When your aura is open, these energies that contain your anger can leave your spiritual energy field. In order to make this happen, you need to remain calm and continue to take deep breaths. Your understanding of why they have hurt you can be very useful in this situation. I have already explained why negative experiences are a necessary part of life, but I would like to review this subject one more time, because understanding this concept is extremely important in your spiritual development.

The good and the positive cannot exist without the bad and the negative. The opposite energies create an environment in which you constantly move back and forth between the good and the bad over many lifetimes. Both positive and negative energies exist within the first four layers of your spiritual energy field. It's important to understand that neither negative nor positive energy create the negative experiences in our lives. Negative experiences happen because the dual energy system creates a feeling of separation between every human being in this world. Separation is the cause of the evil, but separation is not real. It is only a figment of your imagination, or more accurately a figment of God's imagination. This separation was necessary so we could experience ourselves in the three-dimensional space.

It is no one's fault that they behave the way they do. These cycles of good and bad have happened over many lifetimes. You may have done more good in one lifetime and caused much pain and suffering to other people in another life. In order for you to stop swinging between good and bad you will have to reach the vibration of the fifth, sixth, or seventh body of your spiritual energy field, because energies within those bodies have neutral polarity. Once that happens you will experience unity and go beyond experiencing positive and negative. It is the only way to stop this vicious cycle.

I want to make one other point. We are all trying to completely stop the bad in our world. First of all, that is never going to be possible, one cannot exist without the other. But even if hypothetically we could, would you be interested in living in a world where absolutely no bad exists? I know that there is too much bad in our world today, and we need to move from separation to unity and bring balance between good and the bad, but experiencing negative events in our lives is absolutely crucial. Remember that we are here to experience the low, and that experience has to come from somewhere. It comes from the people who give you the negative experiences in your life. Do not be angry with them, as they are only giving you the experiences that you have chosen to experience.

This is difficult to comprehend and accept, so let me give you an example that you may relate to. Let us say that someone in Hollywood has decided to make a movie that is absolutely positive with no bad people or anything negative in it. Do you think that you would enjoy watching such a movie? I promise that you would not enjoy such a movie because it would be boring and lack meaning. How could you have positive without the negative? The positive can only shine in contrast to the negative; one is not possible without the other. Even if you watch a documentary about missionaries who feed the hungry, hunger is playing the role of the bad guy.

Ever since God created this world, it has been necessary for some people to play the bad guy. We all start from the bad and move towards the good. We move from experiencing complete separation to absolute unity; that is the circle of life. Every one of you is somewhere between those two points, so do not judge anyone, no matter how bad they are, because you have been there yourself at some point. It's not really their fault if they are at the beginning of their journey and feel completely separated, so they hurt others. They're giving you the negative experiences you need to help you grow in this lifetime. Their time will come as well. Maybe not in this lifetime, but we are all moving towards the light, so show compassion for people with lower vibration. People would look at a child molester who has raped and killed a child and say that he is evil, but I want to share something: an entity that is evil does not exist. Only an experience of evil exists, and there is a big difference between the two.

When a movie is made in Hollywood, the producer gives a script to an actor that describes the character. This description includes the environment where the character has grown up and been shaped. The actor studies the script and projects the character onto the screen. An actor could play the role of a villain in one movie and play the role of a hero in another movie, but you have to remember that he is neither a villain nor a hero. He is what he is. It's the same for consciousness, but there is no written script here. You are born into a family in a certain environment, with a certain IQ and physical abilities. As you go through life, your parents, siblings, friends, teachers, geographical and cultural influences, and different events in your life shape your character. Some of us are fortunate and end up in positive and better situations, but others who are not as fortunate end up with negative personalities. We are all just experiencing different characters from the beginning of the time, not only as humans, but also as trees and animals. You have lived many lives to get to where you are today, you have been both the good and the bad in many of your lives. Our lives are a movie that started at the beginning of the time, and someday will come to an end when we are all united. Then a new movie will begin again. The circle of life has happened for an eternity, and will never end. This life is just a movie, so don't take it too seriously. Remember that nothing ever dies. We are all eternal, we are God's consciousness, and nothing can hurt us.

There is only one of us

While meditating, or at any time where you feel hurt by someone, remember this understanding that there is only one of us. Each one of us is only playing a role in this movie of life. Have compassion for people who are at lower levels in their spiritual journey. You can be assured that Life will guide them towards the light, maybe not in this lifetime, but eventually they will find the light. We all do. Remember that we are all doing the best that we can. Stop seeing people as individuals. Your parents, siblings, friends, coworkers, and every living thing on this planet is you in a different form. We are all God's soul, **no one else but you exist.**

Every enlightened person who has ever walked on this planet has come to the same conclusion. Jesus said: "But I tell you, love your enemies and pray for those who persecute you" (Matthew 5:44). Jesus said this because he knew that his enemies were literally himself in a different form. He knew that if anyone can get to the point where they can love their enemies, then they will achieve enlightenment. The only possible way to love your enemies is by knowing that your enemies are you in a different form, and so there is absolute unity.

I am not asking you to believe everything that I'm telling you wholeheartedly. Whether you are a Christian, Muslim, Jew, Buddhist, Hindu, Sikh, atheist, or adhere to any other faith, meditation will bring growth into your life. These meditation techniques are secular; they are not prayers and they do not have any philosophical values. They are devices to help you become the master of your mind and emotions. Practice these techniques whether or not you believe in anything that I have said. If Life chooses to give you any experiences along the way and that changes your opinion about anything, that's great. If not, at least you will have learned how to be in control of your mind and emotions.

I have talked about many techniques, knowledge, and insights in the section on meditation, and the art of meditation. There are too many things for you to remember, so read this section several times and take notes for yourself. Choose your preferred meditation posture, and the meditation technique that you would like to practice, and then look at your notes every time you start to meditate until you can fluently remember everything. Continue to re-read this section, and the book in general, from time to time so that these understandings go deep into your consciousness.

Enlightenment

Life is a journey that you have been on from the beginning of the time. Every soul begins from complete separation and moves towards absolute unity; we are all somewhere between those two points. The progression from the beginning to the end depends on the path that we take along the way. It is your God-given right to choose your path as you see fit. Life wanted me to write this book, so you will have some guidance as to how to proceed along the way. The path to God cannot be replicated by anyone, because we are all unique in our own way. You cannot follow the exact same path that I have walked, but you can learn the techniques that Life has taught me and apply them in your daily life in order to walk a direct line towards the light, rather than risk walking in circles.

This section is geared towards people who are interested in learning how to climb to the peak of the mountain quickly. You may not think that you are now ready to take the plunge and go for enlightenment, but you simply don't know what the future holds or when you will be ready. On December of 2005, I was a 35-year-old man ready to join an organized crime family. Spirituality was the last thing on my mind and I had never in a million years thought that I would ever be where I am today. Once you start to meditate, you never know what experiences you may have and when. Read this section attentively, there will be some insights that everyone can use, and there will be some insights geared towards people who want to go all the way to enlightenment. Remember one thing, there is a part of you that will not remember your experiences from this life when you reincarnate. But there is a part of you that remembers everything that has happened to you from the beginning of the time until now, and has been guiding you along the way. You are both of those parts, your higher self and what you know yourself to be in this life. Everything that you are learning will be with you for many lives to come, so learn all that you can and your higher self will tell you what you need to know when the time is right. It could happen in this life or the next ones.

Different paths to enlightenment

Enlightenment is absolute unity; it happens when you become one with All That Exists. You can reach enlightenment in one of three ways.

Enlightenment can be attained through absolute physical balance

The lowest form of enlightenment can be achieved through absolute physical balance. Physical balance is an important aspect of the path to enlightenment in all forms, but absolute alignment and balance in the physical body produces perfect energy patterns that will drop the aura and give you the experience of unity. This form of enlightenment will not come with the wisdom and knowledge of other forms of enlightenment. Even though you will learn to focus your consciousness, you will not become the master of your mind and your emotions. Some forms of yoga are geared towards this particular path.

Enlightenment can be attained through focus

You can become enlightened through performing the meditation techniques that we have discussed earlier, or any other technique where you reach absolute silence. I have talked to many people who meditate regularly and think that they have reached absolute silence during their meditation. Your thoughts have many layers. Even if you silence your mind for short moments, there are many layers of thoughts still within your energy field. Absolute silence only happens when there are no thought patterns left within your energy field. This silence must be maintained without any effort, because any effort that you make will hinder the advent of enlightenment. This is very difficult to comprehend, so I'm going to use a metaphor. In this metaphor, thoughts are clouds, and your energy field and silence are the blue sky. Before you begin to meditate your energy field is like a sky that is full of clouds from end to end; you will not be able to see any of the sky whatsoever. There are thoughts circulating in your mind as long as you are awake. Once you start meditating and improving your focus, you begin to see small patches of blue sky here and there. As you meditate more and more, you see less of the clouds and more of the blue sky. Finally one day, you will come to a point where there are no clouds left in the sky, but **you still have to make an effort to keep the clouds out**. Enlightenment happens when there are no clouds left in the sky, and you have reached complete silence. Once your consciousness lifts off your body, you will experience pure silence without effort, which is nirvana, but once you sleep and wake up you will have to repeat the same sequence again to reach pure silence and nirvana. Your silence is not permanent.

You will become the master of your mind and emotions and attain enlightenment by performing these meditation techniques. Once you have completely silenced your mind, the aura drops and you become one with the universe. Physical balance is necessary for this form of enlightenment, but does not need to be perfected. The better your physical balance is, the easier will be for you to silence your mind, so make sure that you put sufficient effort into aligning and balancing your physical body. In this form of enlightenment, you will have to repeat the same sequence of meditation daily to reach pure silence and nirvana.

Enlightenment can be attained through surrender

This is the highest form of enlightenment. Enlightenment through surrender is meditation plus giving up your will to a master, or life itself. In doing this, the ego completely disappears. It is difficult to express what surrender is. Surrender happens when you completely give up making decisions in your life. Every day you are making decisions about many different things in your life. Your mind is constantly assessing different situations and scenarios happening in your life, and presenting you with various options. Your higher self also presents you with options in the same circumstances. Ultimately for any given situation, you will choose one of those options. People who are more in tune with their higher self and listen to their gut feelings usually make the best choices, because the best option is always given to you by your higher self. This process gets complicated when you consider your feelings and fears regarding different subjects. Making decisions pushes your mind into overdrive, so as long as you are making decisions in your life, you will always have to make an effort to keep the thoughts out.

When you surrender, you completely give up making decisions in your life about important issues. Once you stop making decisions in your life, your mind will have nothing more to do, and as a result will gradually slow down. Even if you completely agree to surrender yourself intellectually, it will take time to completely give up your will experientially.

Surrender through direct contact with Life is extremely rare, but it does happen from time to time. Normally, a seeker will have to surrender to a spiritual master. The problem is that you have to find a legitimate master. There are lots of spiritual leaders who call themselves masters, but they are not enlightened people, so you could easily get lost if you're not careful when choosing a master. The master represents Life itself, so a true spiritual master must have a direct connection to Life itself.

You will find that your mind will fight with the decisions that are made by the master. You will have to continuously make an effort to silence your mind during this process, until you fully surrender. Complete surrender will take years to accomplish. But as long as you are vigilant in silencing your mind, slowly, slowly your mind slows down, until it completely comes to a halt.

You may ask, what is the difference between enlightenment through focus and enlightenment through surrender? The difference is in the quality of the silence, and what is experienced thereafter. Remember when you reach enlightenment through focus, you reach silence by focusing your consciousness, but you have to make a tremendous effort to keep thoughts out. Once you reach enlightenment, your mind becomes silent without effort, but you have to repeat the effort every day to maintain that silence. Your mind will never become truly silent.

Enlightenment through surrender is different. Once your surrender is complete, the mind has completely come to a halt. The silence is pure without requiring any effort, there are no more thoughts coming. You have completely aligned yourself with the master and have never questioned whatever path is put in front of you. To say it simply, if a master tells you to jump off the bridge, you don't ask why, you trust the master enough that you simply jump without any hesitant. This requires a tremendous amount of trust.

In the beginning after the events of December of 2005, Life required my complete surrender. Life also tested my surrender and resolve by asking me to fast for about seven months, eating only 250 g of food once a day, until I experienced death in the hospital.

In this situation I was following Life itself. As mentioned, most people will need a master. The master can give you structure to follow, but you must surrender yourself to Life itself. Life communicates with each and every one of you through people that you know, thoughts, and events. When you surrender yourself to Life, you say "yes" to everything that comes your way. When you try for something and it's not working out, it is not meant to be, so move on to something else. Basically, go with the flow. Whichever direction the water flows, go with it. Life is in complete control of the direction, so if your faith is strong and you trust Life, you go with it. **That is surrender.** It helps if you stop seeing people as people. Everyone around you is God, so pay attention to what everyone is telling you. Pay attention to the events that are happening in your life. When you're not sure, then follow the master and the direction that he has put forth before you.

There is a movie called *Yes Man* starring Jim Carrey, and I suggest that everyone watches this movie. Carrey plays a character who **never says yes** to anyone when he's asked to do something. Through a sequence of events he finally has an epiphany, and decides to say "yes" to everything. Once he starts saying yes, everything begins to work in his favor. Everyone can learn a lot from watching that movie, because it basically describes how to surrender to Life. I have been doing that since December of 2005. Of course there are scenarios where I connect to Life and ask for clarification, but in most cases, I just follow the events. I have also got really good at picking up what Life is communicating to me through others around me. Choose a structure that you want to follow in your life, once you know where you want to go, and then follow the signs that come to you from Life. These signs can come through people that you know, a television program, a magazine that you are reading, or anything for that matter. If you're not sure ask Life to give you clarification. But if you ignore the signs because you don't like the answer, Life will stop communicating with you in that fashion. Remember that your higher self knows your convictions about any situation. So if you go into it thinking you may or may not listen to the guidance, then you will not receive the guidance. But if you go into it with conviction, thinking show me the way and I will follow, I promise you that Life will show you the signs that you are looking for.

I want to be clear about one thing. Surrendering is not about saying yes to everything and expecting everything to turn a positive. Surrendering is about saying yes to everything and accepting the outcome regardless of it being positive or negative.

The reason surrender is the highest form of enlightenment is due to the fact that when you completely surrender and give up your will, your ego completely disappears and you are fully aligned with your higher self. The unity achieved through this type of enlightenment is like nothing else; it is absolute unity. The small part of you will no longer exist, so all that is left is God. Jesus called this state of consciousness: "I and the father are one." The male and female energy within you become one; this is the highest form of unity that can be experienced within the three-dimensional space.

NECESSARY ATTRIBUTES FOR THE SPIRITUAL PATH AND ENLIGHTENMENT

Which people are good candidates for enlightenment?

Who would be a good candidate for enlightenment? This is a difficult question to answer, because we are all capable of so much change. I agree that change is extremely difficult, but if someone is motivated to change, they can completely turn everything around within a short period of time. I am a perfect example of that, so I am not going to talk about who would be a good candidate, rather I would like to focus on the attributes necessary to go all the way.

The perfect candidate for enlightenment is a male who is in touch with his feminine side, or a female in touch with her masculinity. The goal of enlightenment is to reach perfect balance when we activate the male and the female energy within our energy field. I have already discussed how to achieve this goal by bringing the right amount of intensity and calmness to every moment.

Being inquisitive helps. Whether you are going for the path of enlightenment or just an average person trying to evolve themselves spiritually, the desire to know and experience more is the driving force that pushes every one of us to seek. This is why people who are on the path to enlightenment are called "seekers." This seeking should never stop because enlightenment is not a threshold that you pass. Different experiences of unity with All That Exists (Enlightenment) are just points along your journey. In the end, the desire to seek could become a

277

hindrance in itself, because the object of any desire is always in the future. Enlightenment can only happen if you simply are content and present in the moment. You simply "are." This is a paradox that you will battle throughout your journey, until one day you give up running, and then it will happen. It is not that you will stop seeking. But simply, one day you will understand that you have to give up running after it, because you will realize that you have always had it. The perfection has always been within you.

Being tolerant helps. The fact of the matter is that people are going to behave badly, that is a given. We all have some types of deficiencies. We need to develop the ability to let things go. It is the only way you can go beyond the positive and the negative. Tolerance comes with practice. Meditation will help you to silence your thoughts, but perseverance will get you to the end.

It helps to cultivate tunnel vision. Tunnel vision helps you achieve your goals no matter what they are. But for enlightenment, it is absolutely necessary to develop tunnel vision. The path to enlightenment is treacherous and long. You have to fixate on wanting to become one with All That Exists, and nothing more. Enlightenment must become your single focus in life. Tunnel vision is when you see beyond everything else that comes in front of you. Your mind will try to distract you by thinking about sex, fame, fortune, and special abilities. You cannot get distracted along the way, so from the moment you open your eyes in the morning, you must focus to silence your mind, until you go bed at night. You have to want to experience unity more than anything else in the world.

It is very important to be nonjudgmental. In some ways it is better to come from a background of being bad, because if you have not done bad things yourself, you tend to judge people more, which can become a hindrance in your spiritual development. God is both the good and the bad. You do not have to condone the bad behavior, but if you want to become one with God, you will have to accept the good with the bad without judging.

You need to be health conscious. Your body is the medium that you use in order to experience the three-dimensional space. Your body is your temple, and you need to treat it with care and respect. You cannot travel on this path without taking care of your body. As I have said before, the path of spiritual growth and enlightenment is treacherous. You need to make sure that you take care of your body enough to get you along this treacherous road.

You need to become selfless. Life will test you to see if you are willing to sacrifice yourself for people around you. Being selfless is the prerequisite for unity, so be prepared to show you are willing to do anything for anyone. Remember that everyone around you is Life itself, so if you want to become one with Life, you have to show that you are selfless towards all its parts.

You should be a perfectionist. The state of perfection cannot be achieved as long as we are in a physical body. Not even an enlightened man is perfect, but you need to be the type of person that strives for perfection. Life will not accept mediocrity on the path to enlightenment. Enlightenment is the ultimate achievement for any human being. There is no room for a mediocre effort.

You must become submissive. You have to be able to identify with your female energy. In the path of enlightenment Life is the dominant force. You have to be submissive in order to surrender yourself. You cannot allow your ego to get in your way.

You must cultivate patience. This is by far the most difficult. Spiritual growth takes time to develop. You have to be patient and allow energy to build inside of you, while silencing your mind. It's in our nature to want everything to happen fast, but spiritual development is the exact opposite of fast. Remember that it's about the journey, not the result. When you work hard for something it is much more enjoyable and rewarding when you get there. On the other hand, it will not be meaningful if someone just handed you something. The path of enlightenment is about the journey, never forget that. One day you will have to teach others all that you have learned, so be patient and learn from your miss steps. Growth comes from your struggles.

Spiritual path and celibacy on the path of enlightenment

Enlightenment is the highest peak of the spiritual path. Do not set your sights on the highest peak. Instead, you should focus on what you need to do next in order to take the next steps in your spiritual development. Meditate as much as you can and use mantras to get over your fears and shortcomings. Focus on going beyond the duality of this world; focus on going beyond the positive and the negative.

Allow yourself to grow without any pressure. You can still experience the highest levels of spirituality without celibacy. The path of celibacy and enlightenment is not for every soul. You may or may not be ready to go all the way in this lifetime. The best thing to do is to live your life while incorporating the teachings of this book in your daily life as much as possible, and then see where Life takes you. Celibacy and enlightenment is a calling. You do not choose to become celibate and go for enlightenment, the path chooses you. Something keeps growing inside of you as you meditate and aligns you with Life's teachings. Maybe one day, and only if Life sees enough conviction in you, you will be called upon. This calling will usually happen through an event or an unusual experience that you may have with your higher self. Do not expect to have an experience like the one I had. It is not often that Life connects with people through direct contact. It is more likely that your experience will be subtle. This calling is the greatest honor a human being can receive from Life itself. This is a complete book to help you on your journey from the beginning to the end, but you may still need to seek a master to answer your questions and guide you along the way.

Why celibacy is necessary on the path to enlightenment

I do want to talk about why celibacy is necessary on the path to enlightenment. The core energy needs to rise up to the crown chakra in order for enlightenment to happen. Any type of sexual activity causes your energy to move down towards your root chakra. Your energy cannot rise up while it's moving down towards the root chakra. The second issue is that a sexual encounter with a partner results in energy exchange between both parties. The energy that you receive from the other party will not be pure and crystallized. This is similar to adding dirt to water that you are trying to purify. The water cannot become clean and purified if you continue to add dirt to it from time to time. The third issue is that as long as you desire sex, your mind will never stop projecting thoughts of being with another person, and as long as there are thoughts in your mind, you will not reach enlightenment. Men also bleed out energy when they have sex. You cannot fill a glass with water if there is a hole in the bottom of the glass, so celibacy is necessary for enlightenment. One last thing is that Life changes the way energy moves in your body once you become celibate and dedicate yourself to the path to enlightenment. This change happens during the time of celibacy. In essence, Life prepares your body to experience the unity of the male and the female energy within your energy field. This is an important step on the path to enlightenment.

Celibacy and the path to enlightenment are different for men and woman. There are both advantages and disadvantages for both genders. Men only need to stop all sexual activities in order to initiate the rise of energy within their energy field, but for women, stopping all sexual activities will not be enough. Menstrual cycles in women cause their energy to move down once a month during the time of their period. Therefore, a woman cannot attain enlightenment until her menopause is complete. This obviously complicates things for women who want to become enlightened, but it is only another hurdle to overcome. Women can make the necessary preparations by going through all the steps before the end of their last menstrual cycle, and once they transition into menopause, they can take the final steps. The positive aspect of being a woman is that women have more of the female energy within their energy field. Female energy is submissive, so women will find it easier to surrender themselves. On the other hand, men have more male energy, and male energy is naturally aggressive, so they will have a harder time surrendering. In general, men are more egotistical than woman, and the spiritual path is about breaking down your ego. However, the path to enlightenment is usually more challenging for women because of the challenges presented by the timing of menopause onset. That is one reason why there have not been as many enlightened women as men throughout human history. Of course, there are also many other reasons. In general, almost all women in all societies globally have always had no choice but to spend all their time and energies taking care of the needs of others, whether as daughters, wives, or mothers. This has been essential for their very survival in societies where women have no means to survive on their own by working outside of the home. Taking care of others constantly leaves little time to focus on one's own spiritual development. Recently this has changed, and many women are now able to be independent and focus on themselves.

Things not to do on the path to enlightenment

One other important thing to know about the path of enlightenment is to never put any conditions on yourself to continue on the path. You're not ready to be on the path if you tell yourself: I am willing to do everything, but I will never do *that*. Life will not accept any conditions; you have to fully give yourself, unconditionally. Live your life in any way that you want until you reach a moment in time where you feel that you want more than what this physical world can offer you in terms of pleasures. Once you're there, come with open arms and be ready to dig deep and give all you have, because that is what it will take to go along this treacherous road.

Some things you should be aware of

Your spiritual body needs to heal. As part of this healing process, you will experience physical pain. This physical pain is unavoidable. Physical pain brings up to the surface the issues from our past that we need to deal with. This suffering is not without purpose. You have to be patient and continue to meditate while you are facing any type of challenge, including physical pain. Tremendous growth will come out of these situations.

One of the other hurdles to overcome is getting used to the energy of the crown chakra, which is the seventh layer (cosmic body). This energy is so calm that it can only be experienced with a very low heartbeat. This slow heartbeat will also slow down your breathing. Unfortunately, our physical body has a mechanism to go to sleep when you have a slow heart rate and breathing. You will have to be prepared, before you can experience the energy of the seventh body. The same thing will happen when you meditate and successfully silence your mind. At first, many people feel sleepy when they begin to meditate. In that case, you will have to increase the intensity to fight sleepiness. Life could also put forth a sequence of events, where you are deprived of sleep. This is normal, but you need to be prepared, because sleep deprivation will make it more difficult to focus and silence your mind.

Hurdles to overcome: desires and attachments

Two of the biggest barriers in anyone's spiritual development are their desires and attachments to things. Your desires and attachments are the reason you keep reincarnating back to this world, because as long as you have them, your consciousness will continue to lock onto them after you die, and bring you back to life. The cycle cannot end until you are free of them. Many of you might think that it is a good thing, but you have not experienced being outside of your body, so you cannot comprehend the pleasure of being united with Life itself. I assure you that all the pleasures that this world offers pale in comparison with seconds of being one with Life.

Your mind is like an electrical motor. As long as you supply electricity to the motor, it will continue to work. The only way to stop the motor is to cut off the electricity to the motor altogether. The electricity to the motor of your mind is supplied by your desires and attachments. Let me explain to you why this is the case.

Your desires are always about something that you do not have. The object of any desire is always somewhere in the future. Your mind will continue to work and project until you find a way to get there. You will either be successful or unsuccessful. The problem is that if you're unsuccessful, your mind will never stop working, and if you are successful, by the time you have reached your desire, your mind is already fixated on something else. A desiring mind is a sick mind that is never content, so you go on desiring into the next life for many lives to come.

Desires can also turn into attachments. What are attachments and why do we create them? Attachments are everything that you use to support yourself in your life. These attachments could be both positive and negative.

We create attachments because we naturally want to feel blissful and happy. Life can become difficult at times, so we begin to do things to support ourselves. Some people might listen to music and live in a dream world where they can feel happy. Some people get into a habit of drinking or doing drugs to feel blissful and happy for moments in time. Some people get attached to occupying themselves with TV or surfing the Internet, so they're not alone with their thoughts and fears. You could also attach yourself to positive things in life, such as having children, working out and being healthy, or helping other people.

Attachments may be physical objects, relationships, habits, ego, or anything that we can fixate on. For example: money, cars, companions, children, music, looks, health and physical body, your job title and power, or even enlightenment itself. I want to be clear about something: there is nothing wrong with having any or all things mentioned above. But there is a problem if your contentment and happiness depends on any of those things, because everything that exists in this physical world can be taken away from you at any time. You can lose all your money and investments because of something that happens in your life. Your children may leave you, or God forbid die in an accident. Your friendships and companionships could end at any time. You will eventually lose your health and your looks as you get older. No one truly holds any power over anyone or anything in this life. Your attachments to anything in this world bring about the fear of losing them. Your fears are feeding the electricity to the motor of your mind. You're always thinking about how to protect yourself, or what if this or that happens. The only way you can truly be free and blissful is by letting go all your attachments, whether they are positive or negative. Once you have let go of your attachments, then you can have them all because your contentment and happiness no longer depend on having them. You can have all the money in the world if your contentment and happiness do not depend on it. You can work out and do anything in life as long as you are capable of doing it, and once you're physically no longer capable of doing those things, nothing changes because you're not attached to it.

Parents might say, "How can I let go of my children?" It is important to understand that you and your children have come to this life and died hundreds or thousands of times. Your attachments will have no effect on what is going to happen in their lives. Whatever is supposed to happen will happen. Life is the driving force in every soul's life. You have to let go of any notion that you can control what is supposed to happen in their lives. Do the best that you can to guide them, but allow life to take its course, whether it is positive or negative.

This is why a period of separation from everything is necessary at the beginning of the path of enlightenment. You have to give up everything; you have to cut off all the support in your life. You have to find happiness and contentment without anything. You have to find peace with your mind when there is nothing else to support you. This is the most difficult part of the path of enlightenment. Most seekers give up during this period.

I want to give advice to any seeker who survives the separation period. Your mind is very cunning and will easily latch on and become attached to enlightenment. It will project thoughts of becoming enlightened and acquiring special powers, or think about becoming a master and teaching others, or think about the pleasures of becoming one with Life. Remember that projections are projections, no matter the subject. You have to stop all thoughts, whether they are positive or negative, or have anything to do with the path to enlightenment. Experiences will come when the time is right; your projections about those experiences are just like any other projections, so stop them all. Do not allow your mind to use the back door and project thoughts about anything.

Whether you are on the path to enlightenment or are an average person trying to improve, it is better to have the least amount of attachments in your life because the fewer things you're attached to, the more stable your life will be. The goal is to be happy, regardless of what you have or don't have in your life.

I want to be clear about something: once you start meditating, you develop the ability to stop thoughts. You begin to stop the projections that your mind creates, but you cannot suddenly bring your mind to a halt. This can become frustrating at times, because your mind is relentless and it may feel as if you are not making progress. I assure you that progress is being made. Remember that with meditation your energy is rising and will reach the necessary threshold, even though it may take some time, so be patient and you will get there. For example, you may be the type of person who has attachments to money and is worried about not having enough. You go on meditating and stopping all the thoughts about not having enough money, but the thoughts keep coming back until suddenly one day you wake up and you are no longer are worried about money. This transition will always be sudden with everything that you are working on. This is also true for enlightenment. You do not reach pure silence gradually; in fact, it is completely out of your hands. Meditation will help you to stop individual thoughts and slow down your mind. You will even experience moments of silence with **considerable effort,** but this is not nirvana. The transition from having thoughts to having no thoughts at all without any effort will be sudden. Once your higher self feels that you are no longer afraid or attached to something then all thoughts are dropped. Only your higher self has the ability to stop the mind altogether.

I want to give you an example of how Life helps me get rid of some of my attachments. I have always paid a great deal of attention to my appearance throughout the years. I never liked facial hair ever since my teenage years. I also shaved my head when Telly was going through chemotherapy for support. Once her chemotherapy ended, I continued to shave my head because it was more comfortable and looked better on me at the same time. I would groom myself regularly. Once I began the period of separation after the events of December of 2005, Life asked me to only shave and cut my hair once a month. I originally thought that Life asked me to not shave regularly because I'm supposed to not care about how I look. I had seen pictures of yogis from India with long beards, so I let my hair and beard grow. This went on for about a year. There came a time where I no longer cared that I had a full beard on my face or that the hair on my head was long, I no longer cared how I looked. Once I reached that point, Life connected to me and told me that I could shave everything off, and keep it off as I saw fit. The issue was not about whether or not I should have cared about how I looked; the issue was that I was attached to how I looked. My happiness depended on looking a certain way, and once that attachment was gone, it did not matter how often I groomed myself.

You should contemplate to find the things that you are attached to in your life and initiate a sequence of events to cut off those attachments. Once you let go of those attachments, it will be okay for you to have them again. You will only be truly blissful if you have no attachments at all. Remember that Life will take it away from you if you do not work on letting go of your attachments. For example, if you are attached to material things in this life, your higher self will have no choice but to choose a life with few material possessions in your next reincarnation, so you can work on being happy without those material possessions. It may continue for many lifetimes until you get it right. The sooner you do the work, the sooner the cycle will come to an end. This is the meaning of karma. Look around the world and see the lives that exist all around. Any of those lives could be what you will experience in your next life. Work on yourself and be kind, have compassion for people who are less fortunate. Remember that whatever you dish out will come back to you with the same force. Whatever effort you make to better yourself will have a considerable effect on the quality of your next life.

On the path to enlightenment, your conditioning and personality can also become an attachment. You can become attached to your identity and who you know yourself to be. Your job, conditioning, and personality cannot become your identity. Be prepared to drop it all. You have to be willing to drop who you know yourself to be with all your characteristics. Remember that enlightenment is about transformation from the root to the top. Once you have dropped all conditioning and personality, a new self will emerge from within. Remember that you were born a perfect being; the perfection is just hidden below the surface. Once you let go of your personality, conditioning, and attachments, then your true self will emerge.

You have to be aware of one important fact; gaining anything in this physical world is about achieving, and enlightenment is the exact opposite of achieving. Enlightenment is about dropping all the noise and the notions about everything, and finding what is already there. You cannot improve upon the perfection that is already within you. All you need to do is clean up the dirt that you have picked up along the way. Have you ever watched a paleontologist work on a pile of dirt and pull out a perfect bone of a dinosaur? Your inner journey is exactly the same way. Remember when I told you earlier that you are both your higher self and the consciousness that you know yourself to be. One day when you have meditated enough and cleaned up the dirt, a true self will emerge. This self is perfect in every way, and has always been there from the beginning. You will realize then that there has never been two separate parts of you. Both your higher self and who you know yourself to be, have been "you" all along. Simply, **self is experiencing itself**.

Do not expect that at some point in your spiritual development your higher self is going to pop up and say: "Hello, I am here!" Your higher self has always been there. In fact, there is no small self and higher self. There is only one true self who is occupying the body of every human being and creature living on this planet, and that is you and has always been you, the being who is experiencing your life. The one who is looking at the outside world through your eyes. Let me give you a metaphor. Imagine that you are the space that contains this entire universe. Now imagine that you built a house in a small space somewhere in the universe. Now, the space that is stuck within the house is looking out through the windows of the house thinking that it is separate from the outside space, but the space within the inside of the house and outside of the house are not separate. The house only gives the appearance of separation. Now imagine that you have built many houses and the spaces within each of those houses are looking through the windows thinking that they are separate from each other and outside space, but all the spaces in all the houses are one and the same. I told you about the experience that I had in the hospital where my consciousness went in and out of my body three times. One moment I was the space that was the room looking at my physical body on the bed of the hospital, and one moment I was looking at the ceiling through my eyes. Experiencing myself outside of my physical body was one of the most exhilarating experiences of my life. I was one with Life and I knew that I could never die, and I am eternal.

I know that at times it may seem as if I am contradicting myself, but if you look deep enough there is no contradiction. There is a mechanism that I explained earlier in the book using an example of a person (the person who you know yourself to be) who is learning how to drive a car with two sets of steering wheels, brakes, and gas pedals, and the teacher sitting on the passenger side (your higher self). In fact, this mechanism exists so that self can experience itself. One part of you makes things happen and is the creator of all the events in the universe. This part of you is the prime mover, while another part of you experiences those events. The experiencer cannot be aware of the outcome or the prime mover, otherwise life will not be interesting. You would not want to know how a movie ends, or what is going to happen next. It is the only way that the single consciousness can experience itself, but the single consciousness, the one true self, is every one of us.

The prime mover is in control of the movement of every single physical body, while other parts of consciousness experience those movements. We choose what we want to experience, and the prime mover creates a sequence of events so that we can experience what we have chosen. You are both the prime mover and experiencer of all creations at the same time. As I said before, this universe has been created so that self can experience itself.

Some people have difficulty accepting that Life controls every event because it feels to them that they're not in control of their own destiny.

The reason that they feel that way is due to the fact that they still see themselves as individuals. But **you are both the prime mover and experiencer of all creations, you are Life itself, you are All That Exists. You have chosen to experience every event that has been created.** The prime mover is a function of yourself and is there to give you what you have chosen to experience. **You are in fact in control of your own destiny.**

The reason why what I have said may seem different at times is due to the fact that I am speaking to a wide audience who are at different junctions in their spiritual development. I experienced and was given these insights over an eleven-year period. You are reading this book and receiving all these insights over a matter of days. Depending on where you are in your spiritual development, some of the material will resonate with you, but other parts are harder to grasp and even difficult to believe, and that is normal. So meditate and feed the parts that resonate with you, and throw away the parts that do not.

Until now, no enlightened person has ever attempted to give specific details about the inner working of our physical body, the lower consciousness, and higher self, because it is so difficult to describe this unity. My insights and descriptions are not perfect, because unity cannot be described with words – it has to be experienced. I wanted to give you a glimpse of my reality so that you can connect the dots more easily. Enlightenment has been experienced by many spiritual masters for thousands of years, and they have all done their best to describe their experience to people of their time. This description may be similar in some ways and different in other ways, because two people who experience the same event may have a different take on what has taken place. This book is about my interpretation of the enlightenment and unity that I have experienced with All That Exists. I have shared with you as much as I could so that you could use the knowledge to find your own way. I have given you different variations of the same understanding, so that as you grow in your spiritual development you can connect with your higher self and propel yourself forward. Remember that **nothing but God exists, no one but you exists, and there is only one of us**.

All the insights and understandings in this book have sewn the seed in your soul. Now you need to water and feed the seed by meditating as much as possible. The more you meditate, the more this seed will grow, so be vigilant in your meditation. Read this book over and over again from time to time, because as your energy grows and the frequency of your vibration increases, you will comprehend more of the material and also support yourself by re-strengthening your understanding. A true comprehension of a single understanding can greatly propel you forward in your spiritual development.

Be ready to let the old part of you who is angry and fearful die, so that the new you who is confident, compassionate, and fearless can grow and shine. Allow yourself to transform from a small being who is occupying a single body to All That Exists, the God within you. **This is the journey of self-discovery and transformation.**

THE FOURTH PHASE

I knew from the beginning of my journey that Life was teaching me the spiritual path so I could share with others how to progress in their spiritual development. Once I realized that Life wanted me to write a book about what I have learned, I began to think how I could get it done. This was a great undertaking; after all, I had no experience in writing a book. The most I had ever written was business letters, during the time when I went to the British Columbia Institute of Technology to get my electrical engineering diploma. I was not quite sure how to proceed, so I decided to first write down all the material that had to do with teaching meditation and meditation techniques. I then added what I wanted to share regarding the spiritual energy field, and the inner working of our minds. I ended up with about 120 pages of handwritten notes.

After that was done, I sat one day and tried to figure out how I would turn these handwritten notes into a book. I was thinking, how can I tell my story? Should I share with readers that I was involved with an organized crime family? Should I share that All That Exists directly communicates to me? How would I be received? I was overwhelmed, and laughingly asked Life, "Where are you going with this?"

"After many centuries the stars have lined up again such that the human collective consciousness can take a leap forward in the evolutionary process," Life replied. *"This is a time of awakening. You are a spiritual master, a master healer; you will raise the vibration of the planet. The door is open for you."*

I understood my purpose in life, but I also understood what Life meant by saying, *"You will raise the vibration of the planet."* No person can raise the vibration of the planet by themselves. We all need to balance our lives and meditate in order to raise the vibration of our energy field individually, and then come together and unite in order to raise the

291

vibration of our planet together, and deal with the serious issues that are threatening our way of life and existence. Our planet is at a moment of reckoning; powerful forces are separating us from each other. We need to come together; we are only separate in our minds, in reality there is only one of us. All opposite views among people regarding different subjects are part of our mind, not part of our consciousness and soul. Your soul is the single consciousness in all of us. Let go of your judgments and discriminations, no one but you exists. Everyone around you is you in a different body. The common world-view is based on a lie, and the lie is that we are separate. The separation is not real; the only real thing in this world is that we are all one, and there is only one of us.

What you do matters. Not only for yourself in this life, but for the future of humanity and your next lives to come. Your efforts in balancing your life and raising your vibration can create change beyond your physical body. Once you raise your vibration, your energy field affects everyone around you. Individuals who can reach the vibration of the fifth, sixth, and the seventh body not only can significantly affect the vibration of everyone around them, but they can significantly affect the vibration of the planet and the direction in which we move.

It is not enough just to meditate and raise your vibration. We need to get involved in the political process and force our politicians to make the correct decisions for us and for our planet. The problem is that a huge segment of population, who are balanced and in the middle, do not vote and make their voices heard. This has allowed extremists on both sides to decide our fate. Many of you are frustrated and have given up on the political process, but this is not a time for inaction. Life has guided me to give this message to all of you:

"Regardless of your political views, you need to get involved in a political revolution in which special interest groups can no longer lobby a politician."

This is the most important task to achieve in our lifetimes: The complete separation of money and power. Corporations and special interest groups have hijacked democracy in Western societies worldwide. We no longer have democracies in our societies, only illusions of democracy. Corporations and special interest groups are changing the way politicians vote by lobbying them. Do not allow politicians to hide behind the constitution and tell you that the forefathers have decided our fate by writing the constitution. The forefathers are dead, and the people who are alive today should decide the fate of their nations and our planet today. The next generation should decide how to precede when their time comes. Our constitutions need to evolve as we evolve. We cannot continue to operate with constitutions that were written hundreds of years ago. The people in every country should vote on whether it is acceptable to lobby a politician. Moreover, it is time that **we demand the complete separation of money and power, and this should be written into the constitution of every country.** We cannot fix the problems that exist in our societies if politicians don't work for the people of their nation.

Terrorism, religions, and racial divides have caused divisions among the population all over the planet. It is time to move from the evil of separation to the blessings of unity and cooperation. Meditate and raise the frequency of your vibration, balance your life, and get involved in the political process.

I bow respectfully to every brave soul who has taken it upon themselves to embark on this journey of life. I feel you, I am with you, and I will do my best to reach out to you in any way possible to help you in your spiritual journey. Let us come together and write this next phase of our journey as one soul, as one consciousness.

God bless

Homayoun Amin

Proof

Made in the USA
Charleston, SC
15 February 2017